DELIRIOUS

ALSO BY DAVE PRAGER

Poop Culture: How America is Shaped by Its Grossest National Product, Feral House, 2007 (as Dave Praeger)

DELIRIOUS DELHI

Inside India's Incredible Capital

Dave Prager

ARCADE PUBLISHING • NEW YORK

Arcade Publishing books may be purchased in bulk at special discounts for sales promotion, corporate gifts, fund-raising, or educational purposes. Special editions can also be created to specifications. For details, contact the Special Sales Department, Arcade Publishing, 307 West 36th Street, 11th Floor, New York, NY 10018 or arcade@skyhorsepublishing.com.

Arcade Publishing® is a registered trademark of Skyhorse Publishing, Inc.®, a Delaware corporation.

Visit our website at www.arcadepub.com.

For extra pictures, essays about Delhi, and more, visit the author's website at deliriousdelhi.com

10 9 8 7 6 5 4 3 2 1

Library of Congress Cataloging-in-Publication Data is available on file.

ISBN: 978-1-61145-832-9

Printed in the United States of America

To Jenny, with great love, deep gratitude and grudging respect for your Mario Kart skills.

"If you are told 'they are all this' or 'they do this' or 'their opinions are these,' withhold your judgement until facts are upon you. Because that land they call 'India' goes by a thousand names and is populated by millions, and if you think you have found two men the same amongst the multitude, then you are mistaken. It is merely a trick of the moonlight."

—Zadie Smith, *White Teeth*

Contents

(An insert of photographs appears between pages 208 and 209.)

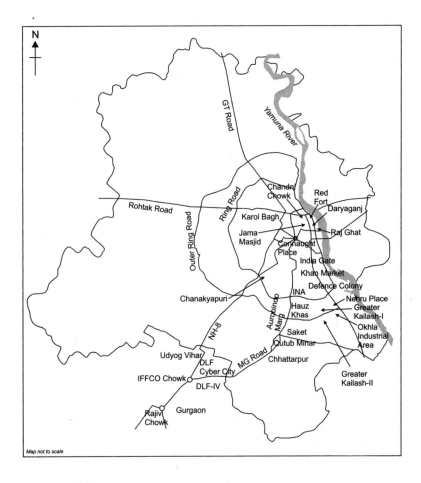

N

Map not to scale

1

The First Morning and Other Mysteries

We knew we would love living in Delhi the moment we heard the door-to-door paella salesman.

Ah, paella! The national dish of Spain. A sumptuous fusion of saffron rice, scallops, prawns, peas, sausage and cuttlefish. We'd expected Delhi to be cosmopolitan, but never did we imagine men would be riding around with giant canvas sacks of paella strapped to their bicycles. In our eight years in New York City, the most exotic street food we ever found was the guy selling gyros on 47th Street. But we had to go to him—nobody ever rode around Brooklyn shouting "fa-laaaaaaa-fel!" and dispensing hummus by the scoop. But after just fifteen hours in our new flat in the Hauz Khas market neighborhood of south Delhi, we already had a guy selling Valencian delicacies right outside our bedroom window.

Lying in our new bed, Jenny and I listened to the cry that was to fill our ears every subsequent morning for the next eighteen months. "Pie-ehhhhhh-AH!" he hollered, riding slowly by three stories below. "Pie-ehhhhhhh-AH!"

We were already half-awake. Our restless morning had begun at sunrise, when the mosque across Aurobindo Marg cranked up its call to prayer through crackling speakers that were loud enough for Muhammad himself to make no mistake about how reverent they were. Soon after that came the honking, as every vehicle began saying 'good morning' to every other vehicle on the road, a call-and-response that would end with goodnight honks only around 11 p.m. And just as we began to wonder if renting a bedroom that overlooked a busy road was a bad idea, the paella man rode by and put all our fears to rest. 'Pie-ehhhhhhh-AH!'

We peeked out the window on his third pass and saw him: thin, wiry, dressed in clothes that had long since been sun-bleached out of whatever shade of beige he'd bought them at, riding a colorless bike with one rag-wrapped bundle strapped behind the seat and another to the handlebars.

"Ah," I said. "That back bundle must be where he keeps the paella." We wondered what the front bundle contained: thyme and saffron shakers? Bottles of 2006 Baron de Barbon Oak-Aged Rioja to pair with the meal? Extra cuttlefish for preferred customers?

And what other culinary delights were to be peddled by? We salivated in anticipation of the crêpe guy. We wondered if the sushi salesman could get fresh ahi this far inland. Oh!

Maybe a gazpachowallah would come around during the hottest months!

That morning, our first morning in our new flat but our sixth in the country (we'd stayed in my company's flat in Gurgaon, the tech hub south of Delhi, five days beyond our realization that we didn't want to live in Gurgaon), Jenny and I lay in bed and listened to the sounds of the city outside our window. We were neophytes in Delhi, and the struggles that would soon confound us—where do we go to buy a wireless router? why does every third car have a sticker promoting "Fun 'N Food Village" in its rear window? how do we call an ambulance at two in the morning?—were still waiting beyond our bedroom walls. We would soon explore the streets of a city we'd never imagined we'd actually live in. We would soon see the full gamut of the human experience on those streets, from joy in the most despairing of circumstances to cruelty perpetrated by those who have everything in the world. We would soon watch dogs get beaten. We would soon see children get saved. We would soon meet holy men and unnoticed women who should be saints. We would soon stumble upon hidden treasures and walk past transcendent sights without noticing a thing. We would soon explore as much as we could manage. We would soon learn as much as we could absorb.

But we would barely scratch the surface. Every time we left our Delhi flat, we'd return home with more questions than answers. Which means we never became "Delhi experts." We'll never be "Delhi experts." Even if the city wasn't constantly changing—even if the Delhi we experienced could be frozen in time so that we could

explore every inch before its next iteration came along—
our grasp of the city would always be limited by the
cultural filters through which we can't help but view
things. All we know about Delhi is what we saw, what
people told us, and what we think we've figured out. No
matter how much we would try to immerse ourselves, our
Delhi would remain a rarefied one: we were comparatively
rich and unmistakably foreign, and the only Delhi we
could possibly experience was the one that aligned itself in
reaction to us.

This was the third Delhi flat in which we'd woken up,
but the first in which the morning symphony was this
audible. In the Gurgaon apartment, the only soundtrack
had been the howls of wild dogs and the pounding of
construction machinery that could induce headaches even
from twenty-three stories up. And in the apartment I'd
stayed in during the month of August, in a neighborhood
called Greater Kailash-II, the morning's sounds were muted,
distant and almost tranquil. (That apartment, obviously, did
not face the road.)

My August in GK-II had been a test: for my soon-to-be
employer, to see if they'd want to commit to me on a long-
term basis; and for me, to see if I'd have the *cojones* to leave
the city in which I'd lived for eight years and the country in
which I'd lived for thirty. They did, and so did I. And just
two days after first landing in the country, I called Jenny in
New York from a yellow STD kiosk in the GK-II M Block
market and gushed, "I think I could live here forever. I
love it here!"

Five months later, I hated it.

Most books about India written by Westerners document an obligatory "personal journey": at first they hate India, but then they "learn to love it." At first they're overwhelmed by the chaos, but then "the soul of the people shines through." At first they're horrified by the poverty, but then they "find spirituality" in every speck of dirt.

Our trajectory in India was different. We loved it instantly and intensely, every bit of it, as frightening and overwhelming and incomprehensible as it was. But then, as novelty turned into routine, we grew disgusted with it all: first the pollution, then the traffic, then the poverty, then the constant fear of getting swindled, and then just about everything that wasn't what we knew back home.

But that wasn't our journey's end. Instead, we were to vacillate back and forth between the two extremes—love India, hate India, love India, hate India—until we found equilibrium. We learned to love the things that should be loved, and to hate the things there are to hate. Most of all, we learned that both these aspects of India—the good and the bad—must be taken together.

We would never describe India as "spiritual," like so many do, because that would mean ignoring all the misery. Nor would we call it "disgusting," like so many do, because that would mean ignoring all its beauty. Our attitude towards India now mirrors our attitude towards our own United States: some aspects turn our stomachs, but others make us soar with joy. India—like all countries—offers both.

★

But all these emotions were ahead of us. The love and the hate, the heat and the cold, the sickness and the worry—all these were still to come. We were still aurally innocent as we awoke in our new flat; and as we listened to these sounds without meaning, our only context was the sounds that we'd left back in the Park Slope neighborhood of Brooklyn, New York City, where we'd lived the previous four years.

That bedroom also overlooked a busy road. Which meant that mornings there also had a soundtrack. Thursdays began with a garbage truck roaring down the street, inching from house to house on its fifteen-minute journey in and out of earshot while one worker drove and the other two trailed behind on foot, lifting and dumping curbside garbage cans into the back of the truck. When the truck was full, they would pull a lever to compact the trash; and on those unlucky mornings when they did so directly in front of our window, the truck's volume would double—and our sleep would be shattered—as its pneumatic presses ground into action. Monday mornings were worse: the twice-weekly garbage trucks were joined by once-weekly recycling collection trucks as well as by entrepreneurial bottle collectors who raced to collect the weekend's empties before the city could pick them up. They rattled stolen shopping carts down the sidewalk, and the bottles they'd already collected knocked together at every crack in the cement.

The song of municipal sanitation was a biweekly performance. But it came on top of a daily morning soundtrack. Neighborhood cars with poor mufflers roared to life. The guy across the street assured himself that masculinity was both equated with and demonstrated by how loud he could rev his motorcycle. The radio station's traffic copter hovered overhead to visually confirm that, yes, the Gowanus Expressway was jammed once again. In winters, the ancient steam pipes in our hundred-year-old brownstone would shriek and bang as the heat kicked in. Summer weekends often began with our neighbor Hector shouting at Sherlock, his tenant and ex-wife's sister's husband, who possessed the loudest laugh we'd ever heard. ("You know what?" Hector hollered during one memorable morning row, "You're an asshole!" Hector slammed his front door, Sherlock's laugh rattled our windows, and our hopes for sleeping past nine were dashed once again.)

We cursed these sounds at first. Hector and Johnny Motorcycle and the New York City Department of Environmental Protection made us pledge to forever avoid front-facing bedrooms. But we soon learned to sleep through it. And we eventually learned to sleep through Delhi's dawn din.

Not that Delhi's night had been that much quieter. The warbling horns of the trucks on Aurobindo Marg (which were banned from city streets during daytime but free to terrorize after dark) were loud enough to invade our dreams. Worse was when the truckers with knowledge of local streets took the shortcut past our flat. Our window was positioned exactly where they'd switch into second gear; the roar of the high end of first gear rattled the house. And if a single truck could bounce our floors, you can imagine how badly we were jolted by the earthquake that hit a few weeks after we moved in, just as we were growing accustomed to sleeping through the truck noise. It was our first earthquake: a gargantuan fright that began as a distant roar before engulfing our whole building in its terrible vibrating grasp. Jenny and I clutched impotently at each other and whimpered.

In retrospect, there are probably better earthquake-survival strategies than just lying in bed and hoping the building doesn't collapse.

(In the half-hour following the quake, too scared to sleep, I resolved to learn the walking route to the American embassy, in case we ever had to make our way on foot through a post-apocalyptic Delhi to the safety of the embassy's hamburgers, Budweiser, and swift repatriation. But the embassy is in a neighborhood of streets and roundabouts that are indistinguishable and bewildering even when the ground isn't spewing lava, so the route proved unlearnable. If the Day of Reckoning had arrived while we lived in Delhi, we'd have just hoped that autorickshaw drivers couldn't distinguish it from Delhi's everyday apocalyptic traffic.)

Delhi's night had other noises we'd learn to sleep through. Dogs, for instance: not as loud as trucks or earthquakes, but far more frequent. Every square inch of Delhi is claimed by gangs of stray dogs who vociferously defend their turf. There is a whole political structure to their world: the Hauz Khas Howlers guard the market against territory incursions by the Aurobindo Maulers while maintaining a dumpster-sharing agreement with the Green Park Greyhounds; the former are allowed access to the discarded chapattis on Tuesdays, Thursdays, Fridays and alternating

Saturdays, during which time the latter take over to ensure that no passing autorickshaw goes un-barked at. The stray dogs live, love and lie on the street; but their docile daytime trotting gives way to snarls and warfare at night, and the evening streets echo with their power struggles.

Most stray dogs are ragged and haggard, with patchy fur and the vacant look of the perennially hunted. An exception was the gang of three who lived outside our building: Bruno, Signal and Snoopy, who were stray in name only. They'd been adopted by our neighbor Anya, a single woman in her thirties who lived in her late grandfather's flat on the floor below ours. The only difference between being "adopted" and "owned" was that they weren't allowed inside the building at night. The three were fussed over and fed far too much. Fat from their lavish life, they spent their days napping, waddling from one nap to another, and biting the tires of passing cars. By night, though, the envy of strays who actually had to work for a living meant that their territory was constantly being encroached. So their vocal cords got the workout their scavenging muscles never did, inevitably right below our bedroom window.

But nighttime was serene as compared to morning, starting at sunrise with the mosque, followed closely by car horns and bicycle bells and paellawallahs. After that came less delicious sounds, like the pigeons who had regular sex on our air conditioner, their claws scratching the metal surface of the window unit, the male cooing pigeon poetry while desperately flapping himself into the mounting position. Or like the workers at the ICICI Bank depository across the street who dropped metal boxes out of armoured cars and threw other boxes inside, their hollow booms observed by a dozen guards who stood around fingering ancient rifles. The sweepers then joined the chorus, pushing a day's accumulation of dust into the gutters so that passing cars and passers-by throughout the day would kick it up to coat the sidewalks and driveways, ensuring the sweepers would have something to sweep again the next morning.

A school bell chimes at nine with the sound of an air-raid siren. Doorbells begin ringing as maids begin arriving for their daily chores, and neighbors begin shouting at maids for being late. One of them clatters up metal stairs outside our kitchen to the servants' toilet on the roof above our heads; soon we hear splashing as he comes back down to bathe with unheated water drawn from the outdoor tap. ("You've spoiled your servants," we heard Anya's mother tell her once, "by letting them wash the dishes with hot water.")

The sound of the servant washing finally roused us out of bed and into the shower. Fortunately, we'd known from our Gurgaon flat to turn on the hot water geyser a half-hour beforehand. We also knew that "geyser" was pronounced "geezer" in Delhi, bringing to mind the image of a grumpy old man complaining from his perch on the wall above our toilet about the electricity we were wasting for the extravagance of a hot shower. It was awkward to bathe with the sound of the servant washing himself on the other side of the wall, but it was clear at that point in our first morning that soundproofing had not been the priority in the construction of our building. It was designed primarily for the summer heat: no insulation, loosely fitted window frames, gaps under doors big enough to allow chipmunks to invade, and exhaust fans open to the outside air—all to create that elusive cross-breeze. It's a lovely feature in the spring and fall. In the summer, though, it lets out our air conditioning; and in the winter, it lets in the smell.

★

The first time we smelled it was during our first night in Gurgaon. We were jet-lagged and bedraggled when we entered Hamilton Court, a massive apartment complex built for the kings and queens of the new Indian economy, where my company had rented a flat to house Jenny and me and all the other expat employees they expected to imminently hire. We dragged our suitcases past the children running about the walled compound and the couples walking laps around the building, through the featureless lobby and up the elevator to the four-bedroom, 4,500-square-foot duplex on the very top floor. The master bedroom, which had been earmarked for Jenny and me, was a 700-square-foot concrete echo chamber. It was bigger than our entire apartment in Brooklyn. And it was completely empty except for a bed, two chairs, a small television and the smell.

The smell got worse as the evening wore on. It was so bad that I woke in the middle of the night convinced that poison gases were leaking from the pipes. This is no exaggeration: I actually shook Jenny awake and hissed, "That smell! Do you smell it?! I think there's some sort of gas leak!" We were the first people ever to sleep in this brand-new bedroom, and I had visions of Ratan, the apartment's live-in servant, finding us choked to death as he came to deliver our morning mangoes. What else but some sort of terrible plumbing malfunction could explain that enveloping odor of rot and death?

It was two in the morning, but I nevertheless forced Jenny out of bed and into one of the other empty bedrooms in the flat. The smell was there, too, but not quite as asphyxiating. And that was where Ratan was surprised to find us the next morning: Jenny grumpy, but both of us alive.

As it turned out, there was nothing wrong with the pipes. That was just how winter smelled. And we learned that the smell comes on every fall, ushered in by Diwali fireworks that create a haze of smoke that seems thick enough to choke out a city-wide infestation of flying insects—which, during the second Diwali we celebrated, actually happened. The smell is the aroma of cow-dung cooking fires, of coal-fired power plants, of brick kilns that almost outnumber cows in rural Uttar Pradesh, of the dead leaves and plastic chai cups that tent-dwellers and security guards burn to keep warm, and of Delhi's millions of cars, trucks and motorcycles that haven't yet been converted to run on natural gas. The smell comes at night; daytime provides a respite. And every day as dusk would fall, we would hope that maybe the weather had finally shifted, that maybe the smell had finally moved on to Rajasthan or something. But then the sun would set and the smell would rise, permeating every corner of the city just like those flying insects did, except the smell couldn't be dissipated by swatting at it. When morning came, the cycle would repeat, much to the dismay of the city's sixteen million lungs.

Until the seasons changed. And the heat began.

★

Delhi's winter surprised us by existing. Packing our suitcases back in Brooklyn, we anticipated eleven months of unbroken heat and one month of unbroken rain. But by the midpoint of our first December we'd purchased two electric heaters and two thick wool blankets to wrap around our shoulders during those moments when we'd exit the narrow arc of air that the electric heaters kept warm. And still the drafts radiated through our windows and wrapped icily around our souls. Walking upon the marble floor—which was intended to echo the air conditioning in the summer—was a barefoot trek across an icy lake, despite the three pairs of socks I would be wearing. (I couldn't find any slippers my size in the market.) Going to the bathroom made us wish our flat had a squat toilet—anything other than sitting on that icy seat.

The dropping temperature had been a gradual revelation. At first, we only needed a comforter for our bed. Then we only needed a sweater around the house. Before long, we were buying hats, and then scarves, and then gloves, and then jackets, and then those electric heaters that we'd also use to thaw our bathroom—without the heater, the bathroom was more useful as a walk-in freezer. Late night rides in open-air autorickshaws made us regret not leasing a car. Huddled together in the back seat, staring at the driver's back through our own fogged breath, we'd envy the surreptitious warming sips he'd take from the small bottle in his breast pocket, no matter the impact they had on his driving.

But winter also brought splendor to Delhi. Driving down M.G. Road on the coldest mornings, segments of the Metro would disappear into the vanishing point, majestically suspended in the sky, more massive and beautiful than they ever seemed on a clear day. The air, thick and still, would be broken only by brilliant flashes of blue as kingfishers flitted across the road. Passing through Gurgaon, the skyscrapers would be hidden behind gray clouds, an invisible presence somewhere beyond the black silhouettes of the electrical towers.

Beautiful as it was, though, this fog was trouble. Every winter morning the newspapers told of canceled trains and flights forced to land in Jaipur and wait on the tarmac for half a day until conditions improved. To combat this smog, Delhi had by 2003 forced nearly all its buses, autorickshaws and taxis to convert to compressed natural gas, reducing air pollution considerably—except that Delhiites added 1,000 new vehicles to the road every day, increasing the total from 3.6 million vehicles in 2001 to 4.8 million in 2006.[1] The benefits of CNG were lost in the volume of new traffic.

And worse than travel delays was the toll this pollution took on health: *India Today* said that Delhi was "India's

---

1. http://urbanemissions.info/simair/SIM-22-2009-AQ-Management-Delhi.html

asthma capital." By New Year's, it seemed like all of Delhi was coughing at once. The rattling hacks of drivers in desperate need of antibiotics shattered the serenity of our foggy rides home.

The weather never went below freezing in Delhi. So it never snowed. Which meant Delhi had all of the misery of winter but none of the fun. But winter was relatively short; so by February the nights were comfortable, the days were pleasant, the winter fog was no longer delaying midnight flights until 6 a.m., and the air was slightly more breathable. With the April heat just around the corner, spring was a frantic rush to squeeze in as many outdoor activities as possible: walks in parks, rooftop barbeques, trips to desert cities in Rajasthan.

The heat began on schedule. And it ushered in a series of dust storms that blew into our house through the same loosely fitted doors and windows that the winter drafts found so conducive to making our refrigerator redundant. A series of springtime storms washed the dust off the trees, quickly transforming the roads into mud that would just as quickly dry in the sun and turn back into tree-coating dust—but not before hopelessly snarling traffic.

And then the spring rains stopped, and only the heat remained.

That was when both my mother and Jenny's father began reading to us from the global weather forecasts printed in their local newspapers, each independently conniving to convince us to move back home. "I see it'll be 110 degrees for you today," they would both say, "but gee, you know, it's only seventy-three in Brooklyn . . ."

By their numbers, April, May and June appeared to be the hottest months. But July and August were worse. Because that's when the humidity kicked in. I couldn't complain too much, as my daily exposure was limited to those moments I'd leave my air-conditioned taxi to dash into my air-conditioned home or air-conditioned office. Jenny had it worse: she commuted by autorickshaw, so reaching her air-conditioned office necessitated a sweaty crawl through unmoving traffic, with her scarf draped around her mouth to filter the dust as well as draped over her arm to block the sun and below her neck to dissuade the driver from trying to ogle cleavage she wasn't revealing anyway.

Still, we complained about the heat much less than we complained about the cold. That's because we knew we were among the fortunate few in Delhi who were never far from an air conditioner, and also because we were even more fortunate to live in Hauz Khas, which had fairly reliable electricity. Power in our neighborhood failed relatively infrequently and then only for an hour or two at a time, and our flat's backup power was sufficient to keep our fans whirring until power returned. As long as we didn't turn on too many lights. Compare that to our friends Scott and Sally, an American couple from Chicago who lived in Shanti Niketan, a few miles and a whole infrastructure west of us: they spent many of their summer nights staring at silent air-conditioners as the (battery-powered) bedside clock ticked slowly towards morning.

But while the heat and humidity wilted us expats, making us pine for a return to the British tradition of moving the capital's business to cool mountain towns for the summer, native Delhiites endured with proud stoicism. That's because they knew something about the humidity that we didn't: it meant the monsoon was on its way.

The monsoon is storied in both ancient and modern Indian culture. It's a giver of life. It brings the rains that feed the crops that feed the nation. The monsoon begins in Kerala in June and meanders its way across the subcontinent, a beloved air mass that's bounced around the country by ocean currents or winds off the Himalayas or whatever other global weather patterns magically ensure it touches every part of the country. The newspapers predict its arrival, debate its strength, and warn of a disappointment for farmers; and the whole of the city scans the skies in the mornings, hope rising with every cloud, every breeze stirring anticipation and joy in Delhi hearts.

Our friend Penny said it best: "I didn't realize why people here loved rain so much until the first summer the rains refused to come."

But eventually, they did come. For us, the first rain brought water spilling into our living room, thanks to the clogged drain on our terrace; we plugged the gaps under the sliding wooden door with our clean towels and sacrificed a few paperbacks to lift the air-conditioners' power stabilizers off the soggy floor. And we were so engrossed in mourning the laundry (which we didn't do ourselves anyway) that we nearly missed noticing that the rest of the city had turned joyful eyes to the sky. We looked out the window, beheld the scene, and then pulled out our umbrellas and went down to the street to watch. Children ran merrily through the puddles. Men held babies in the downpour. Laughing women adjusted soaked saris that clung to their curves like Bollywood song numbers come to life. Motorcycle riders smiled despite their soaking, enjoying the coolness with the knowledge that the sun would soon return to make everything too hot again.

The monsoon delighted all: the adults, the children, the farmers, the mosquitoes and the foliage. Unfortunately, the pavement in the streets also wanted to get in on the action: like a boy tilting his face into the rain, the roads would crack wide open to absorb as much water as they could. But while the boy would eventually close his mouth and move on to school, the roads didn't stop: cracks widened into potholes that swelled into chasms. Water collected in puddles that became ponds and then lakes. Sinkholes transformed whole stretches of road into impromptu Indian Oceans.

This had a negative effect on traffic. And this effect was compounded by the apparent fact that the city saw it as futile to repair its infrastructure while there were still more rains to come.

But potholes weren't the worst of it. When the run-off would overwhelm the drainage, roadside gutters would overflow two lanes beyond their banks. Sometimes entire roads would be cut off by floodwater, as was the case with Aurobindo Marg during one downpour, when a flood stretched from the far end of the street all the way to our building's front door, a hundred meters away. (We grabbed our umbrellas and went out to watch the chaos; as the water receded, manhole covers appeared on the road dozens of feet from the holes they'd covered—the pressure of the run-off backing up in the sewers had literally blown the cast-iron lids into the air.) In Gurgaon, whole stretches of road and pavement that had washed away early in the monsoon remained that way weeks later, forcing commuters to drive over rubble hillocks and through rock-filled gulches to enter the Millennium City.

When the monsoon ended, the heat returned. But it was feeble. We weren't frightened of it any more. We'd seen its worst and the heat knew it. Its post-monsoon effort was a last gasp, a pathetic attempt to salvage some dignity before collapsing into the coolness of fall.

As with spring, fall was a time for outdoor activities, for daytime football without fear of dehydration, for enjoying the terrace on evenings when the breeze blew the gathering pollution into Rajasthan. And by November, the nightly fog was again rolling in, the nightly flights were again being delayed and, as we celebrated our one-year anniversary in Delhi, the smell and the cycle began anew.

★

But back in that first morning in our new apartment, we were still blissfully unaware of the cold that awaited us, the heat we couldn't imagine, the monsoon we didn't understand; we were still even unaware of the household mysteries that awaited us just outside our bedroom door. And we would have remained innocent at least until after our showers had we not heard the next sound to join our Delhi morning chorus: our doorbell rang.

I put on my clothes, exited the bedroom, and opened the front door to reveal a woman I didn't know who began shouting at me in a language I didn't recognize. Tugging her headscarf with a humility belied by her shouting, she mimed shapes I couldn't discern and pointed emphatically out to the terrace.

"I'm sorry," I told her. "I don't understand."

More shouting, waving, gesturing and pointing, all punctuated by sharp tugs of her headscarf.

"I'm sorry!" I told her. "No Hindi!"

The woman paused as Jenny came to the door and stood behind me. As we regarded her faded mustard sari and the big brass ring in her nose, she regarded us: a pretty blonde with brown eyes standing next to a taller, slightly goofy-looking guy who'd clearly gotten lucky in the spouse department. Our puzzled faces were tinged with just the slightest amount of panic. "No Hindi," I repeated again.

She frowned at me. "Something something?" she asked in her language.

"No," I said, relieved. "No Hindi."

She threw her head back and laughed. And then she resumed shouting, and she continued shouting, and she wouldn't stop shouting. So Jenny and I decided to try a different tactic.

"Aha!" I said, nodding with as much vigorous sincerity as I could muster. "Haan, haan! Yes, yes!"

The woman grinned with triumph and marched down the stairs.

We watched after her, shook our heads and closed the door.

The next morning, the doorbell rang again. More shouting, and more gesturing on her part. Again, neither Jenny nor I could wave or mime well enough to convince her that we didn't speak her language.

As the week progressed, she grew increasingly frustrated with our inability to comply with her plainly stated requests, and we grew increasingly frustrated with the scene at the door.

When we stopped answering the doorbell before noon, she started ringing it at one.

Finally, our landlord Shankar explained it: she was Shilpa, and she was there to collect our garbage, which we were supposed to leave for her on the terrace. For this, we were to pay her 300 rupees a month, plus a bonus on Diwali. And Shilpa wasn't going to let us forget it.

Shankar didn't ask what we'd been doing with our garbage up until that moment. Which was good, because we'd spent our first week carting our trash a few hundred meters up Aurobindo Marg to a dumping station that had been constructed in the parking lot of the Swift Car Rental company. Swift's workers had stared at us each time, as if they'd never seen anyone dumping garbage into the garbage dumping station before. Now we realized that they'd probably never seen anyone dumping garbage who wasn't a maid.

Shilpa would ring our doorbell every morning that we didn't leave a bag for her, always chattering away with no acknowledgement that we had no idea what she said. We even tried practising our Hindi on her. "Hamlog Hindi nahin samehajta hoon," we would tell her, reciting what we'd learned in our lessons as phonetically as we could. "We don't understand Hindi."

"Nahin?" she'd cock her head and regard us as if she understood. But each time we were about to rejoice at this communications breakthrough, she'd laugh and then continue her indecipherable lecture anew.

Shilpa provided the garbage-hauling and stair-sweeping services for all the flats in our bungalow, which is what our landlord called our style of building. It consisted of six units on four levels that shared a driveway and a stairwell, plus a seventh flat with a separate entrance around the corner on the main road, three stories below our living-room terrace. We never saw any signs of life in that flat, but during our final Christmas party, one of our guests knocked a wine glass onto their property below. When I went down the next morning to clean it up, the shattered glass was already gone. Which meant that somebody did actually live there, and that his only impression of Jenny and me was that we were vandals who threw trash in their driveway and didn't apologize for it.

The other ground-floor unit, with its entrance just off our driveway, belonged to Dr. T., a throat surgeon in his sixties who boasted to us about having both taught and practiced in New York state. I'd periodically come down in the morning to find him berating my taxi drivers about the sprawling manner in which they parked. Most of our conversations with him were in passing, and almost every single one ended with an invitation for a drink that I always declined—not because I didn't want to get to know him, but because Dr. T. had a terrible timing. He was always inviting me to join him right when I was coming home from work late and just wanted to collapse into my dinner, or when I was actually coming home from work early and wanted to take full advantage of that miracle.

Just past the entrance to Dr. T.'s flat was a swinging iron gate that was locked at night to protect our bungalow's central stairwell from the neighborhood's nocturnal evils. Its padlock was old-fashioned and difficult to open even in the best of circumstances; had there been a fire in the building, I could imagine all of us residents piled up behind it, our faces squished into the gate as we shouted at whoever's trembling hands were fumbling to insert the key while Dr. T. shouted from beyond the gate that we should have replaced that padlock years ago.

Beyond that gate, past the ancient electrical meters nailed haphazardly to an equally ancient piece of mounted plywood, was the stairwell. It was our bungalow's central artery, linking all our individual cells, feeding us our daily ration of maids and deliverymen and chance encounters and overheard gossip. The first landing was stained with grease from where Anya's dogs slept during the day, when the gate was open and they could sneak in. The second landing boasted a nondescript gray door, behind which was our landlord's office. A businessman in his late fifties, Shankar lived in Vasant Vihar but worked in this converted flat alongside a handful of other men and a cacophony of computers, contraptions and piles of paper. We never really understood quite what they did, even though we entered his office a few times every month to ask him a question, report something broken, or hand him our rent check.

Up one more set of stairs was the only landing with two doors. Behind the door on the right was a flat that stood empty almost our entire time in Delhi. One day we were surprised to notice activity as we passed by: noises coming from inside, luggage resting on the landing and, oddly, newspapers stuffed into the crack under the door. A few days later, we met a man coming out of the flat who told us he worked 'in the films' in Mumbai; we shook hands and never saw him again. From then, there were no further signs of activity until shortly before we moved out, when a team of remodelers began to gut the entire place, working for weeks but showing no progress visible from the front door that they always left open. Their only clear accomplishment was to brick up an alcove in the stairwell adjacent to this flat and then tear down the wall behind the new bricks—a land grab that added ten square feet to the flat, and stole ten square feet from the stairwell.

Across the landing was Anya's flat. Its door was labeled with the name and military rank of her late grandfather, who'd owned the flat until he passed away; inside, fading photos of old army regiments still covered its walls. A single woman in her early thirties, Anya worked as a freelance Japanese translator, speaking glowingly of her love of sushi and everything else Japanese. She was the first person in the building we met after Shankar, and she became our conduit to the neighborhood gossip. But it's fortunate that we became friendly at all, seeing as how I managed to mortally offend her during our very first conversation, which took place on the driveway as she was feeding her dogs. When she mentioned in passing that she liked south Indian food, I asked her in all my innocent expat ignorance, "Oh, are you from south India?"

She looked at me crossly. "Do I *look* like I'm from south India?"

"I . . . don't know," I stammered. "I, like, just got here."

Anya had a razor-sharp wit that often left me sputtering and Jenny laughing. She was a wealth of knowledge who helped us understand the culture around us, from the trivial to the profound to the deeply catty. She taught us that one Japanese motorcycle company broke into the Indian market only after inventing "sari guards" to protect women sitting side-saddle from getting their clothes tangled in the gears. She regaled us with stories of the Delhi in which she grew up, a city that even ten years prior to our arrival had "no grocery stores and no takeaway restaurants." And she told us stories of Mr. and Mrs. M.

Mr. and Mrs. M. lived one landing up from Anya and one landing below us. Mr. M. possessed a shock of white hair that fell behind his ears and down to his neck in a manner that, in America, would only have been appropriate for an ex-rockstar or a mad scientist. But as amazing as his hair was, we hardly noticed it, because our eyes were drawn inevitably to his spectacular white mustache that contrasted so heroically with his dark skin. He was a formidable-looking man with a formidable-sounding voice that could be heard up and down the stairwell, through doors, around corners and sometimes in different neighborhoods. Conversations with him were intensely one-sided: whatever opinion or fact we tried to inject was either steamrolled over or interpreted as confirmation of his worldview, regardless of whether it actually was. His wife, Mrs. M., was a frail woman, a tiny figure with an exaggerated tremble who, despite weighing what seemed to be no more than fifty pounds, nevertheless managed to successfully walk Izabelle—their beautiful golden retriever who exuberantly jumped after anybody who passed by— without ever being dragged down the stairs and around the neighborhood.

Mr. M. took a dim view of his fellow Indians, I'm sad to say; and he never grew tired of sharing his dim views with us. Sitting on his terrace in the mornings, he'd spot me when I'd step out to see if my taxi had arrived. If it hadn't, he'd gesture angrily at the empty parking spot and shout how one couldn't trust "any of them," initially meaning taxi drivers but quickly broadening his thesis to encompass his countrymen at large. "Indians are very cunning!" he'd shout at me and the rest of the neighborhood. "Very cunning, very selfish! They park like this!" He'd wave his arms at the nearest parked car. "Not even God can help!"

Mr. M. was always very friendly and helpful to us, and it pains me to present him as a caricature; but almost every interaction we had with him was succeeded by Jenny and me turning to each other and saying, "I can't believe he said that." His heart was in the right place: he just wanted everyone around him to meet his standards of civilization. So from his perch upon his balcony, he waged a one-man war on street-level transgressions. He'd yell from above at cars that parked sloppily, at taxi drivers who had the audacity to wait downstairs for me instead of coming up and ringing my bell, at autorickshaw drivers who didn't help Jenny carry her bags, at boys spitting, at guards sleeping and, of course, at men urinating. Anya told us that she'd seen him on numerous occasions run downstairs and chase peeing men away from the object of their affliction, hollering at their receding backs as they duck-walked away.

Perhaps because he spent his whole day making enemies from above, Mr. M. was very concerned about the neighborhood's security situation. "You can have your stone-clad house, but outside it's worse than Harlem!" he told us. One day he and Mrs. M. grew convinced that someone was stealing light bulbs out of our stairwell, so he unilaterally instituted a policy of padlocking the front gate at 7 p.m., right after Shankar's employees left, instead of at midnight as it had been up until then. Unlocking the padlock was difficult enough from the inside; unlocking it from the outside, as I now had to do every night when I arrived home from work, required contorting my wrist to ease the reversed key into the hole, pressing my face against the dusty iron gate and usually dropping my belongings in the process.

Mr. M. periodically shared his political views with us. He praised George W. Bush and worried during the American election that Barack Obama was "a secret Muslim." And as our time in India grew short and we began considering a number of Southeast Asian cities as our next home, he had some advice: "You should go to Singapore, because in Kuala Lumpur are the Muslims."

With the guilt that one feels when brushing off an elderly relative, Jenny and I politely squirmed out of Mr. M.'s invitations for coffee, mostly because we didn't want to spend our brief weekend leisure time being told how to treat our maid and what "the real problem with Indians" was. But on the day we moved out for good, we did take a moment to say goodbye. At first, we mutually lamented the small amount of time we'd had to get to know each other; but then Mr. M. made it clear that he'd gotten to know us in other ways. "I read that too much wine can cause cancer," he told us, raising his white eyebrows poignantly, clearly referring to the empty bottles we'd leave once or twice a week on the terrace for Shilpa to collect (and, as we were now learning, for him to scrutinize). He looked at us critically. "But . . . you're young, and life is exciting for you right now."

Up one more landing past Mr. and Mrs. M. were two doors. One led to a large, empty roof terrace with clotheslines that we used to dry our sheets; and the other, with a horseshoe nailed atop the frame, led to our flat. A small terracotta Ganesh on the wall—the only other decoration on that landing—smiled patiently at us every time we opened the door to answer Shilpa's morning knocks. Shilpa's visits had become part of Ganesh's morning symphony as well as ours, joining the honking horns and sweeping brooms and shouts of overbearing neighbors and murmur of armed men.

As in Brooklyn, it all became background. Even the paellawallah's morning rounds stopped waking us up with hunger pains. Although that's also because we found out he was shouting "ka-baaaaaaaaad-ai," which meant he was looking for old newspapers and empty bottles to buy. An entrepreneurial garbage collector, in other words. In fact, "he" was probably a "they"—a number of different men bicycled through the neighborhood every morning, shouting their intention to buy rags or cans, or to sharpen knives, or to make keys. And while at first we couldn't understand how people could equate their cries with garbage removal or on-the-spot button affixing, we realized there was an American parallel: Indians visiting America in summertime must be equally baffled that the music emanating from speakers atop a white van can suddenly cause all the children in the neighborhood to run to their parents begging for ice cream money. The kabadiwallah has combined the business model of Brooklyn bottle collectors with the marketing strategy of the Mister Softee truck. Only to our wistful Western ears did it sound like a Mediterranean delight.

Still, the paellawallah idea is a good one. And we claim no patent on it. Some reader of this book will start this service and make a fortune, at least once he figures out where to source cuttlefish in India, and once people stop trying to sell him their scrap paper.

2

Delhi: The Sprawled City

On my very first night in Delhi, jet lag and foot pain woke me at 3 a.m. This was in my company's rented apartment in the Greater Kailash-II neighborhood at the beginning of my trial month in the country, eight days before Jenny would join me from New York and three months before we would move to our flat in Hauz Khas. My feet were a mess of blisters because the brief neighborhood tour I'd embarked upon after arriving from the airport had turned into an hours-long trek once I'd gotten hopelessly and panic-inducingly lost.

It's embarrassing to recall how frightened I was while wandering those unfamiliar streets. But this is the truth: those hours I spent searching for my flat were the most overwhelming of my life. My terror can be blamed perhaps on jet lag and naïveté (I had traveled without sleep for twenty hours to a country I'd never realistically imagined I'd visit), but it was compounded by the fact that I had no

Indian currency, I couldn't get my bank card to work, I carried no mobile phone, I was wearing no sunblock, I had no water, and I could discern absolutely no logic in the layout of the hot streets. Dogs glared at me as I encroached on their shade for respite. Monkeys swung menacingly overhead. Crows perched like death, cawing curses as I passed. Every vehicle on the street seemed to be honking at me. And every person I asked for help pointed me in a different direction.

It took me hours to find my flat again. My neck was as bright and as red as, well, a tourist who didn't wear sunblock. Once safely inside, though, my throbbing fear devolved into quivering malaise and hunger crept forward to assert primacy in my hierarchy of needs, compelling me to knock on my new landlord's door and humbly borrow money for food. And then I hobbled to the market, ate a delightful meal, followed my carefully noted route back home, and gave in to exhaustion even before the sun had set.

Now, eight hours later, I was wide awake and staring at the unfamiliar ceiling. My company had offered me this assignment in India just two weeks prior; and in the rush of paperwork and vaccination and sunblock purchasing that followed, the full weight of my commitment hadn't set in. It was there, in that hard bed, with my sunburned neck gingerly lifted from the pillow and medicated gel slathered on my feet, where angst began to bear down on me. If I were a religious man, I would have prayed for a sign.

Instead, I turned on the television. And there was my sign anyway: *The Simpsons* was on. And it was the episode in which Homer moved to India.

As unlikely as this coincidence may sound, it's the absolute truth: it was 3 a.m., I was in India, and so was Homer Simpson. Springfield Nuclear Power Plant had outsourced its jobs to Bangalore, and Homer was here to train the workers. Against all odds, he was so successful that he was promoted to manage the entire plant.

This, somehow, was exactly what I needed to see: if Homer Simpson could succeed in India, so could I.

Though the rest of the episode descended into nonsense (while Mr. Burns rafted down the Ganges with a group of corpses, Homer declared himself a Hindu god, and the rest of the Simpsons journeyed upriver *Apocalypse Now*-style to stop his madness), I'd already gotten my inspiration from it. I continued watching American sitcoms (I couldn't believe they showed *Friends* in India!) until the sun rose. And then I opened up my map of Delhi, put my finger on the point towards which the city's main roads imprecisely converged, and said to myself, "There is where I will go." I walked outside, hailed an autorickshaw for the very first time, and went straight to Old Delhi.

Nine hours later, I returned home with a deep love for India and the perspective to appreciate how peaceful and quiet Greater Kailash-II actually was.

For both Jenny and me, Old Delhi became our favorite part of the city. Old Delhi is what Westerners imagine when we imagine India: narrow streets, bustling alleys, pressing crowds, bleating animals, and ancient buildings with sculpted stone lattices still visible behind jury-rigged aluminium siding. Humanity's technological progress can be charted in the Gordian canopy of cables strung overhead,

with frayed telephone lines hanging limp like severed
jungle vines over inch-thick power cables, and mobile
phone masts competing with minarets to block whatever
sunlight still trickles down. Every corner turned in Old
Delhi revealed something we never imagined we'd see: a
monkey fight, for instance, or a metal trunk full of severed
goat legs. Women in black burqas sat stoically on bicycle
rickshaws steered by impossibly thin men in impossibly
thin shirts. Porters lugged burlap sacks, bent halfway by the
weight on their backs but still not sweating half as much as
we tourists taking their pictures. A right turn opens up to a
deserted mosque. A left turn takes us into the courtyard of
a nineteenth-century mansion, where a maroon sari swirls
and disappears into the darkness beyond an upper-story
balcony. Children giggle and follow us and ask to shake
our hands.

We'd each recall a different experience every time we
visited: there was always too much to see in Old Delhi for
two people to see the same things. Old Delhi can't be
remembered linearly, but only as sensory bursts, as a mosaic
of fleeting thrills that disappeared before they could be
focused upon: chickens squawking, women squatting next
to vegetables, pigeons cooing, kites flying, children hollering
from the backs of bicycle rickshaws, bangles glinting on
wrists, potatoes frying in giant vats of oil, hawkers shouting,
bells ringing, beards, sweat, sticks slapping on bulls' flanks,
prayer beads clicking, scooters honking, tourists screeching
in indignation, and then suddenly we're both choking and
tearing—we'd wandered into the wholesale spice market,
and they're roasting chilli peppers, and even the workers

are coughing and breathing through their sleeves, only they're carrying fifty-pound bales of dried peppers on their heads as they do so.

Old Delhi has hundreds of thousands of residents, but nobody we asked knew anybody who lived there. Its economy is bustling, but none of the friends or colleagues we queried knew anybody who worked there. Depending on with whom we spoke, Old Delhi either provides the city's economic lifeblood with its wholesale markets, or it's a completely self-contained entity. It's where all roads converge, or it's where no one goes. A few of our Indian friends enjoyed exploring it as much as we did, but many of the people we talked to viewed Old Delhi as the opposite of the India they celebrate. They look with pride on skyscrapers and shopping malls and streets wide enough to actually accommodate cars; Old Delhi, to them, couldn't be torn down fast enough. For the majority of Delhiites, daily life takes place on the periphery, in the sprawl, beyond the Ring Roads. Daily life in Delhi moves around the physical center, and almost never passes through it. The majority of Delhiites live outside the center and are content to ignore what goes on inside.

Like most tourists, Jenny and I never went anywhere those first weeks without a bottle of sunblock in one hand and a copy of the *Lonely Planet* travel guide in the other. And on our first joint trip to the Old City, we followed the book around the area's major sights. We admired the Red Fort, we bought scarves on Chandni Chowk, we climbed the minaret at the Jama Masjid, we ate at Karim's. And then we put the book in my backpack, slathered additional sunblock on our necks, and plunged blindly into the nearest alley until, finally, our eyes glazed from sensory overload, hungry but not yet brave enough to try street food. Wondering why we were the only ones who were sweating, we retrieved the *Lonely Planet* and sought its advice on the nearest air-conditioned restaurant. And that took us to Connaught Place, a half-mile southwest of Old Delhi and a century forward in time.

The very first thing we did in CP was get lost. Which is what we also did on every subsequent visit. CP (as everyone calls Connaught Place) is a set of three concentric streets and radial spokes set around a central plaza. Opened in 1933 by the British rulers as their central business area, it's promoted today as Delhi's top destination for shopping and entertainment. But CP's unvarying two-story colonial buildings, with brightly lit lower floors and dusty windows above street level, offered few landmarks to provide bearings. Each whitewashed block had supposedly been assigned a letter to aid navigation, but none actually displayed their designations anywhere we could see. Some streets were two-way, some were one-way, and some were blocked to traffic and used as parking lots. The sidewalk vendors who sold sprouted lentils, patchwork handicrafts, softcover books, and posters of smiling babies and snarling American wrestlers all added to the confusion, because the same goods were peddled on every block of the inner circle, making it seem like we were passing the same spot over and over again.

The feeling of wandering the Hundred Acre Woods was exacerbated when we started paying attention to the retail outlets: Connaught Place was an infinite loop of Van Heusen stores.

But on subsequent visits, when we looked closer, we saw treasures. Independent antiquity still survived behind the brand names. There were restaurants with both the décor and uniformed waiters of colonial times, ancient tailors and dusty keymakers sitting in alcoves surrounded by antique tools, hand-painted signs that made the area a study in 1950s typography, and two branches of Saravana Bhavan, the most delicious south Indian restaurant in the city.

There were also the elements that support CP's reputation as a shopping-and-retail destination: clubs, restaurants, a nice central park, and a creepy underground capitalistic free-for-all called Palika Bazaar, in which all laws protecting copyright and restraining pornography were apparently suspended. CP was also the closest thing Delhi had to a downtown business district: the city had seeded one of its radial spokes with a small collection of fifteen- or twenty-story buildings that ranged architecturally from striking to shocking. But, just like many of the corporate campuses we visited in the Delhi region, the buildings weren't built with pedestrians in mind. Fences, walls and gates flourished, the buildings were set back far from the street and the ground levels lacked retail—all of which discouraged casual strolling, making the area feel deserted even in the middle of the day.

Soon after we'd arrived in Delhi, we'd hung a map of the city in our living room. ("Why do all foreigners have maps of Delhi hanging in their living rooms?" my boss Murali laughed when he first saw it.) We'd scrutinize our map on weekend mornings to decide which part of the city we'd visit next. "Model Town sounds idyllic." "Friends Colony sounds welcoming." "Let's try a tropical theme: Bali Nagar, and then Sunlight Colony." But in those first few weeks, our gazes returned again and again to the Yamuna River, a big blue north–south swatch cutting through the gray of the map near Old Delhi, Connaught Place and attractions like the Red Fort.

We'd read that the Yamuna was one of Hinduism's holiest rivers. So we imagined a waterfront boardwalk developed equally for leisure and for spiritual matters, with sidewalk cafés overlooking ancient ghats still in constant use, and Segways for rent by the hour. The *Lonely Planet* may not have mentioned it, but cities like London, Paris and New York are defined by and built around their great rivers; why wouldn't Delhi be the same? We noted the proximity to the Yamuna of the great green splotch on our map labeled "Raj Ghat." That green splotch extended all the way to the blue stripe, so we figured that Raj Ghat must be a large park with a splendid view of the river. So that's where we went.

And while Raj Ghat is a lovely park (it was built around the spot where Gandhi was cremated), it was entirely unconnected with the river so nearby. We wandered the paths and read the signs, knowing that a "ghat" is a series of steps leading to water, like the ones that line the Ganges in Varanasi; surely there were ghats around here somewhere, with old ladies selling orange garlands and flickering candles floating peacefully down the river at sunset.

But we never found it. Every path that seemed promising dead-ended in impenetrable woods. Google Maps later showed us that Raj Ghat was a half-mile from the water. Maybe it used to abut the water at one time, before the

Yamuna's cyclical flooding changed its course. If we'd pushed through those woods bordering the park, we would have stumbled onto farm fields—yes, farm fields, there in the middle of the city.

The Yamuna's fertile floodplain is lined with acres and acres of farmland, even as the river passes through the heart of the city sixteen million people call home. (Or perhaps many more—in his book *Delhi: Adventures in a Megacity*, Sam Miller argues that some definitions of the city's limits put the population at over twenty million, which would make Delhi the world's most populous city.) In most global cities, the banks of the city's biggest rivers are the domain of either industry or leisure, but in Delhi, this coveted real estate is reserved for farmers. And the fact that farms buffer the Yamuna for almost its entire journey through Delhi (although the area directly north and east of Raj Ghat was once a massive slum, until its 150,000 homes were razed in 2004[1]) suggests that farmers are so politically powerful as to have forced the city to grow around them.

Aside from when we crossed the bridges on the road to Uttar Pradesh, the only time we actually saw the Yamuna was during our visit to Majnu Ka Tila, the "Little Tibet" neighborhood a few miles north of the Red Fort. Wandering the lanes, Jenny and I caught a glimpse of water through an alley. We eagerly rushed forward, expecting to finally find our boardwalk, anticipating a nice little hiking trail down to the water, assuming that, at the least, there would be a

---

1. http://theviewfromchennai.wordpress.com/2009/10/28/
   images-of-eviction-delhis-yamuna-pushta-in-the-news-again/

riverfront café where we could grab a cold beer. But where the alley broke through the buildings, we stopped short. There were a few rickety stepping stones, there were some farmers, there were some cattle, there was some brownish water in the distance past the fields, and there was the faint smell of the river detectable even this far away. There was nothing any tourist would want to see.

The farmers stared at us. We glumly returned to the market and bought a bootlegged Guns N' Roses CD.

Unlike Cairo or Singapore or Mumbai or New York, where water is a central part of each city's identity, Delhi's river is walled off and forgotten by everyone except those who farm it, the municipal and private entities who dump their waste into it, and anyone who stops to think about where their sewage goes and where their drinking water comes from. (Delhi uses 210 million gallons of relatively clean water[2] from upstream points on the Yamuna for drinking purposes every day.[3] It has to use upstream water because, while the Delhi region is just one percent of the river's total catchment area, the city contributes more than fifty percent of the river's pollutants.[4])

So for all purposes of cultural life and urban design, Delhi is a riverless city, with the Yamuna out of sight and out of mind. Perhaps that's because the politicians who could do

---

2. http://www.unhabitat.org/content.asp?typeid=19&catid=460&id=2170

3. http://www.rainwaterharvesting.org/index_files/about_delhi.htm

4. http://www.unhabitat.org/content.asp?typeid=19&catid=460&id=2170

something to improve the Yamuna's state are too busy sipping gimlets in Lutyens's Delhi.

Lutyens' Delhi is the "New" Delhi that the British built to underscore their conviction that imperial ideals could introduce civility and decorum even to a city as barbaric as they viewed nineteenth-century Delhi to be. Their uninvited benevolence manifested in the razing and remaking of ten square miles[5] of villages, farms and parts of the Old City in the Empire's image of itself: mathematical boulevards on a monumental scale, whitewashed bungalows for proper gentlefolk, monolithic and imposing government buildings, and the uncanny utilization of street design as a tool for maintaining power.

Edward Lutyens, a famous English architect, began designing this New Delhi in 1912. Almost a century later, the area still sings his opera of bureaucracy, his tribute to deaf government expressed in the voice of urban planning. A mile south of Connaught Place, Lutyens's Delhi is impersonal, maddening and exhausting. The wide, featureless streets break off in geometrically precise directions from indistinguishable roundabouts, keeping traffic both busily moving forward and not quite sure which direction forward is. There is almost nothing to see between the roundabouts except for trees and walls; the streetscape almost entirely lacks buildings, houses, shops, vendors, or anything else to break up the monotony, and the trees and walls themselves

---

5. Melvin E. Page (editor), *Colonialism: An International Social, Cultural and Political Encyclopedia*, ABC-Clio, p.415; viewed on Google Books.

are only there to hide whatever is going on behind them—
as are the guards whose mustaches and guns make it clear
that we shouldn't try to find out. The greenery is admittedly
beautiful, but even the trees seem placed to deliberately
avoid providing shade for anyone walking on the sidewalk.

Lutyens' Delhi may be among the most unwalkable
urban landscapes in the world. That's because pedestrians
in the area are confronted with endless, featureless boulevards
that only reinforce how hot it is and how far there is to go
until the next featureless intersection. The design of New
Delhi is calculated to deter and depress anyone not being
driven by a chauffeur already trained to know the way. For
a pedestrian, these streets are without comfort, without
amenity and without end.

And these streets seem to articulate a certain philosophy
of power: that the seat of government is not meant to be
accessible to the people. New Delhi was designed for
empire, but its present democratic occupants don't seem
terribly troubled about being so inaccessible. Today, this
area is where the national government does its business,
and where the powerful enjoy fresh air and quiet streets as
they exchange handshakes and imported whisky and suitcases
full of money. Stringent laws protect the area from new
construction, ensuring that those inside its walls can indefinitely
relax among manicured lawns and cooling breezes.

Delhi crams sixteen million people into a cityscape built
to house and support far fewer. Regulations on building
height have forced the city to retain its low-rise profile
when it so desperately needs to grow upward. But those
who have the legislative power to relieve the pressures of

population density are spared its indignities, spending their time in the one area of the city that actually has elbowroom. Preservationists are right that there is historical value to this area, but wasting this huge and vastly underutilized belt of land on political vanity is a crime. It's beautiful to look at and nice to drive through, but those pleasures don't justify sustaining this lifeless void, this corrupting vacuum. Old Delhi is called the Walled City, but Old Delhi is far more open and welcoming than the Delhi that Lutyens built.

*

We had very little business inside Lutyens' Delhi, but we traveled fairly frequently to Chanakyapuri, just to its west. Chanakyapuri is not technically attributable to Lutyens, but it is almost identical in its spirit of exclusion. It boasts more embassies and swanky hotels than we could visit in a week of lounge-hopping and ambassador-fêting. Dinner in this neighborhood costs more than the guy who drives us there earns in a month. At the entrance to each hotel, a huge valet in full Rajasthani costume—complete with champion mustache—waits for the guard at the gate to dutifully certify that our taxi's undercarriage is free of bombs so he can open the car door for us. To make it past this bouncer, an Indian has to have the clothes, the car and the mannerisms to certify a certain level of status; for foreigners, as our autorickshaw drops us off in dusty sandals and sweaty T-shirts, all we have to do is be white.

Jenny and I periodically patronized these bastions of exclusivity, we admit. The income we earned in Delhi—

which would have made us barely middle class in New York—put us in the highest tiers of Indian society, and we have a weakness for wine that isn't stored in the hot recesses of a state-run liquor store that caters primarily to on-duty autorickshaw drivers. Still, it wasn't entirely possible to enjoy our $50 Japanese yakitori on the same day we'd pay Shilpa, our bungalow's sweeper, $6 for her full month of work.

We learned the importance of going into both Lutyens's Delhi or Chanakyapuri with a pre-planned exit strategy. On the Sunday night that our friend Penny invited us for drinks at the Canadian embassy, we'd stumble back onto Indian soil to the starkest reminder that everyone in this area could afford their own car: no empty autorickshaws were cruising around looking for fares. So silent were those nighttime streets that we heard an autorickshaw approaching from a half-mile away, a little lawnmower engine slowly puttering up the vast expanse of road. Our hopes rose, visions of our pillows tickled our sleepy minds, but then the dark shape in the back seat told us that this autorickshaw was occupied, and that we were best off walking to India Gate to find a lift.

Ah, India Gate! The one location in Lutyens's Delhi that defied Lutyens' best intentions.

India Gate is located towards the eastern end of Rajpath, the vast avenue that is the centerpiece of Lutyens' Delhi. Rajpath originates at Raisina Hill, where the presidential palace, the secretariat building and the parliament all look down upon the masses trudging the long avenues before them. Rajpath is the perfect setting for Delhi's yearly

Republic Day parades, providing a glorious runway to showcase marching men and machines and missiles. On any day not dedicated to the magnificence of the country, Rajpath is, by design, best appreciated from the interior of a horse-drawn carriage, and then only if you have at least two menservants fanning you to keep you cool.

But India Gate didn't turn out as Lutyens intended, because there are few places in the city where everyday people feel more welcome. An Arc de Triomphe-style monument designed to commemorate those who died in service of the British Indian Army, this contribution to the Empire's eternal grandeur has been appropriated by men, women and children as a place to gather when the sun goes down.

It's an inspiring sight. And it's a side of India whose existence the Western media hadn't prepared us to expect. From all the news reports and documentaries we'd seen about India, we were anticipating only extremes: pious thousands bathing at sunrise at the Varanasi ghats; dazzling rainbows of saris drying in the wind; heart-wrenching poverty, blindingly modern malls, catastrophically overcrowded trains. All these images of India are cliché in the West. But what we never expected—because our media had never suggested it existed—were the simple, everyday pleasures of an evening at India Gate: ice cream vendors, laughing kids, strolling newlyweds, teenage boys pretending not to notice teenage girls, aunties glaring at teenage boys, happy parents, kite flyers, toy peddlers, snack sellers, and every other complement to the Indian nuclear family.

It's hard to overstate how unprepared we were for this sight. The Western media perpetuates images of poor

Indians, praying Indians and eagerly globalizing Indians. And because we can't easily empathize with any of those images (the poverty is beyond our experience, the devotion is entirely unlike our churches and synagogues, and the spread of American-style consumerism just makes us uncomfortable), our media had primed us to anticipate the alien and the exotic. And that was the opposite of the scene at India Gate. We never expected to find something so familiar in India.

★

As wonderful and magical as India Gate is, however—not just for the experience but also for its symbolic rejection of Lutyens—it wasn't what we came to India to find. We wanted the India we'd been conditioned to expect: vibrant people doing fantastic things as their everyday routine. So let's travel southward, where we'll immediately get stuck in traffic. Because now we're in south Delhi.

South Delhi's roughly 250 square kilometers are broadly defined by National Highway 8 on the west and the Yamuna on the east. It's an arc of Indian suburbia: privately built bungalows, public housing developments, schools, slums, hospitals, parks, markets, malls, and endless traffic that was exacerbated by (and is now marginally alleviated by) the construction of the southern extensions of Delhi's Metro system. South Delhi's geographic center falls generally in the neighborhood of Hauz Khas market, which is by coincidence exactly where we lived.

Hauz Khas market should not be confused with Hauz Khas village, the arts-and-boutiques district in the middle of the park two miles to the west. Nor should it be confused with Hauz Khas Enclave, the posh landscape of massive houses and manicured gardens to the south. Our Hauz Khas was a residential neighborhood of three- and four-story concrete bungalows, lively street life, and a utilitarian central market in which mom-and-pop stores still outnumbered the modern restaurants and branded appliance retailers that were starting to replace them in so many other markets. The four main shopping streets of Hauz Khas market bordered a central park in which men napped, teens played cricket, and mothers let their kids loose on the sparse playground.

To the east were trendier enclaves like Greater Kailash-I and Greater Kailash-II, where we could eat at restaurants with names like "Diva" and "Nûdeli." To the south were neighborhoods like Malviya Nagar and Saket, where many of our twenty-something co-workers lived. And to the west were wealthier areas like Vasant Vihar and Shanti Niketan, with broad streets, houses like castles, Ferraris parked behind iron gates, and private security guards staring sleepily. Hauz Khas was the ideal neighborhood for us: it was just off the road that led straight to Gurgaon, the satellite city in which I worked, and it was central enough to give us easy access to all points of the city. Although in south Delhi, 'easy access' is a relative term.

There are six or seven major north–south boulevards and about half as many east–west ones that divide south Delhi into distinct segments. And as in Lutyens's Delhi, these boulevards are designed only for driving. Not shopping, not walking, just driving. This single-minded purpose means that most things related to the living of life—residential, retail, recreation, religion—are pushed to the center of these street-bound segments. The focus of each boulevard-bound segment is not outward towards the city, but inward into itself.

The difficulties of traveling between segments reinforce their separation. There are few bridges across the main boulevards, so crossing from one segment to the other requires driving up a traffic-heavy street, making a U-turn, and driving back down to enter the new segment directly across from where we exited the first segment ten minutes earlier. For example, our flat in Hauz Khas market was located just east of Aurobindo Marg. On the opposite side of that busy boulevard was a neighborhood called Green Park, which would have been a three-minute walk away if the traffic on Aurobindo Marg didn't make walking so terrifying. Because we rarely dared to dash across that dangerous street, and because the same journey by autorickshaw would have included a frustrating gauntlet of red lights and U-turns, we hardly ever went to Green Park.

This division by boulevards influences the character of south Delhi's residents. How could it not? Each segment of south Delhi feels distinct in the mathematical sense of the word, like it's completely cut off from the rest of the city. The isolating effects of the street grid are multiplied by south Delhi's neighborhood structure: rings of housing radiate concentrically inward towards central markets, focusing neighborhood life squarely towards the center.

Residents are both figuratively and physically forced to turn their backs towards everything outside. It's introversion by municipal design.

Our preference for a particular style of urban planning is wholly subjective, colored by our years being invigorated by the bustling streets of New York. The main boulevards there are lined by shops, and short residential streets fill in the gaps and make it easy to pass from shopping district to shopping district. New York's neighborhoods align outwards, the borders between them don't deter people from crossing over, and there's a general sense of connection with the city beyond. While we understand that some people find New York's streetscape intimidating or overwhelming, our preference is for pedestrian-scale street life that draws people out of their neighborhoods and into the common spaces. So we can't help but see south Delhi as isolated islands separated by seas of traffic.

★

But municipal psychology didn't stop us. We may not have visited every single one of south Delhi's markets, but we tried. Upscale and downmarket, utilitarian and specialized, modern and archaic, expat and local: we explored enough to learn where to go for Indian food, for Western food, for iced coffee and ham sandwiches, for clothes, for new books, for used books, for people-watching, for bars, for galleries, for movies, for meeting expats, for meeting locals, for buying computer parts. Each market was good for some things, but each market lacked other things, which meant there was no single market we could point to friends visiting for a weekend before their tour of greater India and say, "*That* is where you should go."

Many of south Delhi's markets were built around central parks. The government says the city has 18,000 parks[6] in total, and the ones we visited were testament to how quickly a few trees can cleanse and cool the air. Often walled off to keep out pushcart vendors and hungry cows, they provide grass and shade under which dogs and men can snooze the heat away. Open spaces are commandeered by boys playing cricket. If there's a bench that's even slightly obscured from sight, there's a pair of courting teenagers sitting as close as they dare, whispering secrets away from the prying eyes of the neighborhood grapevine. Men in tracksuits walk the ring path, their dogs being walked a few steps behind them, passing old aunties with sweatshirts over their saris and tennis shoes under them. The few boys who aren't playing cricket are sneaking cigarettes and spying on the lovers. In the bigger parks a policeman may stride casually, his belly preceding him along the paths, enjoying the weight and importance of his bamboo beating stick, ready to smack a mangy dog or drive a beggar back into the streets. Orchid bushes line the paths. Paan masala wrappers flutter in the trees.

The parks were always green. This is another mystery of the city: though Delhi would go months without rain, its flowers never wilted, its trees always provided shade, and its

---

6. http://www.hindu.com/thehindu/holnus/004200906141251.htm

frangipani blossoms smelled eternally glorious. Be it dead of winter or pre-monsoon summer, the city's foliage has adapted just like the people who live here: it flourishes without complaint no matter what the climate throws at it.

Many parks act as buffer zones around Delhi's monuments. These ancient stone tombs or half-millennium-old mosques are everywhere in south Delhi, sometimes protected and landscaped and other times overgrown and squatted in. The stone mosque we passed on our way to the market every day was centuries old and still attracting hundreds of young men for Friday prayers. Just beyond our house on Aurobindo Marg was an ancient village wall that had been repurposed to enclose what looked like some sort of garrison. And when I'd go running in nearby Gulmohar Park, I'd pass a vine-covered ruin that was still recognizable as a bygone stone marvel. (A visiting friend of ours claimed to have been led into its recesses by an amorous local for a brief and unsatisfying tryst.)

South Delhi's heritage included everything from anonymous monuments to Qutub Minar, India's tallest stone tower. The area had urban oases like Deer Park and the Garden of Five Senses, and ancient wonders like Humayun's Tomb—which rivaled, or perhaps even surpassed, the Taj Mahal. Within walking distance of our flat was Siri Fort, a massive ruined citadel now containing a modern sports complex in which one can exercise, play cricket on a proper pitch, shoot an air pistol, and enjoy a milkshake at the on-site coffee shop. One can also attend weddings in the shadow of the Asiad Tower, perhaps the strangest sight on the Delhi skyline: a giant concrete lollipop, built for the 1982 Asian Games, that was once the tallest building in Delhi.

South Delhi is a ghost town after 11 p.m. Streets that had been choked with cars all day are suddenly silent and still, except for when they're raced upon by drunk rich kids in their dads' shiny cars. As midnight approaches, iron gates slam shut across south Delhi to block off local streets from anyone who doesn't live in the neighborhood. Some of the gates are manned and will be opened for innocent-looking travelers who want to pass by, but others are simply locked without attendant, forcing anyone trying to enter or escape the neighborhood to drive around until an unblocked street can be found. The *Lonely Planet* told us that Indians, like Italians and Spaniards, prefer to dine late, but most restaurants seemed empty by ten. The few pockets of nighttime activity—the food stalls at Nizamuddin Railway Station, the parking lots outside the nightclubs, the checkpoints and their dozing cops—are shrouded by nightly fog that dampens the sound and energy of any activity that might try to break the unwritten curfew.

Driving down the hazy late-night roads, ghostly shapes emerge. Bicycle rickshaws parked on the side of the street, their drivers' bare feet sticking out to catch cooling breezes. Ice cream carts assembled in rows, each one with a vendor sleeping on top of it. There is nothing more sobering than passing AIIMS Hospital after midnight, where men and women too poor to sleep anywhere else line the sidewalk while they worry about loved ones inside. My heart was indelibly broken one very late night when we drove past an old man sitting on the ground outside the hospital, staring worriedly in the distance, his frail wife's head laid weakly in his lap. From then on, I always passed AIIMS looking straight ahead and counting my blessings.

★

One reason south Delhi doesn't stay up very late could be because everyone wants to wake up early to beat the traffic.

Jenny's daily commute didn't take her out of south Delhi. She hired an autorickshaw every morning to drive her either to the Saket area (for her first job) or to Lajpat Nagar IV (for her second). She grew intimate with the traffic patterns of these areas, the timing of their red lights, their lyrical street names (Lala Lajpat Rai Path!), and the eternal nightmare that Josip Broz Tito Marg became when the city eliminated half its drivable lanes as a prototype for its Bus Rapid Transit program. Jenny learned the posture necessary to maximize comfort in an autorickshaw: slumping against the seat but always poised to grab a handhold when the driver swerves to miss a vegetable cart by six inches. There were many routes to her office, and each autorickshaw driver had his own shortcut; the various bone-jarring side streets they chose offered a roller-coaster ride that followed a new and more thrilling route every time.

As for me, I took the same road to work every day. The same unvarying route, with the same unvarying traffic, upon which the difference between leaving at 8:15 in the morning and 8:45 was an extra forty minutes stuck listening to cars honk at each other. I had the benefit of closed windows and air conditioning for my commute, but I had the misfortune of commuting to Gurgaon.

Considered part of the greater Delhi region, (even though it's across the state border in Haryana), Gurgaon is an hour southwest of the city on a lucky day but only twenty minutes after midnight. It's where 1.5 million people live[7] and 200 of the Fortune 500 companies have offices.[8] It's called the "Millennium City" by its boosters, and it's promoted as the future of India: a city of gleaming skyscrapers teeming with India's brightest contributors to global capitalism, apartment towers like fists raised triumphantly towards the gods, and shopping malls as far as the eyes can see. And while the city's real estate agents boast about those modern marvels, what they fail to mention is that these heavenly structures are all linked to the humble earth by a dysfunctional infrastructure.

Dysfunctional, that is, where it exists at all.

Gurgaon is notorious for its lack of everything. Insufficient sewers mean flooding houses[9] and wastewater lakes.[10] Its absent solid-waste infrastructure forced the city to dump trash in vacant lots and parkland, creating a situation so bad

---

7. http://articles.timesofindia.indiatimes.com/2011-04-06/gurgaon/29387845_1_literacy-rate-female-population-census-officials

8. http://www.bpowatchindia.com/bpo_news/gurgaon_clean/september-26-2008/gurgaon_ceos_cleanliness.html

9. http://www.expressindia.com/latest-news/sewage-floods-gurgaon-colony/256983/

10. http://www.gurgaonscoop.com/story/2008/12/25/3426/6489

that thirty-five prominent residents had to gather the news media, charter a bus, and drive everybody up to the state capital in Chandigarh to get authorities to pay attention to them.[11] Its abysmal power supply has meant eight- to twelve-hour power cuts[12] and forced any company that seeks productivity to rely on exhaust-spewing generators. (The one outside my forty-person office was the size of a shipping container.) All this is said to be due to the fact that the bureaucrats in Chandigarh are happy to rake in the city's tax revenue but loath to invest it to alleviate the inconveniences of residents who, as these bureaucrats see it on television, live in twenty-first-century castles in the sky.

Jenny and I originally expected to live in Gurgaon. My company had leased and hastily furnished an apartment in anticipation of a stream of long-term expat workers. (I was supposed to be the first, but I ended up being the only.) Our building, Hamilton Court, was Gurgaon's tallest structure at the time: an eighty-nine-meter, twenty-five-story concrete monolith that so perfectly represented the typical Gurgaon apartment block that the *New York Times* actually referenced it as an archetype. ("India has always had its upper classes, as well as legions of the world's very poor," the *Times* wrote in 2008. "But today a landscape dotted with Hamilton Courts, pressed up against the slums that serve them, has underscored more than ever the stark

---

11. http://www.hindustantimes.com/special-news-report/india-news/C-mon-Gurgaon/Article1-341670.aspx

12. http://www.thaindian.com/newsportal/business/power-cuts-turn-posh-gurgaon-areas-into-urban-chaupals_10060033.html

gulf between those worlds, raising uncomfortable questions for a democratically elected government about whether India can enable all its citizens to scale the golden ladders of the new economy.[13]")

Though it only took one full day in Gurgaon to decide we didn't want to live there (the night of the smell scare, and the next day when we realized that it was impossible to go anywhere without calling a taxi and waiting a half-hour for it to come), it took us five more nights to find a flat in Delhi to which we could escape. It was more than enough time to understand that Gurgaon was not what we were seeking for our life in India. Gurgaon was a cloud of construction dust punctuated by dust-covered construction sites. Private developers had operated here in a total governmental vacuum, lacking both regulatory oversight to check growth and municipal infrastructure to support it. My office was originally located in one of a dozen skyscrapers clustered around the corporate hub called DLF Cyber City, each one at least ten stories tall, employing tens of thousands of people in total, with more buildings under furious construction. All these buildings and employees were serviced by a single four-lane road that, while I worked there, functioned as a parking lot for eight hours a day. When I first arrived in Gurgaon, Cyber City's landscaping was being torn up to build overhead power lines that were necessary because they either hadn't built underground cables, or because they'd built them with no thought for the capacity a dozen high-rise buildings would need.

---

13. http://www.nytimes.com/2008/06/09/world/asia/09gated. html

A year and a half later, as I was leaving India, the ground there was being torn up again, this time to accommodate monstrous sewer pipes to collect the massive amounts of waste these buildings were somehow not anticipated to generate.

Gurgaon is one of India's most prominent technology hubs. It's home to countless multinational companies trying to get a foothold in India's rapidly growing market. It's also home to many of the upwardly mobile men and women who are riding India's wave of growth, which is why its main boulevards are lined with malls boasting all the brands we would see in Times Square, and even the drop-off area at my office building was designed around the convenience of the glitterati thronging to the trendy restaurants built into the ground level. At nine o'clock on a Friday night, I'd wait in the drop-off area for my driver to negotiate the sea of chauffeured imported cars dropping off short-skirted socialites and the biceps-of-the-month they'd be clinging to. As numerous as its malls are its towering luxury apartment blocks, and their aspirational names—Windsor Court, Regency Park, Silver Oaks, Oakwood Estates, Royalton Towers—hint at the philosophy behind Gurgaon's development: Gurgaon is what a few private developers think a Western city is supposed to look like.

But while they've focused on the monolithic aspects of modernity, they've neglected the human-scale parts of it. Forget walking. Gurgaon is a city designed for valet parking.

My view of Gurgaon is probably unfairly influenced by what I endured there: a job that stressed me, an office environment of exhaust fumes and uncomfortable chairs, and a commute that sapped my will to live. When I reflect on Gurgaon, I remember the dead crow I passed on my ride to work every day, hanging by one foot from a power cable above the repair shops just east of DLF Cyber City, its wings spread wide as an upside-down avian Christ. I don't know how it got stuck to the cable, but it hung there for months—outlasting the fall heat, the winter chill, and the dust storms that would shred the giant billboards across the street.

But I know that a lot of people love Gurgaon. So I'll contrast that crow with what I usually saw next on my commute. As my taxi would pass to the swampy area beyond the crow, a glorious blue kingfisher would flutter across the road or perch on a telephone wire: a reminder that beauty, too, is in Gurgaon. For many people, Gurgaon is the soul of a newer New Delhi: it's where the rich and the successful live, where business leaders ink deals far removed from the politicians' sticky fingers, where artists entertain in living room salons, and where music blasts until early in the morning. For those who like to see and be seen, and who like to know they're on the forefront of India's future, Gurgaon is it.

But we didn't move all the way to India to live in the DLF Corporation's vision of America. While we also look forward to India's future, we came to experience India's past and its present. So every time we entered Gurgaon, our goal was simply to get out as quickly as possible. We never fully explored it. We didn't even know there was an Old Gurgaon until after we'd left India.

Which leaves north Delhi, east Delhi and west Delhi. Except we didn't explore those areas, either. The *Lonely*

Planet, *Time Out Delhi* magazine, and the various English newspapers all focused our attention almost entirely on the diamond-shaped swath of land between Old Delhi and Gurgaon. So for west Delhi, north Delhi, Rohini, Dwarka, Faridabad, Ghaziabad, Noida and Greater Noida, our experience only included a few meetings and dinners, and it progressed no further than marveling how big north Delhi was as we drove through it on our way to the hills.

So many sights we didn't see! So many monuments we didn't visit! So many neighborhoods we never walked!

Still, we did spend eighteen months reading and wandering and asking everyone we met for their must-see suggestions. And while we saw so little of the city by geographic standards, I think it's unlikely that our overall impression would have changed if only we'd visited Baba Nagar or Vishnu Garden or Ashok Vihar Phase III.

And our overall impression is this: Delhi is a city without an overarching narrative. It is an amalgamation of neighborhoods that are linked by municipal decree but without a shared sense of destiny.

Delhi has no unifying story. Delhi is a blank slate.

Which isn't a bad thing. That means that Delhi is whatever you make of it. Every person defines Delhi for his or her self, and no two Delhi struggles are the same. At any given point, your experience will be the exact opposite of my experience, and we'll both be right.

Delhi exists in a kind of quantum state: in Delhi, all things are true at once.

3

Transportation: How to Get Stuck in Traffic

A lucky expat has no need to read this chapter, because he has no hassles getting around Delhi: his car and his driver, both provided by his company, are at his disposal from the moment he wakes. In fact, his driver may already be in his kitchen as he steps out of the shower, buttering his toast and cutting his mango and arranging his newspaper just so.

Ah, the life of a lucky expat! There's his driver now, wearing either a blue driver's uniform or a snappy pink polo shirt depending on how long he's been driving expats and how well he's been paid for it. The driver knows his job consists of just two main duties: to drive his boss around and then, from the morning meeting to the whisky nightcap, to wait with the car (with the air conditioner off so as not to waste gas) until the boss is ready to be driven around some more.

An expat can determine how much his company values him by the make of the car and the English proficiency of the driver they provide. If good ol' Dharmender expertly narrates the sights as the expat glides silently past Qutub Minar in his Honda City, the firm is obviously expecting the lucky expat to inject life into the quarterly numbers. But if surly Ajit jerks his Tata Indica to the roadside to spit paan juice and ask the fifty-paise paniwallah the way to Gurgaon, the less lucky expat should begin to wonder if his boss shipped him to India only because firing him would have taken too much paperwork. At red lights in his Honda City, the lucky expat's worth as a corporate cog is validated by the buffer other drivers give his vehicle for fear of scratching it. (No one takes risks around cars that could conceivably contain politicians, the most feared of all Delhi's threats to life and limb.) Meanwhile, in his Tata Indica, with motorcyclists knocking his side mirror as they jockey for position, the less lucky expat will wonder if the smell of gasoline that fills the air when the car isn't moving is the more insidious part of his ex-boss's master plan.

I had neither a shining City nor a rusty Indica, for I was a luckless expat. My company provided me with no transportation at all, a fact that surely says *something* about my value to the company, although I dare not dwell on what. (I can't complain too much, though—at least I had a lucky expat's salary to feel guilty about when my co-workers would buy me a round of chai.) While Jenny and I didn't own a car in New York either, that city's comprehensive public transportation meant we didn't need it. But during our time in Delhi, the Metro was still under construction south of Raisina Hill and the buses were crowded, slow, and not at all tourist-friendly. We would have loved to have bicycled in Delhi (we were avid bicyclists in New York, and Delhi's flat streets and unpaved gullies hold the promise of a great bicycling city once bike paths are built, sewage is rerouted, and traffic is calmed), but bicycling seemed suicidal even before taking into account the traffic fumes.

So with no car, no motorcycle, no Metro, no buses and no bicycles, Jenny and I relied mostly on two forms of personal transportation: taxicabs and autorickshaws.

An autorickshaw (which Delhiites call an "auto"; every time we told a story involving a "rickshaw," our Delhi friends assumed we were talking about the bicycle variety) is a ubiquitous, utilitarian three-wheeled open-air vehicle, with a green metal body, yellow canvas roof, and just enough horsepower to chug up a Delhi flyover without requiring the driver to get out and push. They're the cheapest and most convenient way to get around, assuming the definition of "convenient" does not extend to air conditioning or shock absorbers or windows to roll up in the face of bus fumes. All the autos in Delhi are identical, which means either they all come from the same manufacturer or, if there is indeed competition in the industry, all the factories making them are working off the same blueprint. Variation comes only in accruements added by aesthetically minded drivers: Shah Rukh Khan and Kareena Kapoor looking sultry in heart-shaped stickers on either side of the rear-view mirror, or life-sized cut-outs of midriff-baring Bollywood heroines tucked behind the clear vinyl covering the inside panels. More than once I've been scared silly by the sudden appearance of a face when I turned my head: a starlet I didn't initially notice purses her lips back at me, positioned there to keep the driver company when he sleeps, as drivers often do, stretched out on the back seat, his bare feet sticking out the window as he snores in preparation for the morning rush.

About 50,000 autos ply the streets of Delhi, driven in shifts by an estimated 100,000 drivers,[1] most of whom can be recognized by their matching button-down shirts and pants that vary in hue from dull blue to dull gray. Beware those drivers wearing clothes that deviate too much towards middle-class fashion: khaki pants, a button-down shirt and a garishly patterned sweater on a driver revving his auto outside a tourist attraction imply a ride in which he'll speak perfect English, gain our sympathies by describing his daughter's college fees, charge 150 rupees for a forty-rupee ride, and ignore our requests not to stop at his "uncle's" paper factory so he can get a commission if we buy their crafts.

According to Delhi lore and confirmed by a story from the BBC, all of Delhi's auto drivers are male, but one—a woman named Sunita Chaudhary.[2] Against literal 100,000-to-1 odds, Jenny actually rode with her once, agreeing to a rate twenty rupees higher than what any other driver would have charged to support Sunita's fight against patriarchy. Even though Sunita wore the same colorless

1. http://www.thaindian.com/newsportal/health/a-club-of-honourable-auto-rickshaw-drivers_100141685.html
2. http://news.bbc.co.uk/2/hi/south_asia/3541394.stm

uniform as her male counterparts, she revealed herself to be the most aggressive auto driver on the road. And so terrifying was Sunita's style even to a veteran auto passenger like Jenny that when, as improbable as it sounds, she actually chanced upon Sunita a second time, Jenny chose to give her nerves a break, toe the patriarchal line, and go with the male driver Sunita was literally elbowing out of the transaction.

The most important advice we could give to those traveling by auto was to ignore the *Lonely Planet*'s suggestion to patronize only those that use the meter. The official meter rate, fixed when we lived in Delhi at "4.5 rupees for every kilometer after the first,"[3] is less than half of what we would reasonably expect to pay. In fact, any driver who agreed to go by the meter was probably planning a route from GK-I to GK-II via the Taj Mahal.

Because opting for the meter was asking for trouble, every autorickshaw journey began for us with fare negotiations. It was easy to negotiate if we knew where we were, where we were going, and the market rate for getting there. But, for our first week of rides in Delhi, being ignorant as we were of the geography and everything else, the fairness of our fare was entirely up to the honor of our driver, and how adept we were at fooling him into thinking we knew what we were doing.

We realized eventually that no auto ride should ever cost us more than 100 rupees, provided we were sticking to

---

3. This changed in mid-2010 to Rs 19 for the first two kilometers and Rs 6.50 per kilimeter thereafter. See http://www.delhitraffic police.nic.in/auto-taxi-fare.htm

south or central Delhi. I was not armed with that knowledge on my second day in Delhi, when I put my fledgling bargaining skills to the test and negotiated a ride from Connaught Place back to GK-II for 180 rupees—well over twice what I should have paid—and basked in pride for having talked the guy down from the 200 he quoted. Of course, any auto driver who finds a tourist that ignorant of market rates is going to try to push him for all his worth. When we reached my destination, I handed the driver two bills and asked for change. The driver turned around in his seat and started begging me to let him keep the remainder. And I mean *begging*—pleading, moaning, eyes tearing, hands clasped in front of him as he invoked his gods and his children and his poverty and my wealth, all for that extra twenty rupees. But I set my jaw firm, and I saw the twenty rupees change he reluctantly placed in my palm as glowing validation that I was a clever traveler who knew how to drive a hard bargain.

So I can't blame him. The average auto driver is not a tourist-swindler by practice, but simply a pragmatic opportunist who seizes a chance when he spots it. After all, he typically earns barely 200 rupees per day once he's done paying rent for his vehicle[4] (few drivers own their vehicle; most rent them from exploitative financers in a situation that one charity likened to "bonded labor"[5]); so if he can

---

4. http://www.nyayabhoomi.org/auto_general/income_
    expense.htm
5. http://www.financialexpress.com/news/90-delhi-rickshaws-in-
    grip-of-automafias-ngo/430333/

find a rich foreigner who might add fifty percent to his daily take, he'd be foolish not to give it a shot.

Once we knew that we should never pay more than 100 rupees, the fare we'd negotiate for any trip depended simply on balancing the variables: the distance we wished to travel, the time of day (autos are entitled to apply a 'night charge' of twenty-five percent after 11 p.m., although most start claiming it around sundown), the availability of alternative autos (if we had no other options, we had no bargaining leverage), the proximity of our destination to other potential fares, the necessity to cross main roads and take U-turns, the number of people in our party, the sweatiness of our shirts (as a measure of our desperation for a ride), and the color of our skin (foreigners always pay more).

★

Negotiating with autos could often be a frustrating experience. In our worst times, it could be so enraging as to make us dread leaving the house. Negotiating can make tourists bitter and angry and distrustful of everyone they meet in the country. For some tourists we spoke to, the fact that they always had to negotiate—and always felt constant paranoia about being cheated—actually ruined their experience in India.

The way to avoid all that is to see fare negotiation for what it truly is: a pantomime. A game. A source of fun.

We predicated our philosophy of auto negotiation on the assumption that no self-respecting driver will pass up an opportunity to squeeze a few extra rupees out of a dumb foreigner. Our strategy, then, was simply to make it clear that we're not dumb foreigners. So we weren't negotiating to pay forty-nine rupees when he wanted fifty—our efforts were simply to prove that he couldn't fool us, so he might as well not even try.

Negotiating with autos is a game. And when we had fun playing it, we won.

Sometimes the game was played by shouting and waving our arms and gesturing angrily at the road as the driver shouted and waved and gestured right back. Sometimes it was played with polite propositions and sad smiles and weary refusals. Sometimes it was played by turning a crowd of drivers against each other, getting them to beat each other's best price. Sometimes it was played by taking one driver aside and quietly coming to agreement so he wouldn't lose face in front of his peers. Sometimes it was played with laughter and smiles and a good time all around. But at almost no time did we play it with genuine anger. Any antagonism showed by either party was usually feigned on both parts; the façade would drop the moment agreement was reached. A negotiation may have been fraught with frowns and scowls and groans and wild hand-waving, but with a single formal head bobble of acceptance, the veil of false emotion would be lifted and we'd all be happily on our mutual way.

This is one of the most striking aspects about traveling in India. During our year and a half, people regularly tried to overcharge us because that's how the game is played; but once we showed that we were too smart for them, the pantomime ended and the other party showed genuine interest in our presence and pleasure at our company. Compare that to our experience in Egypt, where taxi drivers and trinket vendors were pleasant to us only as far as our tourist dollars would take them. Resentment clearly bubbled under the surface of every transaction. One trinket vendor in Cairo's Khan el-Khalili market let his anger boil over as I negotiated with him for a brass reproduction of the Sphinx in the spring of 2004. "I hate George W. Bush!" he suddenly burst out as I counter-offered with half the price he quoted, just as the *Lonely Planet Egypt* suggested I should. "I hate the whole fucking American army!" I quickly put down the Sphinx and took my negotiating skills elsewhere.

Such antagonism was never displayed in India. The closest we came to feeling hated was when we took a picture of a bunch of men in a Pune neighborhood that turned out to be the city's red-light district: the steely gazes fixed upon us in that photo make it pretty clear that none of these guys wanted documentation of their presence in that location. Even then, though, no outward anger was actually displayed.

By the time we left India, we were skilled at bringing the negotiation ritual to fruition as quickly as possible. Once we established a driver was negotiating in good faith (if a driver quoted above 150 rupees, we'd laugh politely and walk to the next one), we'd propose a fare with the knowledge that most drivers find the pantomime satisfactorily fulfilled when they're able to raise our offer by ten or twenty rupees. So if we wanted to pay fifty, we'd suggest forty. He'd respond with sixty, and then we'd split the difference with a friendly "Theek hai?" and off we'd head into the exhaust clouds.

The game was easier to play once we understood a little Hindi, knew the market rates, and developed the courage to walk away even when no other autos were in the area. Walking away was, in fact, perhaps the strongest negotiation technique. In cases when our price was fair but our driver wasn't, turning and leaving usually accomplished what staying and arguing could not. The driver would call after us or drive up next to us with a gracious final offer that we'd humbly accept.

The game was also easier to play when we kept it in perspective. Sometimes there was no point of arguing over ten rupees with a man who may be wearing the only shirt he owns.

★

Our jovial approach to auto negotiation was not the only method. We spent a few days during our last week in Delhi living with our friends Tom and Michael, and our proximity gave us an opportunity to study Tom's system. His approach seemed based on an assumption exactly the opposite of ours: that every driver in the city was out to cheat him. Tom's strategy was to pre-empt the driver's inflated fare by refusing to negotiate, period. He would simply get in the auto and tell the driver where to go without discussing the price at all. And off they would go, with the driver fantasizing about how much he'd get paid by this gora who didn't seem concerned with money while Tom steeled himself against a confrontation when they arrived. As the driver would pull to the curb and imagine buying himself something indulgent, Tom would shove some money into his hand and begin to walk away. The driver would count the bills and feel his imagined fortune shatter around him.

An argument over the fare would almost inevitably ensue. But this one, unlike the arguments Jenny and I experienced, involved genuine antagonism. "No," declares Tom, arms crossing, voice dripping, eyes narrowing. "Forty rupees is the fare." The driver protests. Tom repeats himself, slower, as if speaking to a child: "No, forty rupees. Is. The. Fare." The argument continues and profanities fly in multiple languages until two angry people finally part ways.

In the instances we rode with Tom, the fares he paid were fair. They were exactly what Jenny and I would have negotiated to pay, and exactly what the driver would have happily accepted had he not spent the duration of the ride fantasizing about all the money he was about to earn. Though the driver hadn't necessarily been cheated, he felt like he had. The antagonism flowed. So did Tom's anger. Tom's expectation of fighting a swindler became a self-fulfilling prophecy, a vicious circle, a bumpy auto ride to hell.

Tom isn't a jerk. Far from it. And his strategy isn't born out of misanthropy. Rather, it springs from supply and demand and Tom's unforgiving misfortune of living on a street rarely taken. His neighborhood had a low supply of autos, which any auto driver passing through would exploit in negotiations to his full advantage, knowing that Tom wouldn't refuse his offer because he had no other choice.

Tom surely had dozens of trips in which he seethed over a fifty-rupee premium extorted by a canny driver; his strategy evolved out of unfortunate necessity.

Which isn't to say cheating doesn't happen. It does, and it's certainly happened to us. Some auto drivers stopped for gas on the way home and asked us to pay. Some auto drivers dropped us in Nizamuddin East and said it was Nizamuddin West. Some auto drivers drove us to their "uncle's" crafts factory instead of our destination. And some auto drivers demanded more money than we'd agreed upon, telling us they said "eighty" when we heard "thirty" and then refusing to accept the bills we held out for them. In these cases, we discovered that the best strategy was to throw the money with exaggerated rage on his seat or in his lap and then stomp away while cursing to the heavens. Then we'd dash around the corner and giggle about how well we'd just won the game.

(Very rarely, though, that rage wouldn't be completely feigned. Sometimes our frustration at being taken for a sucker got the best of us, and we'd shout things that made the whole street turn and stare.)

Aside from the rare instances when it was reprised at the end of the journey, the negotiation game ended and the pantomime ceased the moment the fare was agreed upon. But when the negotiations concluded, the terror began: our lives were now fully entrusted to a man who's sole goal was to deliver us to our destination with his two costs— time and fuel—minimized. While we wanted to arrive at our destination quickly as well, we also placed a certain premium on getting there alive.

This is where our incentives and those of the auto driver come into conflict.

The prevalence of autos on the road may explain the millions of gods in the Hindu pantheon. Because even we non-Hindus found ourselves invoking every deity we'd ever heard of and making up more on the spot as our auto drivers, relaxed in their seat with one bare foot casually hooked over their knee, leaned on their horns and steered into openings in traffic hidden from our vantage points by the looming headlights of oncoming buses. We imagined a god of seat belts who would wrap his divine arms around our waists to keep us ensconced in the vehicle as we careened around corners. We drew up elaborate plans for a shrine to the god who reached down from the sky to perform the split-second act of Tetris necessary to allow four lanes of traffic traveling four different directions to pass safely through the same intersection without regard for the traffic light. We swore to reject all worldly trappings, drape ourselves in orange robes, head up to the Himalayas, and spend the rest of our days meditating on the divine goodness of whichever deity ensured that the careening BMW full of rich kids who'd spent their evening drinking imported scotch and abusing waiters at Urban Pind missed us by a comfortable three inches. Thanks be to our newly invented gods who watched over us! We arrived at every destination with our pants mostly unsoiled, the driver oblivious to our terror and eager to get us on the sidewalk so he could terrify someone else in his quest for good gas mileage.

We were surprised to realize that of his two chief assets, the auto driver values his fuel more than his time. This observation seemed counter-intuitive until the third or fourth dozen time a driver deliberately chose a route through packed alleys, over dirt roads adjoining Metro construction, or down the eternally jammed Bus Rapid Transit corridor. There were certainly faster routes they could have taken in these instances—proceeding to the next boulevard beyond the BRT line, perhaps, or sticking to the main roads even if they were slightly longer—but the drivers always chose the gas-maximizing route, even at the cost of time they could have been using to drive another passenger.

While auto drivers have an uncanny ability to ferret out the bumpiest shortcut in any neighborhood—indeed, they seemed proud to apply their knowledge of the back streets—that doesn't mean they had an encyclopedic knowledge of the city. And while every driver assured us that he positively knew our destination, there were many times when they did not know how to get there at all.

But they always got us there anyway. That's because Delhiites have developed an amazing method for locating places they don't know how to find: they ask other people who *also* don't know how to find it.

Here's how it works. On any given stretch of road, one can always find a passer-by who knows his immediate area perfectly and whose knowledge of the geography beyond diminishes in direct proportion to distance. The omelettewallah standing outside Hauz Khas market, for instance, could give us an exact route to Hauz Khas A Block (just a hundred meters north) and a good nudge towards Hauz Khas B Block (on the other side of the market). He could give us a general route to Green Park, the neighborhood to the west, but he'd have no insight into finding Green Park E Block. For that, we'd just follow his gesture towards Green Park and then find someone who knew the immediate area over there to ask again.

And that's how a Delhi driver does it: he asks a succession of people with no knowledge of the destination until we're collectively guided right to it.

We first experienced this system on our second day in Gurgaon, when we hired a taxi to take us to a very specific location: Building 6 of the India Habitat Center, Lodhi Road, Delhi. Our driver, who had assured us on the phone that he knew exactly where to go, immediately pulled up to a passer-by just outside of our building after he'd picked us up. We couldn't understand the conversation, but we heard enough key words to get the gist. "Do you know where Building 6 of the India Habitat Center is?" the driver asked.

"No, bhai."

"Do you know where the India Habitat Center is?"

"No."

"Do you know where Lodhi Road is?"

"No."

"Do you know where Delhi is?"

"That way, bhai," the passer-by said, gesturing towards a certain road.

And off we went towards Delhi, driving up M.G. Road until we found ourselves at a major crossroads. Our driver pulled over and asked somebody else. "Do you know where Building 6 of the India Habitat Center is?"

"No, bhai."

"Do you know where the India Habitat Center is?"

"No."

"Do you know where Lodhi Road is?"

"That way, bhai," the passer-by said, gesturing towards a certain road.

And so it went, until we found Lodhi Road and then found the India Habitat Center; and it continued even after we got out of the car, as the guard pointed us in the rough direction of Building 6 and a final passer-by finally pointed us to its main entrance.

If we'd have drawn concentric circles around each of the passers-by we'd asked, we'd have found their geographic knowledge decreasing as the circles got bigger; but by overlapping their circles, we created a series of points that led us exactly from our home to our destination, in spite of the fact that nobody but the final passer-by knew where our destination was.

So we never worried that a driver wouldn't be able to find our destination when we got into his auto. We knew the collective knowledge of Delhi was always pointing the way.

In fact, our only real worry when we got into autos (aside from a truck imprinting the Ashok Leyland logo into the side of our head) was whether or not our driver would have change. Because every so often, a driver would pretend he didn't have any. And far more regularly, the driver genuinely wouldn't. If we suspected the former, we'd simply stay seated in his auto until he realized we weren't going anywhere, at which point he'd discover three overlooked tens in his breast pocket. If it were the latter, he'd walk around the area soliciting nearby vendors and passers-by until he found someone willing to break a big bill. We'd watch from the back of the auto, sympathizing as he went from person to person asking for change. We knew what he was going through: nobody in Delhi wants to give away his or her small bills.

We suspect that there was once a time in Delhi when small bills were genuinely hard to come by. Today, we think, change hoarding is perpetuated by habitual inertia rather than currency shortages. In autos and at stores, we'd get groans when we'd present a 500-rupee note and flat refusals when we'd present a 1,000. We learned to cherish fifty-rupee notes, which are the easiest to get people to break. One day, early in our time in India, Jenny grew frustrated with hoarding and pleading, and convinced a bank to exchange five thousand rupees into fifties; the joy we felt holding that bundle of small bills was matched in intensity only by our unwillingness to part with even a single one.

On one of our last days in Delhi, Jenny and I found ourselves in the opposite of our normal role: an auto driver was asking us for change. We were just leaving Humayun's Tomb, a sight I hadn't seen in all my time in Delhi (Jenny had visited without me eighteen months earlier). We'd walked briskly past the tourist-hunting drivers who were demanding 150 rupees in their clipped British English and Cliff Huxtable sweaters to take us forty rupees down the road, knowing that foreigners can never win the negotiating game if it's played in front of a tourist attraction. So we were nearing the main street to find a fairer playing field when an auto driver in a regulation colorless blue uniform approached with a 500-rupee note outstretched before him.

We could see his auto parked outside the parking lot, far away from the Huxtable clique, with a family of Indians standing next to it. They were tourists just like us, anxious to get out of the sun and into the sight, waiting while their driver sought change for their fare. Jenny and I had never in our entire time in Delhi successfully gotten an auto driver to break a 500; and from the trouble this driver was having—each of the assembled Cosbys had already rejected him—we knew it might be an impossible task.

The driver spoke no English, but we were veteran enough to recognize the pleading look on his face. With our countdown to Singapore at T-minus forty-eight hours, we were relaxing our iron grip on our small bills. I found change, and I gave it to him, and his face showed immense gratitude and relief. We followed him back to his auto and then, with the Cosbys glaring, negotiated a trip to our destination for a reasonable forty rupees. Then, once we arrived, I handed him the 500-rupee note he had given me and asked for change.

His jaw dropped, his eye bugged, and he began to groan in protest—until he saw my face, and we shared laughter and backslaps all around.

This particular experience raises an important point: this particular experience was not unique. We had as many moments of delight with auto drivers as we had bad experiences with them. Many drivers were good for friendly conversations about American politics, in which they invariably praised Bill Clinton for his visit to Delhi in 2000 while offering less kind words about George W. Bush. In one unforgettable case, the auto driver who took Jenny's mother home from a museum began with an obligatory offer to take her to his "uncle's" factory; when she gently rebuffed it, the driver switched to a conversation about her life in America that was apparently so interesting that he offered to share his lunch with her when they arrived so they could keep talking.

By and large, auto drivers are good people. A number of them graciously helped us unload shopping bags, or pointed out sights as we drove by, or, in one case, helped me stuff two rolled-up mattresses into the back of his auto so I could return them to my colleague Dipankar's house. I sat up front and shared his seat, my arm around him for balance, chatting the entire way to C.R. Park.

In the best cases, our driver/passenger relationship morphed into genuine teamwork. His Hindi would shoo away aggressive street children and our skin color would deter bribe-seeking cops. We'd both shoot our hands out of the auto to signify imminent turns. Both the driver and I would hang our heads out of the auto and shout curses at some particularly egregious traffic offender, laughing together at the gape-mouthed stare of whomever had wronged us.

Our good auto experiences more than balanced out the bad. But the bulk of the bell curve consisted of unremarkable episodes of negotiation and transaction that bookended journeys of mundane terror: the usual close calls, the typical religious supplication, the average amount of whiplash.

While my parents still describe their harrowing auto journeys as their "favorite part of our visit," for us it was just another day in the city.

Delhi is said to have 5.5 million registered vehicles[6]—one for every two-and-a-half people, and ten percent of India's total.[7] And it seemed to me like they were all on M.G. Road headed to Gurgaon every morning. Many of my co-workers encouraged me to get a motorcycle, telling me they were cheaper than cars and more nimble in heavy traffic. But few thoughts terrify me more than driving a motorcycle on a Delhi road, especially after my friend Nishant gave me a ride home on the back of his bike following dinner with friends. The journey from the restaurant in South Extension to my home in Hauz Khas was a mere two miles, but I spent the entire ride gripping the seat so tightly I feared I'd tear the handles off (which made me more frightened, given how counterproductive that would have been to my goal of not smashing onto the pavement). The potholes that seemed so mundane in the back of an auto loomed like chasms in front of us.

Strangely, all I could think about during that ride was what my parents told me they saw from their tour bus window somewhere in Rajasthan: a cow in a field got spooked, ran across the road, cut in front of their bus, jumped the median, and landed on top of a car coming from the opposite direction. And there on Nishant's

---

6. http://news.bbc.co.uk/2/hi/south_asia/7035826.stm
7. http://timesofindia.indiatimes.com/news/city/delhi/Delhis-flyovers-cant-cope-with-rising-traffic/articleshow/4961488.cms

motorcycle, as buses brushed our shoulders and bugs splattered in my face, my long list of terrors was absurdly headlined with the fear that a cow would fall out of the sky and land on us.

Nishant once said, "You can live more in five minutes on a motorcycle than most live in a lifetime." I couldn't agree more. Multiple lifetimes flashed before my eyes during that ride.

★

So why didn't I have a private car like so many other lucky expats? Because hours after Jenny and I got off the plane in Delhi, we discovered that my boss-to-be's promise of company-provided transportation had evaporated like paan spit on a hot Delhi street. We were left with a bitter red reality: we were not going to live the life of the lucky expat, lounging in a service apartment and training our driver to cook us Kraft macaroni and cheese. So once we found our own flat, I had to find my own ride.

A motorcycle was obviously not in my cards. And while I could have leased a car and hired a driver, I was daunted by the expectation of overwhelming bureaucracy necessary to acquire the car and unwanted responsibility of maintaining it. I also knew I could have called Radio Cabs or Easy Cabs or any of the other corporate taxi companies rapidly multiplying in the city, but their increased reliability is matched by their higher fares. So I decided to see if I could work out a deal with the local taxi stand.

We walked up to the large canvas tent next to Aurobindo Place market, just across Aurobindo Marg from Hauz Khas. The boss's name was Birender, and his fleet consisted of black-and-yellow Hindustan Ambassadors that doubled as mosquito-breeding grounds, neutrally colored Tata Indicas that always seemed to have one wet seat, and a couple hulking SUV-like Toyota Innovas for driving tourists around Rajasthan or taking more discriminating customers home from the mall. Birender's roster of drivers was staffed accordingly: a few reckless young guys for the short trips, a couple of middle-aged men reliable to be less impatient and more safety-conscious, and one or two well-dressed, well-paid English-speakers to ferry the tourists through the desert. Most of these guys were from Birender's village in Rajasthan. Birender would employ them for a few months to drive around the big city, make a lot of money, buy some name-brand jeans, and return home with enough savings and status to attract a better class of wife.

Birender himself was a large man with a prosperous businessman's belly. He usually wore suit pants and neatly tucked button-down shirts. He had salt-and-pepper hair, a powerful square jaw and an expensive mobile phone that he would reverently place on the nearest surface to ensure it was noticed.

"My god is Krishna," he told us as Jenny and I shook hands with him for the first time. We were standing inside his office, which was a cramped wooden structure attached to the canvas tent in which his drivers lived. The drivers had leapt to their feet as we entered the tent and asked for the boss. Now, as we chatted, they walked in and out of the doorway to pick up this paper or that, pretending not to listen to our conversation.

"Krishna," Birender told us again, his eyes urgently searching our faces for a reaction to the significance of that statement. "My god is Krishna."

We eventually reached agreement on the terms. I would call Birender's stand every morning I wanted a ride to work, and I'd pay 750 rupees to the driver when they dropped me off at home in the evening. "This is Mr. David," I was to say when I called. "Pickup, please." Birender would then dispatch a car and driver to drop me at my office and collect me again at the pre-determined time.

What was unusual about our agreement was that the driver would not spend the day parked on the street waiting for me. This was less because I didn't want to pay for the drivers to wait, and more because I just couldn't bear the guilt of some poor guy sitting in his car all day, staring at the clouds, shifting in his seat, sometimes napping, sometimes twitching restlessly, his life trapped in boredom because it was shackled to my schedule. So Birender's drivers would drop me off and fight traffic back to Delhi, where Birender would keep them busy until it was time to pick me up again.

Even then, it gnawed at my conscience when a driver would arrive before I was ready to leave. On the all-too-frequent nights I'd find myself working later than I'd expected, I'd rush out to the car and give the driver money for dinner. "Khana kileyea," I'd tell him in my broken Hindi, passing him fifty or a hundred rupees for dinner, depending on how long I expected to make him wait. The drivers surely preferred the days when I worked late.

It took me some time to establish a routine with Birender. Calling the taxi stand in the morning those first months, I often had to explain who I was, where I lived and where I wanted to go; and when I'd send the driver back to Delhi after dropping me off, they often concluded I was canceling my pickup at night.

But eventually our rhythm established itself. I learned to call as soon as I stepped out of the shower, knowing that the driver would then arrive just as I was finishing breakfast. "This is Mr. David," I would whisper into my phone while Jenny slept in the next room. "Pickup, please." But when I would whisper too softly—which usually happened twice a week—Jenny would wake to the sounds of me bellowing "This! Is! Mr. David!" over and over again until they finally understood. It was a much less pleasant wake-up call for her than the car horns or kabadiwallahs or pigeon sex on our metal air conditioner that would have roused her otherwise.

Birender typically sent the same blue Indica to take me to work every day. I'd try to sleep or read on the way to work in the mornings, but the bumpiness of the road and the shoddiness of the shocks usually precluded both activities. Until my last six months in Delhi, Birender rarely sent me the same driver more than twice a week. I suppose that none of his guys wanted to drive to and from Gurgaon during rush hour, so the "Mr. David duty" was probably a rotating chore. Which meant I grew familiar with most of his employees.

One of those drivers was Ajit. Square-jawed, terrifying behind the wheel, and with a perpetual snarl on his twenty-year-old face, Ajit spent his first day as my driver shouting gleefully at me the entire ride home. "Me you Hindi!" he hollered. "You me English! Straight! Seedha! Left! Bayain! Right! Dayain! You me request every day, me you Hindi you me English! You my only friend!"

When we would reach a breakthrough in vocabulary—"Cow?" "Gaay!"—he would get excited and start dancing in his seat. He'd take both hands off the wheel and point upwards to punctuate his hip thrusts, closing his eyes in ecstasy and throwing his head back but somehow managing to open his eyes and grab the wheel and slam on the brakes at exactly the right instant to avoid a herd of gaayain trotting casually down the road.

The third time he drove me, bored at the pace of our vocabulary lessons, I got the bright idea to teach him English curse words. "Choothia? Bastard!" I told him. "Lund? Dick! Gaand meh le lo? Kiss my ass!" Ajit loved it. He laughed and howled and danced and screamed and repeated my words in shrieks, each new abuse eliciting an equally elaborate reaction from him.

And then he grew quiet and contemplative. He turned to me, looking me directly in the eyes as I sat in the back seat and the car barreled down M.G. Road. "You, you wife. Lie . . . bed? Lie bed?"

I knew what he was getting at. I also knew that he drove Jenny on errands from time to time, and I was uncomfortable with the idea of him glowering at her in the rear-view mirror with this prurient fact confirmed in his mind.

I played dumb, hoping he'd get the hint. "Kya? Huh? I don't understand. Tati? Shit!"

Ajit refused to be drawn from his line of questioning. He screwed up his face in concentration, searching for a phrase he desperately wanted to find. "You, wife! Bed! Lie bed? You—" And then he made a gesture I didn't recognize but immediately understood, pounding his fist into his hand with an unmistakable crudeness of rhythm. "You, wife?"

What else could I say? "I suppose so, yes."

Ajit howled and danced his victory dance, honking and weaving and pointing his fingers towards the heavens in celebration of my good fortune.

★

Ajit disappeared a few months into our stay. I assume he returned to his village to experience marriage and whatever that hand gesture meant to him. And while other drivers came and went, a few remained constant enough for me to recognize their idiosyncrasies. There was an older man who was similar in build and facial structure to Birender, but with blacker hair and a less pronounced belly, whom we think was Birender's younger brother. There was a frail old man who hunched over the wheel with his hands impeccably at ten and two, driving slowly and carefully and, at the end of the ride, trying and failing every single time to get me to pay him thirty-five rupees for a non-existent border toll he had a fake receipt for. There was Sanjay, a young man with stern Nepali features, who was always exactly twenty-five minutes late in the morning and always exactly forty-five minutes late in the evening, every single time. I politely tolerated his tardiness for months and then warned him a dozen times that "I'll tell Birender if you do it again." One day I actually followed through on what even I believed to be empty threat. I called Birender and asked him not to send Sanjay to drive me any more. And Sanjay never drove me again.

But a few days later, I exited the office to find him waiting. Then I realized he wasn't waiting for me, but for another co-worker. And then I realized further that he was working for a different taxi company. I was horrified to know that I actually got him fired, but relieved that he'd at least made some contacts among the taxi stands near my office on those rare days he was the one actually waiting for me.

And then there was Ajay. About a year into my partnership with Birender, my rotating cast of drivers gave way to consistency, and Ajay became my daily driver. He was twenty-two years old and a keen student of popular fashion. His hair was long and styled and oiled to a gleaming sheen. He had an earring in his left ear, a mobile phone flashier than Birender's, and a fashionable green jacket that I thought was an important brand until I read what its stylized logo actually spelled out: "Important Brand." Ajay was trouble. He was always late. He was always disrespectful. He would mutter at me under his breath. He would snort at my Hindi. He would inevitably argue about the route, declaring that M.G. Road was "too jammed" and insisting that we should take the national highway. Not that he cared about making better time—he just wanted to floor it for the few kilometers beyond the toll plaza that were always smooth sailing. (As if I hadn't tested the route a dozen times: it's true that that one stretch of highway was always clear, but the off-ramp gridlock at Vasant Vihar invariably ate up any time we saved.)

Ajay was visibly unhappy to be slogging to and from Gurgaon twice a day. (I think the other drivers foisted the "Mr. David duty" on him because he was the youngest.) But at this point I knew my time in Delhi was short, and I didn't feel like finding a new taxi stand. So I endured Ajay. And since he clearly wasn't interested in helping me learn Hindi, I'd spend the ride home with a DVD on my computer and my headphones on my ears, ignoring Ajay as he talked on his mobile or, as was surprisingly often the case, to himself. Sometimes he'd play music on his mobile. At first he'd surreptitiously insert a single earbud that he thought I couldn't see, until he realized that I didn't care. Then he just put his mobile on speaker. During the quiet moments in my movies, I'd hear "*Om Shanti Om*" or "*Billo Rani*" drifting from the front seat.

Sometimes, if I'd forgotten my headphones, I'd play music out loud on my computer. Ajay would mock it from the front seat, repeating the lyrics in a mean-spirited wail. Periodically, though, he would grow quiet and listen, and I'd think that I'd finally reached him. So during one miserable jam, with Ajay staring silently at the unmoving tail lights in front of us, I decided to offer an olive branch by sharing something of my home culture. Stretching my Hindi as far as it would go, I said, "Ajay! Yeh ghanna subzi acha hai!" I thought I was saying, "This song is the best!" (I now know I was saying, "This dense vegetable is nice!")

He looked at me blankly in the rear-view mirror. So I just pressed play and cranked up the volume, and the sound of Guns N' Roses' "Appetite for Destruction" filled the cab.

I sat back and smiled with self-satisfaction at introducing Ajay to the very greatest rock album America has ever produced.

It was during the lull between "Nightrain" and "Out Ta Get Me" when I heard the chorus from "Pappu Can't Dance" coming from the front seat. Ajay was playing his music on his mobile as loud as he could to distract himself from the monstrous din I was blasting in the back seat.

I got the hint. I put on my headphones and turned on my DVD. Ajay was much happier to be ignored.

★

The Indicas in which I traveled were not designed for comfort. Nor was Birender investing the money I paid him into shock absorbers. So it would be a pleasant surprise those few times when I'd come down to find a shiny white Toyota Innova waiting for me, its deep bucket seat promising a luxurious ride. On these occasions, Birender himself would be at the wheel. Birender spoke decent English, so we'd chat about mundane things for the first part of the ride until he'd focus his attention on his mobile and I'd enjoy the comfort of the seat and the convenience of a seat belt I didn't actually have to dig between the crumb-strewn seats to find.

One time, though, I came down from the office to find
Birender waiting in the Innova with a stranger in the
front passenger seat. Birender assured me, with an
uncharacteristically boisterous voice, that we'd just be
dropping this guy off on the way home. They chattered
happily as we drove into an unfamiliar part of a nearby
residential neighborhood, and when we reached his friend's
house, Birender produced a bottle of whisky. He poured
them both a plastic cup. And then they stepped out to buy
an omelette from a nearby vendor.

Still belted into the back seat, I watched him walk his
exaggerated swagger and laugh his rowdy laugh. And I
realized just how he'd spent his day in Gurgaon.

Birender returned ten minutes later and offered me a
whisky-filled cup of my own. I declined. And then he
looked at me, as if realizing for the first time that his best
customer, sitting in his best car, might not be so keen about
being driven home by a drunk.

"Mr. David?" he asked through the car window,
his friend watching from the darkness behind him. "Are
you unhappy?"

He paused. And then again: "Are you unhappy?"

"Yes," I said, trying to sound curt. I was unhappy. And I
knew that in the employer/employee hierarchy, my next
step should have been to give him a rigid dressing-down in
front of his friend and the omelettewallah and anyone else
who passed by. But I am at heart a timid American who
always ascribes too much consideration to the history of
Western colonial oppression, the reputation of foreign
tourists, and the self-esteem of those over whom I may

hold power. Even in this instance, when all justification was on my side, I passed on the opportunity to assert my indignation.

Instead, I retreated into passive–aggressive silence. I hoped that staring vaguely out the opposite window would communicate my feelings. Also, I refused his offer to share some of his omelette.

Finally, they finished their whiskies and parted ways. Birender drove us back towards M.G. Road, breaking the silence only to inquire repeatedly as to whether I was unhappy. (I still was.) I pretended like I was ignoring him, but I was watching him quite closely to evaluate his driving faculties. Inwardly, I rehearsed what I'd say if I decided he was too drunk to drive. Should I command him to let me out, and then hitch-hike home? Or should I insist that he let me take the wheel myself? (Although it was probably more dangerous for me to drive sober on M.G. Road than for him to drive drunk.)

I was so focused on visualizing my heroic leap forward— picturing myself wrestling the wheel from his hand and steering us out of the way of an oncoming water tanker— that I didn't even realize we'd stopped moving. We were parked at the tollbooth on M.G. Road. Birender was staring at the tollbooth collector. The collector was staring off into the distance. Behind us, cars had begun to honk.

I normally pay attention when we approach tollbooths so I can pass money to the driver before we reach the window. But I'd missed this one, wrapped up as I was in my own imagination. And Birender, clearly eager to get back on my good side, had already pulled a roll of bills out of his jacket and handed forty rupees to the collector. Birender was now due five rupees change.

The tollbooth collector was making no motion towards his change drawer.

I couldn't blame the collector for trying. Birender doesn't dress like a driver, he dresses like the businessman that he is. ("I own two mobile stores," he told me on one of our more pleasant rides home. "I have two buffaloes and one cow in my village. I'm buying a plot near the ISIC Hospital bus stand in Vasant Kunj—one hundred square yards, twenty-five lakhs!") So the tollbooth collector, seeing Birender's wad and Birender's finery and me in the back seat letting my driver do the paying, must have assumed that a rich driver driving around a rich passenger isn't going to care about five measly rupees.

The tollbooth collector stared straight ahead.

With a cold lack of emotion that belied none of his intoxication, Birender stared at him and waited.

There was no anger on Birender's part. Nor did the tollbooth collector pretend to hunt for change. This was another pantomime: one simply stared at the other, while the other simply stared straight ahead. Behind us, more cars packed into the toll lane and leaned on their horns. And suddenly I had a new worry, beyond Birender's drunkenness: would the drivers behind us grow angry? Would their honking turn into shouting, and would their shouting turn into one of those riots I read about in the papers and in *Shantaram*, in which the Indian mob makes snap decisions of guilt and innocence and exacts bloody revenge on whomever they decide is responsible for whatever travesty they've beheld? Would they surround our Innova, rock it, overturn it, ignite it, and dance in the light of our flaming bodies? Or would Birender's silver tongue convince them that we were the victims, turning the mob to pelt the tollbooth collector with stones the size of five-rupee pieces while the khaki-clad cops rested on their beating sticks and watched without expression as he writhed on the floor of his tollbooth and begged for mercy?

The pantomime continued. The honks grew louder.

And then, suddenly, the tollbooth collector conceded. Five long minutes after we got there, five rupees magically materialized in his hand, and we were on our way.

When we arrived home, Birender asked me one last time if I was unhappy. I didn't respond. I just handed over my fare for the day, plus thirty-five rupees to cover the toll.

I didn't expect an apology, and Birender never offered one. The next day, I called for my pickup. Birender sent a driver in an Indica. Things were back to normal. Birender knew that unhappy or not, I wasn't going to seek a new taxi company. It was far too much trouble to teach a whole new taxi stand to recognize a voice on the other line when it whispered, "This is Mr. David!"

4

Culture: The Inscrutable Indians

It was that sweltering August Saturday, my first afternoon in India. My company's head of HR, Mahua, had picked me up at the airport, deposited me at my new flat in Greater Kailash-II, bid farewell until Monday, and disappeared into the flow of traffic. Jenny wouldn't be joining me for eight more days. Aside from the flat's landlord and its servant, I did not know a single soul in India. I was on my own.

And it was lunchtime.

After getting lost, getting sunburned and eventually getting over my fears, I finally found myself in GK-II's main market with food on my mind and my landlord's money in my pocket. I took a few laps to evaluate my eating options and decided that Nathu's Sweets was the least intimidating of the market's restaurants.

Intimidating? Yes. I was intimidated by the restaurants.

I've always been nervous walking into a restaurant for the first time in a new country. In Panama, in Egypt, in Vietnam, even in the UK, I've always hesitated at the door of the first restaurant of the journey, always afraid I'd commit some terrible faux pas in my ignorance of the local customs, and that the whole restaurant would stop in mid-chew to laugh at me. It's a silly fear, and it's unsubstantiated by any actual experience, but I nevertheless endure it. My mind is always racing as I walk through the door: should I sit and wait for the waiter? Should I order at the counter? Will they be able to understand me? Will I be able to understand the menu? Will I accidentally order something disgusting? Will I accidentally insult them, and if so, will they spit in my food?

I feigned a casual walk past Nathu's Sweets a few times, peeking in the window for any behavioral clues. Then I bravely walked in and courageously sat down.

A waiter handed me a menu. So far, so good. But though the menu was in English script, it was full of Hindi words I didn't recognize. What if channa meant "rotten turnip"? What if gobi meant "goat anus"? What if aloo meant "spat-upon chicken liver"?

Eventually, I settled on something that sounded exciting, delicious, and unlikely to contain the brains and eyeballs that *Indiana Jones and the Temple of Doom* had conditioned me to expect from authentic Indian cuisine. Now my only worry was that I'd do something stupid while I ordered.

The waiter came over to my table. I swallowed and pointed at the menu. "One 'south Indian thali,' please."

The waiter cocked his head at me . . . mockingly?

"Uh, one south Indian thali?"

"Gee," said the waiter, who looked about fifteen years old. He cocked his head again, a sharp jerk to the right. A gesture that seemed to drip sarcasm. A gesture that seemed to say, *Nice order, asshole.*

What was wrong with my order?

I looked down at the menu. "And . . . a 'sweet lime soda.'" He didn't answer. He just jerked his head again. *Sure*, his head jerk told me, *that's just what a douche bag like you* would *order.*

"Uh, a sweet lime soda?"

"Gee," he repeated, moving his head in a manner I could only interpret as, *Ha! That's the whitest order I've ever heard.* He walked away, leaving me wondering what I'd done wrong and exactly how many members of the kitchen staff would spit in my food.

The food was delicious, fortunately, and free of both goat anus and human spit. I called for my check and paid without incident. But the question of why the waiter had hated me hung over my head as I walked home. And he wasn't the only one: in many of the subsequent restaurants I'd visit over the next couple of days, the waiters would treat me the same. I'd give my order and they'd jerk their heads as if an epidemic of neck spasms was going around. One thing was for sure: whatever I was doing wrong, at least I was being consistent about it.

★

Jenny and I began studying Hindi as soon as we got settled into our Hauz Khas flat. And the more Hindi we learned, the better we could decipher the country around us. Once we discovered that "dil" translates to "heart," for example, we understood half of the Bollywood song titles that came out. And once we learned a few curse words, I understood what my drivers were saying about me on their mobile phones as they took me to work. (I'll assume they used "choothia" to mean "heck of a guy" like Michael Jackson used "bad" to mean "good.")

To supplement my taxi drivers' lessons, we took formal Hindi instruction from a tutor named Manoj, a college student studying German and Spanish who peppered his Hindi lessons with examples from his other passions. ("Repeat in Hindi," he'd instruct us. "'Chancellor Merkel is in the market.'" "Chancellor Merkel market may hay," we'd intone back, our pronunciation as accurate as my spelling.) Learning the language proved to be physically exhausting for us; I'd end each lesson sweating from the complexities of vocabulary, conjugation, gender variation and word order, never mind the subtleties of semi-silent n's and rolling r's and everything else Hindi had to trip us up. With much practice, we grew capable of carrying on grade-school conversations—"Aap guessa hai? Mera naam Dave hai. Market kaha hai?"—that evoked polite indulgence on the part of passers-by before they'd respond to our questions in English. Their English was always far more proficient than our Hindi.

Strictly speaking, it wasn't necessary for us to learn Hindi. Enough people spoke English that even if the local tailor couldn't explain what had happened to the shirt I'd given him to mend, he could easily grab someone off the street who knew the English translatation for the words "lost forever." But we're proud we made the effort.

And we're delighted to share some key wisdom we learned: that there are three Hindi words that every traveler should know.

The first word is "chalo." It means "let's go," or "get going." It's the imperative form of the verb "to go"—a command that's conjugated to imply that the speaker respects the status of the person to whom he's speaking. It's what polite children say to parents when it's time to leave for the movie, to drivers when it's time to hit to road, or to co-workers when it's time for the meeting to start. "Chalo" signifies that the time for talking has ended, and that now is the time for action. The doctor will see you now. We'll move forward on that proposal. I'm finished with my meal. Chalo.

In familiar company, with friends at a bar or family at a restaurant, chalo takes on an even greater depth. That's when everyone exhorts everyone else at the table with three variations of the command verb form: "chal," "chalo," "chaliye." "Let's go, dude," "Come, my friend," and "Oh, good mister sir, would you be so kind as to commence this journey?" This grab bag of verb forms and respect levels combines familiarity and ironic formality, and those three words echo around the table as everyone meets everyone's eyes and agrees that it's indeed time to go. In all our time in the city, no three Delhiites were ever seen to stand up from a table without a rousing chorus of chal-verb variations all around.

I was told by my friend Sandeep that using verb forms to respect status and indicate politeness may only be useful in certain parts of the country. "In Mumbai," he told me, "we all just say 'chalo,' and we indicate politeness by how many curse words we include in the sentence."

The second critical Hindi phrase for the Delhi traveler is "theek hai." Pronounced almost with a hard "T" sound as if talking about a lovely teak table, it's just as easily articulated by a mush-mouthed American as "tee-kay." And that's convenient, because it translates almost exactly like "okay" in American English. How are you? Theek hai. It's the stock answer to any salutation; but it's also quite useful for concluding transactions, signifying acceptance, and communicating satisfaction. Theek hai, I agree to that price. Theek hai, I'm happy with this mango. Theek hai, I slipped on cow poop and knocked my head on the ground but I'm just fine, thanks for asking. In a country of body language so inscrutable that an affirmative nod can look like a dismissive chin jerk, "theek hai" works as both a question and an answer when body language isn't clear. "Fifty rupees, theek hai?" "Fifty rupees, theek hai."

Our third and most indispensable Hindi word is "bhaiya." While it translates literally into "elder brother," it's used to politely hail any strange man as the Hindi equivalent of "Excuse me, sir," or to address him in mid-conversation.

It's innocuous piece of vocabulary, in other words. Until it's wielded by an Indian woman. In their hands, "bhaiya" is a weapon of coercion unparalleled in Western linguistics.

Jenny observed the power of "bhaiya" while watching friends negotiate with autos, seeing housewives beat down a stubborn vegetablewallah, and studying clever co-workers as they convinced recalcitrant art directors to meet impossible deadlines. A woman takes a simple "bhaiya"—"buy-yaa," as it's transliterated—and bends it around the fulcrum of the "y," modulating the final syllable to do her dastardly bidding.

Making it short and sharp expresses contempt. ("Who do you think I am to quote me such a price?") Adding a long, upward-fluctuating suffix feigns shock. ("You would take such advantage of the sweet, innocent girl standing so humbly before you?") And when a woman gives it an angry cadenza up and down three different octaves—think John Coltrane at the end of *Giant Steps*, an animal howl, a fire from a woman's belly that can singe the quivering beedi right out of the hapless auto driver's mouth—"bhaiya" chastens even the most determined foe. A well-wielded "bhaiya" convinces a man that this woman's outrage has reached his mother's shamed ears back in his village, and that his long-departed ancestors are preparing all the lightning in hell to descend upon his head should he not drop ten rupees off his price.

★

Even as we practiced our Hindi on others (and even as Jenny learned to wield a passable "bhaiya" of her own), other people practiced their English on us. This included auto drivers shouting conversation from the front seat to office boys shyly relaying messages from the finance department. We were happy to indulge anyone who made the effort—including the cursing boy we met on a walk just beyond the northwest reaches of the Old City. The chaotic lanes had given way to streets at right angles that nevertheless retained the capacity for surprise: an ice factory? a cluster of stores selling supplies for science teachers? a tree draped with movie film that, upon close examination, revealed frame after frame of Shah Rukh Khan? On one of those streets, a boy on a bicycle pedaled furiously towards us, slowing as he came near and whispering as he slipped by: "Fuck!"

He braked after a dozen feet. He put his feet down and turned to gauge our reaction. He was eight years old, his hair neatly combed, riding a new bicycle that still had its factory shine. Jenny and I kept walking; and the boy, emboldened by our lack of anger and the fact that we showed no signs of chasing him, reversed direction and tentatively pedaled by again, still a few deliberate feet beyond arm's reach. "Fuck you!" he whispered, this time with more confidence.

Laughing out loud, we continued walking. He circled around for another pass.

"I want to fuck you!"

This time we gasped, and our reaction clearly pleased him. He stopped behind us with a smug look on his face.

"Me?" I asked, pointing to my own chest in mock horror.

"Yes!" he hollered. Then he stood on his pedals and launched himself down the street behind us. When we looked after him, he had stopped once more and was clearly deliberating with himself. Finally, his deliberations ended, and we could hear him approaching from behind yet, gravel crunching beneath his tires. This time he was shouting: "I want to fuck you-oooo!"

"Me?" I asked him once more. "Are you sure?"

He skidded to a halt, took a deep breath, and then screamed loud and high and sustained, "Yeeessssss!!!" His shout trailed off into cackles, and then he rode around a corner and was gone.

★

Being cursed at on the street didn't bother us. In fact, it kind of made us homesick for New York.

Just like we closely studied Delhi culture, so too did we mimic the attitudes of the New Yorkers around us when we first moved there. We quickly learned the importance of the "subway stare," in which we'd keep our eyes focused blankly in front of us no matter what a militant preacher might be screaming nor what a musty hobo is doing in his pants. Above ground, we honed our ability to match surly gum-chewing drugstore cashiers sigh for melodramatic sigh. We came to relish bicycling over the Brooklyn Bridge solely for the opportunity to shout at tourists who strayed into the bike lane. And we exalted in hollering "Exkooze me!" at anyone blocking the subway doors, affecting Brooklyn accents we may or may not have practiced in front of the mirror.

Outsiders generally interpret the New York attitude as offensive. But as we learned to project it, we also came to understand its artificiality. The New York City attitude is a deterrence. It's a pantomime. It's adopted simply to encourage muggers and perverts to find other victims. And it's wholly superficial: once an interaction progresses to the point where a New Yorker understands that you're not intending to mug or grope, the pantomime ends, the subway stare focuses, and the friendly New Yorker eagerly explains which subways go to 59th Street. There's nothing a New Yorker loves more than telling a tourist which subway to take.

But even though Delhi is twice as big as New York, we never felt any big city attitude from its residents. Delhiites were overwhelmingly friendly to us. Perhaps that's because New Yorkers each see themselves as the lead actor in a play with eight million cast members, so every interaction implies commensurate drama. The isolation of Delhi's neighborhoods, on the other hand, means that people relate to the larger city with a small-town attitude: suspicious of outsiders, but welcoming to foreigners.

Whatever the reason, Delhiites were overwhelmingly polite and engaging with us. They'd smile, they'd say hello as we walked by, and they'd stop us for impromptu conversations. And they were eager to help us whenever they thought we needed assistance. Like when Jenny was waiting for the fruitwallah in the market to attend to her: one lady interpreted Jenny's patience as paralysis and took it upon herself to negotiate on Jenny's behalf. She barked a series of rapid and forceful Hindi phrases, gesturing dramatically at Jenny and her pomegranates as if to say, "You dare represent the whole of Mother India to this innocent tourist by charging fifty rupees for your lousy fruit?" Jenny was embarrassed as passers-by stopped to watch the exchange, but she didn't protest too much— after a flawlessly executed "bhaiya!" finished off the lady's harangue, Jenny ended up spending half of what she'd expected to on her produce.

The helpfulness of Delhiites was extremely useful when we were lost or when we were being harassed by a beggar we just couldn't shake. But there were also times when well-intentioned citizens would step in and accidentally make things worse. They'd appear from nowhere to berate an auto driver for offering what seemed like a perfectly acceptable fare to us, shaming him into a lower price that ensured we'd have an argument at the other side of the journey. Or they'd insist to the driver that the foreigner was obviously confused, and that she surely meant "Hauz Khas Village" every time she said "Hauz Khas Market." One police officer grew angry that Jenny and I had to negotiate with autos at all. Seeing us bargain with a driver outside Basant Lok market, he dashed over and pointed his beating stick menacingly at the meter. The driver swallowed and nodded, and the cop saluted us with satisfaction as the driver glumly drove us on our way.

But we knew what would happen next: the driver would go the long way to run up the meter. Not keen on visiting both Tughlaqabad Fort and the Delhi Ridge on our way back to Hauz Khas, I waited until we were out of sight to lean forward and suggest a flat rate. The driver brightened, switched off the meter and swung a quick U-turn to head in the actual direction of our destination. All three of us ducked our heads as we passed the indignant officer.

We tried to appreciate everyone who helped us. But there were times when our New York attitudes would reflexively assert themselves before we could stop them.

Rudeness wasn't our intention; it's just that after eight years in New York City, rudeness was our instinctual response. Sometimes we'd snap at people brushing past us on the sidewalk before recalling the different standards of personal space. Or we'd sigh dramatically at cashiers who didn't attend to us with a New Yorker's haste. Or, as happened when one old man slipped past me as we dawdled at the entrance to the India International Trade Fair, my mouth reacted before my brain did, letting loose with an "Exkooze me!" that would inspire Marty Markowitz to name a street in Park Slope after me.

The old man jumped a mile and bowed an apology as deep as the East River, and I was flooded with a sense of shame that I'd never felt after shouting at the elderly back in New York.

*

We understand that our impression of Delhiites was unique because we are foreign: Indian tourists may have an entirely different sense of the Delhi attitude than we do. Although it can't be that bad, because we saw plenty of Indian tourists visiting their capital city. There's a middle-class India that thrives far beyond Saket Select Citywalk Mall, we learned, and many of them are just as interested in their nation's attractions as we are. And as they'd come to Delhi from around the region, these domestic tourists had the same goals that we foreign tourists did: they wanted to take pictures of things they can't see at home.

But while our list includes sidewalk tailors and roadside shrines, their list includes Western tourists like us. So as we'd rest in the shade at the Red Fort or Jama Masjid, it wasn't unusual for a mother to place a baby in our lap and a father to take our picture. Nor was it unusual for mustachioed middle-aged men to start conversations that always culminated in photo requests. ('From which place?' they'd ask with a genuine interest never shown by jaded Saket Citywalkers. 'You like India? Yes? Take picture?') Gangs of college-age girls would crowd around us, giggling as they'd stroke Jenny's hair, give us their email addresses and invite us to visit their hometowns. Only teenage boys rarely approached us directly. Instead, they'd walk by while pretending to scrutinize an SMS as pretext for holding their phones at picture-snapping angles.

(Our worst experience with teenage boys was at Jama Masjid, the city's central mosque. They'd loiter at the top of the forty-meter minaret, watching for female tourists to enter below. Then they'd file down the claustrophobic stairwell as their victim climbed up, their hands held innocently at a level that just happened to be perfect for surreptitious breast-brushing.)

At first we were offended by all this unwanted attention. We wondered how people could be so rude as to take pictures of us as if we had been posed there by the Ministry of Tourism. Jenny initially made sport of teasing the men who approached her, agreeing to "take a picture" and then pulling out her own camera and snapping shot after shot of the baffled men until they left her alone. Sometimes we'd scowl and chastise people who approached us with their cameras at the ready.

But as time went on, and our own photo album swelled with pictures of vegetable vendors, wandering sadhus and streetside omelette makers, we realized how hypocritical we were being. If we found the people around us to be fascinating, beautiful and photo-worthy—subjecting them to the sudden blink of our black lens and then disappearing without so much as a moment of eye contact—it was disingenuous not to accept ourselves as objects of equal interest. We vowed to happily accept photo requests from that moment onward, putting broad grins on our faces while anybody who pleased put their arms around our shoulders and stared into the cameras. We made ourselves equally open to the people who just wanted to shake our hands, even those who seemed more interested in shaking Jenny's hands than my own.

After some time, we realized that it was much nicer when people asked permission to take our photo as opposed to when they attempted paparazzi-style photos from afar. Which taught us that we owed our own photographic subjects the same consideration. Instead of suddenly stopping, snapping and speeding off, we began requesting permission for pictures and then thanking our subjects and showing them the output on the screen. Not only did that make our interactions with people more satisfying, but our photos got better as well.

*

Though we knew very little about India before we moved there, we'd always heard that religion was an integral part of the culture. So it was nice that Diwali—which, along with Holi, is one of the most widely celebrated Hindu holidays in north India—came less than a week after we settled in Hauz Khas. My office held a pooja, which gave us our first up-close experience with Hinduism, including getting our foreheads marked with red and orange paste and red threads tied around our wrists. (We proudly wore those threads until they fell off as proof that we were having more authentic experiences than all the other bare-wristed Western tourists.) We also attended a pooja at my co-worker Shweta's home, where we learned that the prayers were just prelude to Diwali's main event: the fireworks.

When we think of fireworks, we picture America's Fourth of July displays, which are coordinated by cities and overseen by fire departments. But in Delhi, the responsibility for buying and lighting Diwali fireworks fell to the people. In the days before Diwali, the markets had filled up with so many fireworks that anyone could acquire enough firepower to bring down a tank. And in the nights leading up to Diwali, the skies echoed with sleep-shattering explosions as people previewed their caches.

Diwali itself was beyond anything our eardrums were prepared for.

Explosions began shaking the windows the moment the sun set. The twilight cityscape was transformed into Baghdad during the first night of shock-and-awe. Panicked pigeons flew everywhere. Smoke clouds danced pink and green as colored sparks fountained up from between the trees. Professional-caliber shells exploded far too low for safety. Blasts flashed in the distance and rumbled by seconds later.

Tremendous detonations responded from right next door. Most of these fireworks seemed intended not for color or light, but for sound alone, without any visual aesthetics to offset the momentary deafness. As we ate our dinner on Shweta's terrace, our plates bounced in our laps with every bomb the neighbors set off.

After we helped Shweta's friends and family unleash their arsenal upon the night, our drive home was a tour through an urban war zone. Our taxi crawled slowly through streets as sudden flashes threw fleeting humanoid shadows onto the trees. A bomb would explode right in front of us, and our driver would then rush forward before someone could light another in our path. On the main road, the smoke was so thick that visibility could be measured in inches. Headlights would suddenly appear far too close for safety, slashing thin slits through the fog before disappearing into the darkness just a few feet away. It took days for the smoke to clear and for our ears to stop ringing.

And we enjoyed every minute of it.

Jenny and I were raised in the stifling formality of synagogue and church. To us, religious ceremonies were somber and rehearsed affairs. My Saturday morning services were spent singing the exact same prayers in the exact same order, standing and sitting at the same points in the service as we did every other week. There were only two variables: the subject of that week's Torah passage (which was read in Hebrew, though, so I couldn't distinguish it from any other week, anyway); and the moral of that week's sermon (which was generally delivered so drearily that my mind drifted within moments). Jenny's experience was similar, except everything was in English and her congregation would kneel instead of stand.

In both our cases, our parents put us in our nicest clothes and herded us into the pews where, with the stern glares of which only parents in a house of god are capable, we were warned with no uncertainty to keep our damned mouths shut. In the silences between the prayers, even breathing too loud was enough to attract the wrath of Mom. Woe unto him who sneezed in any moment of serenity: the sound of that transgression would echo off the unforgiving walls while every head in the pew turned to deliver the stink eye.[1]

These dreary experiences defined what we expected from all religion: forced formality and coerced reverence. And we figured that Hinduism, in all its impenetrable mysticism, would be even more so.

But we were wrong. Never mind the fireworks—the poojas we experienced were a vibrating fusion of songs and chants and symbolism that couldn't be more different from our own religions. At all the poojas we saw—for consecrating new offices, for celebrating weddings, or even for paying tribute to a god from a sidewalk shrine as we walked by—there was none of the regulated veneration so prevalent in the religions in which we were raised. A congregation

---

1. And glory be to the old man who farts in services! His impromptu organ solo bounces around the sanctuary and brings tears to the eyes of every man and child who tries desperately not to let his wife or mother see him giggling. He's suddenly truly reverent for the first time all morning as he prays with all his heart not to burst out laughing, or at least not to be the first one to do so.

would gather loosely around idols or pictures while a pandit chanted and sang, often interrupting himself to tell someone to toss flower petals here or throw puffed rice there. People would wander in and out of the ceremony at whim, chatting with their fellow faithful, answering their mobiles, sending SMSes, and breathing as loudly as they pleased. Anyone not directly engaged in reverence simply went about their business. Unlike our childhood services, where the old ladies would tut-tut at trucks passing on the highway three miles away, nobody seemed to have any problem filtering out the background distractions.

And unlike at our synagogues and churches, there didn't seem to be a script. Every ceremony seemed to progress solely at the direction of the pandit. In fact, from the way people watched the pandit for cues, it seemed like no two ceremonies were ever the same.

Even funerals proceeded without the structure we'd expect in the West. As we watched bodies being cremated on the Ganges at Varanasi or at the Pashupatinath temple in Kathmandu, the deceased's family was solemn and serious, but life beyond them continued as normal: sadhus chatted with each other, laborers stacked wood for future burnings, dogs sniffed around, and men spoke on their phones. Nobody seemed to be on their tiptoes but us.

We eventually understood that in the West, religion rarely extended beyond four stained-glass walls. But in India, religion is everywhere. It's inside and outside of temples, it's behind cash registers, it's in front of sidewalk shrines, it's in alcoves built into bedroom walls, and it's in idols Velcroed to taxicab dashboards. Even mosques extend religion beyond their boundaries: the faithful who arrived too late to fit inside our local mosque during Friday afternoon prayers would just kneel on the sidewalk outside. Which meant that if every Indian tiptoed around every religious expression like we were accustomed to doing, nobody would get anything done.

So while the pious would worship, everyone else would go about their business. And there's something to be said for spirituality that flows even as life flows all around it.

The more we learned about Hinduism, the more overwhelming it seemed to us. Seemingly simple questions— "How many gods are there in Hinduism?"—would be answered by a dozen different people in two dozen different ways. We concluded that the lack of definition to the religion *was* the definition of the religion: from what we could tell, Hinduism was a religion in which any expression of reverence was accepted as canon. With millions of gods, who is to say what is or is not the right way to worship them?

So Hinduism is what a Hindu says it is. Westerners may see that as a tautological definition, but that's what we observed: not a single religion with a billion adherents, but a unifying label for the billion different ways a billion different people express their spirituality.

★

After Diwali, the next major Hindu holiday we celebrated was Holi. And like Diwali, Holi began with a pooja at the office. But I was in a meeting that ran late, so I missed it. By the time my boss Murali and I returned to the office, the pooja was over and everyone had gone home except for Navin and Sanat, two of the youngest employees at the company.

As soon as I sat at my computer, Navin rushed up to me with an orange cardboard box. "Have a sweet, Dave!" he smiled, mischief in his eyes as he held out a box of round orange pastries that were slightly smaller than ping-pong balls. I took one and picked off a bite-sized piece with my fingers. That revealed a shiny black lump glistening at the center of the sweet.

"No, Dave," said Navin, now grinning far too broadly to be trusted. "Eat the treat in the middle!"

Sanat popped his head up from behind Navin's shoulder. "Make sure you eat that part, Dave!"

So I did. It was bitter. Navin and Sanat's cackles attracted Murali, who beamed proudly upon learning what I'd just done. "That's bhang," he told me after I'd swallowed. "You should have three more to make sure you have a *really* good evening."

I only had one more. But it was still enough to give me a good evening indeed.

That's because bhang is a narcotic preparation made from the cannabis plant. Although drugs are illegal in India, bhang is sold by certain government shops for religious uses. And while Holi is known even in the West for the colored powders and dyes people throw at each other to celebrate it, it turns out that bhang is just as important a part of many people's Holi celebrations.

The next day, we hailed an autorickshaw to travel to a Holi party at a massive farmhouse in Chhattarpur, in the distant south of the city. As we drove, we saw glimpses of our Holi to come: shirts stained with splotches of color, a man with bright pink skin, teenagers throwing water balloons from their cars, and wandering cows with their hides completely painted over. But somewhere close to the party, we got lost; we could hear the sound of heavy electronic music but we couldn't find it. Figuring we were close enough, we dismissed the auto and followed our ears on foot. And as we walked through this unknown neighborhood, a group of five or six teenage boys approached us with Holi fun in mind.

We'd both dressed for Holi in white Indian-style outfits we'd bought specially for the occasion. Jenny wore a simple white pajama top and I sported a thin white kurta that came down below my knees. And these teenagers knew that such pristine whiteness on Holi called for immediate action. After politely asking my permission, each teenager solemnly dipped his fingers into a bag and, with faces deep in concentration, carefully smeared colors onto my forehead: surreal greens and vibrating pinks straight out of a Grateful Dead poster. Then each one gave me a deep and joyful hug before walking on, and the electric colors on their shirts rubbed off on my own.

A few minutes later, we finally found the party. And the moment we stepped through the farmhouse's gate, our white clothes were a distant memory. Just inside the gate was a table stocked with Holi ammunition that dozens of people were gleefully throwing into friends' faces, smearing into strangers' hair, and tossing at each other by the bucketful. The pictures I took at the event (I'd studiously wrapped my

camera in plastic before we left the house) record how our
Holi unfolded. In the first picture, the left side of my face is
caked unearthly green from the handful of powder someone
threw point-blank at my ear, while a spattering of pink and
yellow descends down to my dye-soaked kurta. Jenny's
photos show that she began the party with an instant
foundation of yellow upon which other colors were layered
as a complement; only in the last photo does it disappear,
covered up by an exuberant burst of red everywhere but
for a yellow slash near her hairline.

Our final picture from the party shows the two of us
together, both of us smiling with glazed eyes, our hair
matted with color and speckled with grass, grinning
stupid smiles that could mean one thing: we were both
absurdly high.

The bhang I'd been given at work was just a warm-up.
Servants had been wandering this party bearing terracotta
cups of green water. Sweetened bhang, as it turned out.
Supposedly, there had also been bhang in the desserts and
even in the ice cream, which explains why we spent the last
hour of the party sitting on the pink grass and staring at the
green people, unaware that we were directly in front of the
DJ's ear-shattering speakers because we were too obsessed
with one particular long-haired, bearded Indian who, but
for his skin color, was a perfect doppelgänger of our friend
Ryan. From the pictures we reviewed later, we learned
that we actually followed him around the party taking
surreptitious photos with the camera at hip-level. If he
didn't notice us stalking him, it was only because he'd
enjoyed as much bhang as we did.

When we'd finally had enough, we somehow found an autorickshaw to take us home. We have no photographic evidence from this ride, but Jenny recalls feeling utter terror as a convoy of open jeeps passed us somewhere near Mehrauli. In the backs of the jeeps, massive men held giant guns and stared cruelly down at us. Her squeals attracted the driver's attention, and at a red signal he abruptly turned in his seat and stared long and hard, contemplating the pink and green foreigners who were smearing Holi colors all over his back seat. And then he began laughing—gently, pleasantly—and for an eternal moment we were sliding through the tunnel of his gaze. And then the signal beyond him turned as green as my left ear, and his laughter ascended into fading flute music as he faced forward again and jerked the auto back into drive.

We remember the rest in snippets: Hauz Khas market was surreal in its emptiness; the hike up our stairwell took hours; and then we were showering, and then we were eating a dozen bags of potato chips, and then we were showering again, and then it was tomorrow.

Jenny's hair was green for days. And for weeks I found red stuff every time I cleaned my ears. I can't say we learned any more about Hinduism, but we sure learned to love Holi.

★

Of all the aspects of Indian life we'd hoped to experience in Delhi, we were most excited to attend our first Indian wedding. Everything we knew about them came from movies and from our friend Heather who had been lucky enough to travel all the way to India for the experience. So we expected five-day feasts in which every invited guest took a week off from work to enjoy an uninterrupted flow of homemade food. We expected 3 a.m. wake-up calls for intricate ceremonies involving choreographed elephants and ring-bearing monkeys. We expected rituals so elaborately rehearsed that any deviation from the millennium-old inflections would, in accordance to some ancient moral code, force both families into a year of mourning.

Our experience, of course, was different. First of all, weddings only seemed to be multi-day events for the closest family members. And from what we could tell, the participants spent the bulk of those days sitting in folding chairs, holding half-finished plates of food, comforting the bride's mother as she broke into sudden wailing hysterics, listening to the bride's brother shout at the caterer, and waiting for someone to figure out what was supposed to happen next. While there were multiple ceremonies that happened over those five days, Jenny and I were only invited to experience two of them: the weddings themselves, and the mehndi ceremonies, which took place the night before the wedding.

The mehndi ceremonies we attended were relaxed and intimate affairs. Though open to both genders, they're probably akin in their pampering and animated gossip to an American bridal party getting their hair and nails done. The bride and her closest female friends and family sat on stools as young men hired for the occasion patiently squeezed henna into elaborate patterns on their arms and legs. We watched as peacocks, parrots, and other symbols and figures materialized within the complicated webs of drying dye. ("The mehndiwallah also hides the groom's initials somewhere in the henna," my colleague Mahua told me, "which the groom has fun finding on the first night.") The designs created by these henna artist opened our eyes to the potential of the medium: they were far more beautiful than what the hennawallah who sat in the Hauz Khas market glooped onto the forearms of our visiting American friends.

We enjoyed the mehndi ceremonies more than the weddings themselves. That's because we actually got to interact with the bride and groom during the mehndi. At my co-worker Sharbani's mehndi ceremony, for instance, Jenny and I chatted with the happy couple while multiple generations of aunties laughed uncontrollably every time Sharbani dragged me out to dance my flailing bhangra. If there were any formal rituals, none of the guests seemed expected to pay attention to them. Instead, Sharbani would quietly disappear from her henna application along with her fiancé Tapan for what we assume was a blessing. She'd reappear a few moments later to corral everyone onto the dance floor for another round of laughing at me, while the henna artists put down their tools and waited patiently for her return.

Like the poojas we observed, the weddings we attended were far less ritualized and rehearsed than those in the West. At our own wedding, Jenny and I had jettisoned many of the ritualistic elements (our ceremony itself was all of five minutes long), but it still followed a script honed by tradition and Hollywood: we had a formal presentation of the bride, ceremonial family photos, and an official announcement of our entry into the reception as "man and wife." And like most American weddings, ours was still meticulously scheduled down to the eleven minutes we allocated for guests to eat their salads. American weddings may vary based on religion and personal tastes, but almost every one will still have somebody consulting an itinerary and throwing a fit if things go off-schedule.

Which couldn't be more different from the weddings in India we attended. We saw no visible signs of schedule or structure, and almost no interaction between the couple and their guests. Instead, the guests just busied themselves at the buffet while the bride waited out of sight for the groom to show up. Nobody seemed to know what time the groom would actually arrive on his horse-drawn carriage, and nobody seemed concerned when midnight passed and there was still no sign of him. When he did eventually pull up, heralded by a brass band in parade uniforms, the street outside the venue would fill with men dancing furiously while the bride's mother wailed and, above it all, the groom sat and looked terrified. A few ceremonies and blessings were tossed at the groom as he made his way from the carriage to join his bride on a raised dais, but the dancing throngs quieted down for none of them. And as the betrothed and their families prayed or chanted on the dais, guests would come and go as they pleased, snapping a few pictures with their phone before heading back for another plateful of golgappas.

"There is no structure in a typical Indian wedding," Mahua confirmed. "Just awareness about a bunch of customs that have to be undertaken. Those things just fall in place."

At only one of the weddings we attended were the majority of guests still present when the bride and groom finally began to receive them. We all rushed to hand them flowers and compliment their outfits while uncles and aunties dragged cousins and business relations up to pose for pictures. Aside from that, the weddings we saw were all buzzing vortices of celebration swirling around a bridal nucleus that was almost wholly removed from the happiness pulsating in their honor. The new couple just looked dazed and unhappy as they were led around the event. (And apparently their disposition is also part of the tradition: the bride is meant to appear devastated that she's saying goodbye to her family, and the groom is obliged to look terrified of his wedding night obligations.)

It's no wonder that Sharbani was much more concerned that Jenny and I come to the mehndi ceremony than to the actual wedding: at the wedding itself, there was no allowance for her to enjoy the presence of her friends. In fact, as we walked into her wedding with a few of our mutual friends, we saw Sharbani and her family performing some sort of ceremony in the main room. Following our friends' lead, we stopped and watched for no more than a few minutes before we all dashed to the buffet.

I don't remember speaking to Sharbani at any point during her wedding. But I guess that's okay—that's what the mehndi was for.

★

Jenny and I dated for four years before we lived together, and we lived together for eighteen months before we got married. Sharbani and Tapan got married after having spent no more than a few hours actually being face-to-face.

It wasn't exactly an arranged marriage. Nor was it precisely a love marriage. It was instead a union of both: a traditional institution modernized by new technology, changing mores and cheap airfare. Sharbani and Tapan found each other on one of the matrimony websites that are replacing the matchmakers who show up at prospective families' homes with binders full of photos and bios of potential matches. They began their relationship by speaking on the phone a few times, which went well enough that Tapan decided to fly from Bangalore to Delhi to meet Sharbani and her family. In Delhi, they shared two hours of conversation in the company of Sharbani's parents, followed by a chat at a coffee shop the next day. The next time they saw each other was in Bangalore, when Sharbani and her mother flew out to finalize the details of their marriage.

"I had the right to say no," Sharbani said when I asked if her parents would let her reject any matches they proposed. "My parents always respect my decisions." So while this was not an arranged marriage as we expected from the movies (in which two families meet and bargain in the bride-to-be's living room, and the girl sees her new husband only when she is called in to present tea on a silver tray), it was not a love marriage in any way Jenny and I could relate to.

But they love each other now. In fact, this is the most heart-warming aspect of Sharbani's story: after they agreed to get married, Sharbani and Tapan began to court each other. Sharbani flew to Bangalore to surprise Tapan for his birthday, meet his friends, spend time with his mother, and join Tapan on walks around the neighborhood in which they'd soon live. Together they drank coffee, ate dinner, and gave each other gifts; and then, as Tapan drove Sharbani to the airport for her return flight to Delhi, the betrothed couple held hands for the very first time. "I'll miss you," Tapan told Sharbani. They didn't see each other again until he flew to Delhi for the wedding.

Their story contains all the elements of a Western marriage, but in a different order: first came the engagement, and then came love, and then came the courtship.

In fact, of all the married couples we met in Delhi, only a few conformed to our expectations of Indian marriages. Some of our friends met along a traditionally Western trajectory: they dated, they fell in love, they got married. One couple we knew had a unique twist to this story: the man and his wife dated surreptitiously for years with the knowledge that his parents would never agree to a love marriage. So when the time came, they got a trusted friend to innocently suggest this girl as a potential match to the boy's parents. To this day, the boy's parents have no idea they got scammed.

But not every story was so romantic. One of my co-workers had his marriage all set until the girl backed out—because, according to the rumor mill, her parents found a guy with a higher income, a more promising career path, and a car of his own. (My co-worker only had a motorcycle.) And when a sister of one of Jenny's co-workers chose to marry for love—against her parents' wishes—the father cut off all ties with his daughter. He forbade anyone in the family from contacting her, and he refused to relent even when the sister called from the hospital with a new baby in her arms. Only when Jenny's co-worker went on an all-out hunger strike did her father finally relent to accepting his estranged daughter. Years had passed in the meantime.

But of all the things we learned about marriage in India, our biggest surprise was that arranged marriage was not dreaded. In fact, most of the people we spoke to were in favor of the system. *Newsweek* reports that ninety percent of all urban Indian marriages are arranged.[2] Before we came to India, we would have expected that statistic to mean that ninety percent of all urban Indians were coerced onto the altar, but that wasn't the case. My co-worker Sonia told me that while most Indian girls grew up dreaming of love, they nevertheless looked forward to an arranged marriage. That's because, while Bollywood movies do indeed glorify love marriage (the hero and heroine fall in love, her father promises the heroine to some jerk, and then the hero wins over the father at the end), those are just fantasies. It's analogous to American boys who grow up fantasizing about winning the Super Bowl: we'd all love to have been America's greatest athlete, but we're still perfectly content with how life turns out even if we don't become the next John Elway.

Jenny and I cannot imagine a relationship based on anything but our own choices. It's safe to say that both of us would have preferred to live our lives searching for love

---

2. http://www.newsweek.com/id/137472

than to have our parents find it for us in a database. But a proponent of arranged marriage would wonder why we'd leave such an important decision to the whims of mere emotion, without a dispassionate examination of the potential spouse's career trajectory, religious compatibility and family background. The odds of finding true love are actually seen to be better in an arranged system because they seek the ideal spouse scientifically; we just stumble through life, hoping that our perfect match just happens to be sitting on that bar stool over there. What could be a more irrational way to make the most important decision of our lives? No wonder that in America, forty-five percent of marriages end in divorce; in India, that number is around one percent.[3]

Still, this rational approach to marriage has an emotional cost. One of my co-workers was head-over-heels, stand-up-in-a-restaurant-and-shout-it in love with her boyfriend. But when she told her family about him, they gave her a stark choice: if she married him, they'd disown her. Unlike Jenny's co-worker's sister, she couldn't choose love over family.

In America, love is more powerful than blood. Americans will marry against their parents' wishes, or sometimes explicitly to spite them. But in India, family is everything— and for this particular girl, and for so many others, family is the only choice.

★

---

3. http://www.divorcemag.com/statistics/statsWorld.shtml

As Jenny and I orbited Delhi culture (observing from a distance, touching down for a closer look, retreating to analyse what we saw), the inscrutable slowly acquired clarity. The things that baffled us from the first day began, with repeated observation, to obtain significance. We came to understand and even mirror some of the cultural nuances, which in turn led to deeper engagement with the country around us.

Indian standards of personal space, for example. This cultural nuance was especially difficult to accept, because it required adjusting to more than just being pressed against in queues. I had to develop a much higher threshold for touching, hugging, and other forms of nonchalant guy-on-guy contact that would violate all norms of masculinity back home. Loose hand-holding was perfectly common among buddies. As was it common for guys to wrap their arms around each other in casual friendship. Male co-workers would sit on each other's laps when there was nowhere else to sit, and this act had no greater significance beyond pointing out that we needed more chairs in the conference room.

So while at first I'd jerk away when my colleague Dipankar would give me surprise back massages—picture Angela Merkel's reaction to George W. Bush kneading her shoulders—I eventually learned to appreciate it for what it was and what it wasn't. (Which allowed me to surrender myself to his skilled hands—my god, can that guy give a back rub.)

In fact, male-on-male contact was sometimes used to signify hypermasculinity, which is exactly the opposite of how Westerners interpret it. When two teenage boys would see Jenny coming down the street, they'd clutch at each other's waists and sing softly in her direction. To them, this was probably the height of macho; but for Jenny, she couldn't help but giggle as she interpreted it through her own cultural perspective.

The cultural acceptability of guy-on-guy contact permitted dance floor moves that, as signs of manly posturing, were hilarious only to unenlightened us. I'll never forget one office party—a night of booze and madness in the office canteen—when the pulsating music inspired a particularly large colleague to dangle a particularly small colleague upside-down over his back, with the large one holding the small one by his right foot as they paraded around the dance floor and writhed their rear ends against each other.

As our time went on in Delhi, other gestures also acquired clearer meaning. Body language that we'd been unable to interpret when we first encountered it fell into patterns as we saw it again, until implication slid into place and the movement suddenly meant something. Sitting at Sagar Ratna's in Defence Colony, for instance, Jenny elbowed me to lift my face from my dosa to watch a distinguished old lady in a muted salmon sari stand gracefully as her grandchildren spilled out of their chairs and, one by one, genuflected before her as if to—what? Were they bowing?

Clarity came as we saw this same act performed by sycophants stooping before politicians and beggar children prostrating themselves on the floor of our stopped autorickshaw. This was how Indians showed respect: they'd touch someone's feet.

However, just because we understood a gesture, it didn't mean we knew how to use it. I once tried to touch Mahua's feet as a humorously exaggerated reply to some minor HR-related favor she'd granted me at work. But as I stooped before her, she grabbed me to prevent me from following through. I then guessed that this was also part of the ritual: maybe truly humble people prevent others from debasing themselves in their honor? This was what I expected the next time I tried it, as another show of ironic gratitude, this time directed towards my co-worker Sonia. I bent down and then halted halfway in my stoop, waiting for Sonia to grab my shoulder. Except Sonia made no move—perhaps she felt I owed her this respect, or maybe she just thought I was reaching for a fallen pen. Either way, I was suddenly off balance and unsure whether it would be ruder to pull away or to start groping her shoes. In my hesitation, I was spared one humiliation only by another: I fell over.

Other guestures Jenny and I observed required far less coordination to mimic, like touching our foreheads. This reverent gesture, commonly seen in temples, was also performed by co-workers to show mock respect and by shopkeepers to show genuine thanks for the first sale of the day. Another gesture was the way our office guards would salute us as we passed, raising their hands to the vicinity of the forehead with their palms facing out; the crispness of the motion suggested that it was derived from the military. There was also a loose-fingered doorknob-turning gesture that vendors and shopkeepers would perform at us to communicate "maybe" or "kind of" or "I have no idea what you're saying." And there was an apologetic gesture that was performed by touching one's chest with one's fingertips, although I only ever saw my co-worker Soumya perform this; it could be that this was just his personal habit. He'd make that gesture every time my feet would accidentally brush his, which was quite often because I'm apparently as clumsy at controlling my own feet as I am at touching others'.

And then, of course, there was the head bobble.

The Indian head bobble has been written about everywhere from the *Lonely Planet* to *Shantaram*, a novel about the Bombay underworld that is as ubiquitous on the tourist circuit as multicolored hippie jodhpurs. However, the guidebooks generally describe only its most exaggerated form: as a signal of vigorous affirmation that's enthusiastically performed by shoeshine boys outside the Taj Mahal who know how adorable Westerners find it, and how much they tip when they see it.

But there are subtleties and variations of the head bobble that go far beyond the reservation confirmation of the five-star hotel clerk. The head bobble can mean "hello," or "thank you," or "you're welcome." It can communicate peaceful intent among two men whose eyes meet in a cash machine vestibule. Auto drivers use a curt derivation of the bobble to end a fare negotiation, rotating their heads laterally in a manner that I'd usually misinterpret as Delhi shorthand for a Brooklyn-accented "Get da fuck out of here wit' your 'fifty rupees to Khan Market!'" Only after I'd start walking away would they call after me and clarify their meaning.

More inscrutable than that was my boss Murali's head bobble habit: a singularly incomprehensible motion that defied everything I thought I knew about head bobbling. He'd close his eyes and shake his head horizontally as I'd present work to him; to my Western eyes, it appeared as a combination of refusal and ecstasy. In my first weeks of knowing him, I had to clarify numerous times if he hated my ideas or if he was getting off on them.

And then there was the office boy at work, who would accept my lunch order ("Veg or non-veg?") with a sharp jerk that finally brought clarity to the mysterious gesture performed by the waiter at Nathu's Sweets on my very first day in Delhi. He wasn't saying "gee"—he was saying "ji," which meant "yes, sir." And his gesture, which I'd interpreted to be disdainful because I had no other context for it, was just another variation of the head bobble. It turns out that I don't order food like a douchebag after all.

5

The Food: Oh My God, the Food

Jenny and I moved to India for the food.

When we first considered going abroad, Jenny was more interested in China. But when I thought back to all the weird dim sum we'd encountered in New York City's Chinatown—every roll and dumpling wheeled past our table seemed composed primarily of gelatinous seafood—I feared we'd spend most of our meals in China staring distrustfully at our plates and then heading off in search of McDonalds. Our experiences with Indian food, on the other hand, left us wanting more every single time: more ghee on our naan, more raita on our biryani, more trips to the buffet.

We first learned to love Indian food at the touristy restaurants that once clustered on East 6th Street in the Village. We soon grew beyond their mulligatawny-and-curry set meals to frequent Lexington Avenue vegetarian restaurants and downtown dives popular with taxi drivers. We once bicycled to Jackson Heights, the Indian neighborhood in Queens, and ate so much that we were physically unable to ride back home; we fell asleep on the subway with our bicycles chained to our legs, our bellies distended and joyfully churning, dreaming of what curries and kormas must taste like when they're not dumbed-down for the American palate. One year, my co-worker Sunita invited us to her home for a Diwali party; and for the promise of home-made Indian food, we actually traveled to Jersey City. After that journey, moving to India only seemed slightly more drastic.

When we fantasized about life in India, we didn't imagine ringing bells and honking horns. We imagined the food. And we specifically fixated on the real deal: we wanted to eat someone's mother's home cooking.

And soon after we arrived in India, we hired a woman named Ganga to cook and clean for us three days a week. In her early thirties with two school-age children, Ganga's English skills had helped her ascend into the well-paying niche of working for foreigners. But Ganga could have spent her days lying on our couch eating bonbons for all we cared, because we were really only concerned with one aspect of her resume: that she cooked for us.

We were in India, eating someone's mother's home cooking. Every single day.

Consider where we were at that moment in our lives. We'd just packed up our apartment in Brooklyn, enlisted a half-dozen friends to lug everything we owned into a storage locker in Queens, taken a fifty percent cut in our income, said goodbye to everyone we knew, flown 7,000 bleary-eyed miles over twenty-four cramp-legged hours, spent five frantic days in Gurgaon trying to move out, and plunked down twice as much for a flat as a person with darker skin would have paid for it. But the first taste of the first dish Ganga made for us—paneer in a creamy tomato-based gravy—made it all worth it.

And every subsequent bite we'd take for the next eighteen months was an equal joy. Every Monday, Wednesday and Friday, we would put 300 rupees on the counter as we left for work and return home to three freshly cooked entrées waiting in our refrigerator. For just six dollars, Ganga would buy everything she needed to make us enough for two lunches and two dinners—eight full meals—and still have change left over. As a native of the state of Andhra Pradesh, her culinary portfolio was north Indian with a Hyderabadi flair: paneer makhani, aloo gobi, rajma masala, malai kofta, egg curry, masala baingan (lord, how we miss her masala baingan!), sautéed bhindi with crunchy onions and just enough fire to justify an extra spoonful of her creamy boondi raita, vegetable biryani, palak paneer, and much more. Even her white rice, spiced with fragrant cloves or mixed with browned onions, was delicious enough to eat on its own. Sometime during her career she'd picked up presentation skills as well, and our Tupperware full of dal makhani would be topped with a decorative swirl of cream, a garnish of cilantro and a few slivers of raw ginger artfully arranged at oblique angles to the rectangular container walls.

When we first interviewed Ganga for the job, we asked her to cook for us whatever she would for her family. She assured us that she'd dial down the spice for our sensitive Western taste buds. "No!" we protested. "We want it exactly like you'd make for your family." She looked worried, and I think she imagined Jenny and I running around the apartment holding ice cubes to our tongues, smoke coming out of our ears, making plans to fire her as soon as we could talk again. But she did as we asked, and a few months later she told us that none of her friends believed that her foreign clients could handle food as spicy as she was known for making it.

I gained ten pounds in my first couple of months in India, all thanks to Ganga's food. Every morning, I'd load up the four metal canisters of my electric tiffin (a Thermos-like lunchbox that warmed its contents when I plugged it in) with what was probably a pound and a half of food. There was so much food that I'd have to plug in the tiffin an hour before lunchtime because it would take that long to heat up. One day my tiffin short-circuited and melted under my desk, which was a blessing for my waistline because I actually had the self-discipline to replace it with a smaller one. But even during those days when I was gorging on four full canisters I still ate every morsel and wished I'd brought more. (I was so embarrassed when my co-workers would gape at the size of the mound on my plate that I began opening just two canisters at a time; I'd wait until nobody was looking to surreptitiously open the other two.)

We were living our dream with every meal. But the very culture that facilitated my gluttony also provided a steep impediment to it: when it comes to food, Indians like to share.

My first introduction into India's culture of food sharing came on my third morning in the country. I'd sat down to meet with Murali, the creative director of the ad agency at which I'd now be working. Later described by Jenny as "boisterously bombastic," Murali was the kind of guy who became the immediate center of attention in every room he entered. I was assigned to be his Creative Group Lead for copy, which meant I'd oversee the department's day-to-day operations so he could spend his time smoking cigarettes with the clients. (Murali believed that far more business was conducted during cigarette breaks than in actual meetings. And judging from the way he and the client would return from the smokers' balcony slapping each other's backs and informing everyone of the decisions they'd made, he was quite clearly right.)

I shook hands with Murali and sat on his couch. We chatted as he opened a plastic container and took out his breakfast: a kebab of some sort, with meat and vegetables wrapped in a paper-thin roomali roti. He dipped it in some green chutney and prepared to take a bite, and then paused to say something before it made it to his mouth. And as he spoke, one of my new co-workers appeared at the door, grabbed the roll from Murali's hand, bit off a third of it, placed it back in Murali's hand, and walked away.

The co-worker hadn't said a word. And Murali hadn't even looked up to see who took his breakfast. Murali just dipped the remainder of his kebab in the chutney and, this time, managed to take a bite of his own.

What I'd witnessed, I'd soon learn, was not out of the ordinary. In my office and in those in which Jenny worked, anybody's food was everybody's food. Anything that was on the table—whether brought from home or ordered from McDonalds—was open for anyone to grab a few spoonfuls or take a few bites. If someone had sent the office boy out to buy samosas from the chaiwallah, nobody needed an invitation when he returned to rush over and eat one. Many desks had water bottles with their owner's name on them, but anyone thirsty would simply reach for the nearest one. And anyone walking by my desk while I was stuffing my face with Ganga's finest felt no social compunction against grabbing my fork and helping themselves to a bite or two.

Once I knew this, I would make a big show of offering my food to anyone within earshot. I wanted to fit in, after all. But behind my smile, I'd grit my teeth as my precious baingan bharta would disappear from my plate.

This communal approach to food was as much about sharing company as it was about sharing sustenance. Nobody ever wanted to eat alone. Jenny's co-workers would coordinate their daily schedules to ensure they all ate lunch at the same time. And while official business in my office was conducted in English, the conversation in the canteen was almost entirely in Hindi, a more casual language for the laughing and gossiping that danced around me as I fake-laughed when everyone else did, wishing I could participate while quietly studying who was taking from my plate so I could take equal amounts from theirs. Such was the power of this social occasion that even those co-workers who hated each other would joke together over their shared dal.

(But I soon gave up on community lunches. I preferred instead to eat at my desk while reading the *New York Times* online. I know that some co-workers found my mealtime isolation to be aloof, or even arrogant. But their lunchtime camaraderie made me homesick for my friends and family who were nine-and-a-half time zones behind me, asleep and unavailable on instant messenger at that time of day. The *New York Times* was the next best thing.)

★

One of the few items that my co-workers would never want to share was the carrot sticks that I'd snack on to avoid the temptation of pre-lunch raids into my tiffin. So naturally, I made a big show of trying to share them so people wouldn't realize how stingy with my food I really was. And I'd tease my co-workers Anurag or Soumya when they refused, telling them, "In America, it's considered an insult to my ancestors if you refuse to eat my vegetables." They'd reluctantly agree and then scrunch their faces as they chewed. "Who snacks on raw carrots?" they'd ask me.

Well, nobody in any country truly enjoys snacking on raw carrots. But in India, they actually tasted better than they did in the US. In fact, all of India's fruits and vegetables tasted better. That's because in the States, fruits and vegetables are bred to meet Americans' demand for unnatural perfection. Consumers prize produce that looks uniform and shiny like it rolled off a factory floor; taste is a secondary consideration. We have huge white onions that weigh a pound each but are bland enough to eat like apples. We have perfect pink tomatoes with flawless skin and tasteless flesh. We have green peppers that form rows of identical spheres but taste indistinguishable from celery.

In Indian vegetable markets, the imperfection of unmediated nature is on full display: the vegetables are smaller, uglier and more frequently blemished than those in America. But they're far more flavorful. The tomatoes may be splashed with green and yellow patches, but they crunch deliciously in a salad. The onions may be golf balls instead of softballs, but no American onion has ever been sharp enough to make me cry when I cut it. And even plain green peppers—called "capsicum" in the local markets— were so full of flavor as to almost taste spicy.

The superiority of Indian vegetables reflects the demands of that particular marketplace: Indian shoppers care less about the vegetables' appearance than about their flavor and value. They typically bargain for their produce with the sellers, which means an ugly tomato that tastes the same as an attractive one may actually be more desirable, because the flaws are a point of negotiation. Jenny and I would watch dramatic back-and-forths between vendors and housewives, with the housewife pointing out the flaws in his offerings while the vendor extolled their hidden virtues. She'd demand a lower price and he'd plead for her to consider his daughter's upcoming wedding. He'd root through his stock to pick out items to fit her expectations, and she'd reject them immediately and berate him for trying to pawn off his lousy produce on her. She'd then haughtily pick out her own selection, which is what the vendor knew she'd do anyway.

(A blogger called Thequark sums it up well for us. "A vegetable-buying experience is not a mere act of give and take, or a supply meets demand," he wrote, "but rather a creative fiction between two talents and an eye for picking out the right kind of vegetables. It's the buyer's talent to negotiate, and you would not believe the kind of arguments thrown to the vendor to reduce the price—you certainly wouldn't find them in game theory or other economic texts. It is the vendor's talent to not let price go down, to ensure he is not left with the worst lot if every one picks the freshest ones. Try picking out fresh ladyfingers individually and face their wrath!"[1])

Jenny and I never felt comfortable bargaining for our produce. That's mostly because we had no idea what to consider a good price, and also because we always forgot to consult the newspapers' price tables to know a good deal when we saw one. So instead of bargaining, we'd bluff half-heartedly and hope the vendor would take pity on us. "How much?" We'd ask him, handing him a basket of carrots.

He'd throw a few more carrots into our basket before weighing it and quoting a figure. "Seventy rupees."

"Seventy rupees?!" we'd repeat, feigning incredulity. "Come on, man!"

"Haan ji," he'd tell us, "seventy rupees. One kilo, seventy rupees."

"Really?" we'd demand, our hands on our hips, our heads cocked, channeling George Jefferson.

---

1. http://ourdelhistruggle.com/2010/01/25/finished-manuscript/#comment-2893

"Haan ji."

"Oh." Pause. Defeat. "Oh. Okay. Here's seventy rupees."

Beyond our lack of market rate knowledge, we couldn't bring ourselves to argue over individual rupees with men who spent their nights sleeping on cots outside the very stands they spent their days working in. Besides, we didn't think the vendors were cheating us that much.

Although in that second belief, we may have been alone. Our neighbor Anya regaled us with horror stories that mirrored a nationwide mistrust of the food chain: rumors that they inject syrups into melons to make them redder and sweeter, that they put chemicals on apples to ripen them quicker, that fish sellers have some sort of illicit lotion they use to make rotting scales shimmer like new. The newspapers periodically reported even further horrors of food adulteration: steroids or oxytocin injected into plants to make them look fresh and fluffy,[2] vegetables coated in wax or pesticides to make them shiny,[3] brick dust added to chilli powder,[4] and many other tales to make shoppers indignantly view each transaction with the suspicion that the vendor is out to poison them. From that perspective, every trip to the market is undertaken with the underlying fear that one misjudged mango or under-

---

2. http://www.indiastudychannel.com/resources/73074-Harmful-chemicals-fresh-looking-vegetables.aspx

3. http://timesofindia.indiatimes.com/Delhi/Govt-arms-itself-to-check-vegetable-adulteration/articleshow/4646131.cms

4. http://timesofindia.indiatimes.com/Cities/Allahabad/Adulteration-on-rise-during-summer-season/articleshow/4693574.cms

examined cucumber might turn their children into Frankenstein's monsters.

We assume that most people have at least one preferred vendor in their local market whom they trust to keep the prices reasonable and the produce non-toxic. We held secret try-outs when we first arrived, seeking reasons to prefer one vegetablewallah over the other but failing to spot any points of distinction. Eventually, we settled on the vegetable stand diagonally across the sidewalk from where we bought our mobile phone top-ups simply because he usually had the biggest queue; we assumed that meant he had the best stuff. But when we mentioned to Anya which veggiewallah we preferred, she was surprised. "Why would you choose *him*?"

When Jenny explained that his goods attracted a crowd, she laughed. "Those are all maids! He's known for writing fake receipts so they can skim a few rupees off the top!"

★

Like most American tourists, Jenny and I were obsessed with avoiding the local water. That's why we were so horrified when we saw *Slumdog Millionaire*. We'd strutted into the theater with the cockiness of veteran travelers, but we both gasped out loud as we watched Salim, while working in the Bombay restaurant, fill a bottle of Bisleri water from the tap and then reseal the tamper-proof cap with super glue.

It wasn't the refilling that shocked us. It was the resealing.

We closely scrutinized every drop we drank to ensure we didn't ingest raw municipal water. In our Hauz Khas flat, we relied on the musical electric water filter our landlord had installed; it played an eight-bit version of Beethoven's *Für Elise* as it operated to protect us from all waterborne threats. But outside of our kitchen, our entire line of defense consisted of confirming that the tamper-proof cap hadn't been tampered with. We'd put our full faith in those caps to protect us from bottles that had been refilled and resold because we'd never conceived that it was possible to spoof the seal. On the rare instances when we were sold a bottle that opened without tamper-proof resistance, Jenny and I held an immediate whisper conference. Depending on how many people were around for us to look silly in front of, we'd either hand the rejected bottle back to the vendor and demand another, or accept it with no intention of drinking it and then look for another vendor out of sight of the first.

The only time either of us ever knowingly drank from a suspicious bottle was on one extremely hot day when Jenny was touring the Red Fort without me. The sun was an angry god, all the shaded seats were occupied, and the water in the bottle looked so cold and delicious that she decided not to worry about how easily the cap had come off. Of course, she got sick.

Many brands of water add extra security by shrink-wrapping plastic around the tamper-proof cap. The plastic, too, is usually a good measure of purity, except for when we bought water from a vendor outside of Raj Ghat: the plastic slid right off. My parents were with us at the time, so

I switched into my tough-guy act to impress them, protesting loudly to the vendor about his attempt to poison us. The vendor stared blankly, so I shook the bottle and gestured sharply at the cap. The vendor exchanged a glance with the guy manning the adjacent ice cream cart, but said nothing. After a helpless moment that I attempted to disguise as a manly stare-down, I slammed the water bottle on his cart and walked brusquely away, knowing that I'd taught him a lesson: he could keep his water *and* my money.

Traveling up the sanitary continuum from peddlers to restaurants (from filthy plates to obscene bills), we became wary of water for a different reason: the fancier the restaurant, the more they'd charge for bottled water, and the more likely we didn't need it at all. Any five-star restaurant charging a 1,500 percent mark-up on a fourteen-rupee bottle of water will also provide filtered water for free, grudgingly, if one asks, and if one doesn't mind the waiter's disdainful sniff.

Ultimately, though, we knew that we wouldn't be able to avoid local water forever. Too many times we watched our pure Himalayan bottled water get poured into a glass so freshly cleaned that there was still a quarter-inch of city water in the bottom. We decided to see this as for the best. We were in Delhi for the long haul, so a wet glass here or a moist plate there would help prime our stomachs for that sleepy morning when we accidentally opened our mouths in the shower.

★

Many travelers avoid water altogether by drinking beer. In fact, we read in one of our travel books that drinking local beer helps the stomach acclimatize to new places, which was all the excuse we needed. While there wasn't much choice beyond Heineken, Guinness, and a handful of identical-tasting lagers (Tiger, Fosters, Carlsberg), the beer scene was dominated by Kingfisher. We'll always remember India's most popular beer for the legendary hangovers it brewed: our morning headaches would hammer at our skulls even before we went to bed the night before.

The reason Kingfisher was so proficient at ruining our mornings after, we were told, was that they added glycerine to keep it from spoiling in the heat. I suppose we should thank them for beer that stays fresh no matter how hot the unplugged refrigerator in which it's stored, but sometimes it felt like we were spending as much on Paracetamol the next morning as we were on beer at the bar.

Travelers in Goa have developed a trick to remove the glycerine: they turn the Kingfisher upside-down into a glass of water. The chemical will seep out while, thanks to the magic of atmospheric pressure, the beer itself stays in the bottle. It's an effective trick (and it's satisfying to watch that loathsome glycerine weep into the glass), but when there's a dozen bottles on the table and as many people racing to top up their mugs, who doesn't suddenly feel like *this* might be the one time they're immune to the Kingfisher curse?

Whenever we'd order a bottle at a restaurant—be it water or beer—the waiter would hold it out for us to check its temperature. At first, though, we didn't know that's why they were extending it to us; only after observing others did we learn that they expected us to touch the bottle to confirm it was cold. Which meant that we spent our first weeks assuming that waiters were presenting us our water the way a sommelier presents wine. ("Oh, yes," I'd say, bending over to scrutinize the label on the bottle of Kinley. "That's a fine brand. Very nice. A product of the Coca-Cola Company, I daresay. Jenny, would you care to taste?")

Aside from Guinness, most beers were extremely affordable. They'd cost around forty-five rupees for a big bottle in the liquor store and only two or three times that in a reasonably priced restaurant. But the best combination of taste and value, to my palate at least, was whisky. India offered a variety of mid-range brands I'd never heard of (Teachers, Vat 69, Blender's Pride, Royal Challenge) that were indistinguishable to my uneducated tongue from the imported blends. But I learned the hard way to beware anything claiming to be high-end that wasn't priced as such. In the upmarket liquor store near GK-II, I came across a single-malt Scotch priced at one-sixth of the cheapest bottle of imported stuff. The clerk assured me that it was legitimate, and the stiff cardboard tube was indeed printed with pastoral Scottish scenes, so I bought it and drank a single glass that evening.

That single glass was the only point that my diet had deviated from Jenny's in the previous three days. So there is no other possible culprit for my subsequent food poisoning, which was so severe that I was pooping blood by the end of the week.

We generally avoided Indian wine after a few educational bottles taught us all we needed to know about its taste and its subsequent hangovers. Indian wine is a relatively new industry. It needs a few more years to mature before it'll compare favorably with imported brands—even though the state-run liquor stores are doing their best to level the playing field by storing imported and domestic bottles on dusty shelves in sweltering stores. Half of the imported wine we splurged on turned out to be vinegar.

These government liquor stores seemed almost purposely designed to make buying booze as dehumanizing and frustrating as possible. (After all, the government would surely want to discourage the rampant drunk driving that plagues Delhi after sundown.) To buy booze at the Hauz Khas market's liquor store, we'd have to shove through a narrow doorway clogged ten people deep and past the counter where surly employees slapped into their customers' hands the most undeserving fifty-rupee plonk ever to have the label "whisky" applied to it. In the back of the store, where nobody ever seemed to go but us, bottles of wine were covered with months of dust. Outside the shop, autorickshaws screeched to a halt; their drivers would dash in with exact change in an outstretched fist and their free palm itching for the bottle that would warm them better than any blanket on the cold winter nights. We learned very quickly not to hire any auto driver who was parked in front of the liquor store. Although in retrospect, it may have been better to be driven by someone at the beginning of their nightly binge than after they'd already spent a couple of hours working on it.

In all the times we went to the Hauz Khas market liquor
store, Jenny was the only woman we ever saw buying
booze. Which worked to our favor, because the men
always let her jump the queue.

The more respectable members of the community looked
down upon liquor stores. One day I chatted with my
neighbor Dr. T. as I was leaving the house to pick up some
beer. When I told him where I was headed, he remembered
that he, too, needed some booze to entertain an evening
house guest. He took a few steps towards the market with
me, stopped, and thought better of it.

"No," he said, "I can't go to that store. Too many
people know me here." He got into his car instead and
drove to a liquor store in a neighborhood where he'd be
more anonymous.

★

We drank about as much alcohol in Delhi as we did in
Brooklyn, which meant we'd finish perhaps a bottle of
wine a week and a bottle of harder stuff every couple of
months. We'd put our empties on the shared terrace along
with the rest of our garbage for Shilpa, the building's maid,
to remove in the morning. One day, while hanging our
laundry, we stumbled upon a cache of our bottles hidden
under a ledge, behind a pile of bricks. Shilpa had been
stashing them.

Anya told us why: our trash was Shilpa's revenue stream.
She only earned 300 rupees per month from each of the

flats in our building, so she supplemented that income by going through all our trash and selling the good stuff to the kabadiwallahs. Shilpa was hoarding the bottles, Anya said, because the more she sold at one time, the better the price she'd get for each one. Obviously, Shilpa had recognized our consumption patterns and was holding out for us to continue them. Or maybe she knew Christmas was coming and that our holiday party would mean a celebration for her as well.

"You didn't peel off the labels before you threw them out, did you?" Anya asked. "If you did, she couldn't have resold them."

The labels were the key. Unlike the afterlife of plastic water bottles, which amounts to simple recycling (cooking oil, after all, comes in the same kinds of bottles as mineral water), the post-consumer economy for liquor bottles is driven by something else: the desire to look wealthy without necessarily being that way.

Liquor is big in India.[5] And foreign whisky is especially coveted: India drinks forty percent more whisky[6] than the US. My commute through Gurgaon took me past dozens of billboards promoting Ireland's finest export with vague headlines about "living the good times" and "making it" alongside photos of bikini-clad beach-goers or Saif Ali

---

5. http://economictimes.indiatimes.com/News/News-By-Industry/Cons-Products/Liquor/India-tops-Diageos-growth-markets-in-H2/articleshow/4127158.cms

6. http://www.mg.co.za/article/2006-03-03-battle-for-the-worlds-largest-whisky-market-india

Khan looking smugly satisfied with the good times he was living as a direct result of making it.

(Technically, those billboards weren't advertising booze. Dwarfed by the giant logos or bouncing breasts would be a few words set in tiny type that explained what the ad was *actually* promoting: "Cricket gear," said the ad for Seagram's Royal Stag in letters perhaps two percent as tall as the whisky logo. "Music CDs" said the ad for Bacardi rum, implying that the bikini girls were having such a sexy good time only because of what they were listening to. I presume this technique allows Bacardi to skirt some law banning liquor advertising by pointing to the words and telling the regulators, "No, it's all perfectly legal. We're just advertising our latest tunes!")

All over the city, billboards assured the citizenry that one could be seen as classy and sophisticated only if they drank the right brand of booze. And this is why Shilpa was hoarding our bottles: to help people whose aspirations weren't matched by their incomes. These people knew that there were a few markets in the city in which vendors sat surrounded by empty bottles of booze. We stumbled upon one of them near Shanti Niketan: haphazard piles of cheap vodka bottles, neat rows labeled for mid-range rum and, in the spot of honor, well-preserved bottles of whisky that had been shielded from the sun, their labels intact and clean, often accompanied by the fancy printed cardboard tubes in which they were originally sold. The people who bought these bottles would presumably refill them with cheap swill so they could flatter their guests into thinking they're being served the good stuff. The guest's eyes would pop when he sees the green Johnnie Walker label, and the host would hope he's too bedazzled to notice that the first sip is already making his head hurt.

I hope that Shilpa negotiated for the full value of that empty eighteen-year-old bottle of Glenfiddich single malt scotch I'd bought at the duty-free. Because somebody at the demand end of the empty bottle economy would surely pay a lot of money to serve 200-rupee rotgut from it the next time his father-in-law paid a surprise visit.

★

Despite the joy we felt every time we opened the refrigerator and beheld Ganga's latest creation, there were still times when homesickness or actual sickness would make us crave food that tasted like home or behaved in ways our stomachs could predict. Which is when we would be grudgingly happy that the viruses that have transformed every American suburb into the gastronomic twin of every other American suburb are even infecting Delhi: Ruby Tuesday and TGI Friday's and Bennigans and other chain restaurants are sprouting like boils, blemishing the subcontinent with the blandest outgrowths of American culture that, nevertheless, were occasionally just what we needed. And while we accept that there's nothing worse than traveling halfway across the world and then visiting the same restaurants we ate at with our high school friends, that's where life lead us to celebrate our third wedding anniversary. (We just really wanted a beer that wasn't Kingfisher, and the Ruby Tuesday in GK-II had Corona on their menu.)

Fortunately, when the urge hit for imported flavors, Delhi also had options that weren't global chains. There was excellent pizza at Flavors, near the Moolchand flyover, and decent Mexican food at Sancho's in South Extension Part II that was cooked by an actual Mexican chef (until he left the country, reportedly because the food in India didn't agree with him). If we wanted to go more upmarket, the Smokehouse Grill near GK-II was as close to a steakhouse as Delhi could get without serving actual beef, although filet mignon of buffalo was on the menu. When we needed something guaranteed not to agitate our endlessly churning stomachs, Subway's subs were reliably identical to those served two continents away. And every so often we'd get one of the coveted invitations to dine in the various embassy restaurants, where we would eat authentic cheese in the company of underdressed expats.

If we were combating a particularly virulent outbreak of homesickness, we might head to a five-star hotel. Not that we patronized such places at home; in fact, we deliberately avoided any scene that would turn people away for wearing sandals or, for that matter, could accurately be described as a "scene." But in Delhi, we needed periodic respites from the city, and while the guilt of driving past beggars and slums and sidewalk-sleeping laborers on the way to 400-rupee Kingfishers was hard to reconcile, it usually evaporated in the lavender haze of the lobby flower arrangements.

Most five-star hotels have multiple five-star restaurants, and a few of those are transcendent. Bukhara in the ITC Maurya is rightly famous. Bill Clinton said it made him "wish he had two stomachs" (although I have had meals at

Taco Bell that have made me wish the same thing). But Bukhara is famous for the wrong dish: its storied meat plates blurred together in my mouth and inflicted upon me my first-ever meat headache; but its dal makhani was so creamy that it almost tasted like chocolate. The Oberoi's 360 restaurant offers a delicious variety of Japanese-inspired everything, but the Oberoi's Italian restaurant was no better than Flavors, despite being three times as expensive.

Many of these hotels also offer Sunday brunch extravaganzas. At the Oberoi 360, a mere 2,500 rupees got us all the food we could eat and all the wine or champagne we could drink; but it turns out that we couldn't eat enough to hold us over for a week, which is how full we'd hoped to have been to justify the cost of the indulgence. A more cost-conscious alternative is the Metropolitan hotel, where brunch is only—*only*—1,800 rupees. Their selection was smaller and skewed Japanese, which was fine for a sushi lover like me: there aren't many oceans near Delhi, so this was one of the few places I trusted the fish. (Seafood in Delhi was probably the one thing I was more wary of than the water.)

To supplement Ganga's food, Delhi offered plenty of other Indian options. (I'll refuse to admit that we ever chose to eat out when we had Ganga's food in the fridge— I miss it so much, I don't want to contemplate having ever passed it up.) Jenny favored Park Balluchi in Hauz Khas village both for the food and the jungle park atmosphere; it was there where she decided that paneer tikka kebabs, roasted in a tandoori oven with blackened spices encrusting milky sweet paneer, and then wrapped in roomali roti with red onion and mint chutney, was one of the world's perfect dishes. (We discovered that the paneer tikka at Saket's Citywalk mall food court was nearly as good, although we're embarrassed to have eaten there so often.) Excellent north Indian food could be found everywhere from the upscale Punjabi By Nature chain to the tiny Chulha Chonka in Lajpat Nagar IV, which specialized in sarson ka saag, a delicious forest-colored sludge of mustard greens that was only available in fall and winter.

Back in New York, even as we dreamed of diving head first into a vat of chicken curry, we remained ignorant of the diversity of Indian cuisine. Never mind not knowing the difference between Mughlai and Punjabi—we didn't even know there was a difference between north and south Indian styles. But we are quick students, and it didn't take us long to appreciate the nuances of the cuisine. When we got tired of heavy Mughlai gravies—such dishes should only be enjoyed in moderation, in interest of both palate desensitization and waistline expansion—we'd head over to Sagar Ratna in Defence Colony. Their south Indian specialities included dosas with potato filling and uttappams that were embedded with coconut meat and roasted tomatoes and served with bottomless bowls of sambar. But our favorite south Indian restaurant was Saravana Bhavan in Connaught Place. It was too far north to casually visit, but we rarely missed it if we were in the neighborhood.

One of Delhi's biggest concentrations of upscale restaurants was in Khan Market. The Big Chill had good Western food, and Chokola in particular served one of the few passable Western breakfasts in the city, which is why the

Democrats Abroad organization regularly met there during the US election to discuss which one of us was in love with Candidate Obama more.

The inner alley of Khan Market, where many of the restaurants are located, had crumbling sidewalks and oozing manholes that were at aesthetic odds with the area's supposed position among the most expensive commercial real estate in the world. Nevertheless, it also boasted a few terrific kebab shops that were mobbed late into the night; I arrived home many evenings with Salim's mutton burra still smeared on my face. Despite the muddy cobblestones and dangling power lines around Salim's, I was never nervous about eating there, because there was always a line of customers that testified to their salubrity.

And this judgement reflects a certain bit of folk wisdom that American tourists pass along to one another: if a restaurant or street vendor has a line of customers, its food is probably safe to eat. The logic behind this rule is that locals intrinsically know who serves good food and who spoons out cumin-sprinkled botulism. We adhered to this rule religiously, despite its inherent inconsistencies: on some days, the bored-looking Nepali vendors in Hauz Khas market who were selling momos—what Americans would call Chinese dumplings—would have a half-dozen people clustered around their stalls, while other days they stared glumly at the passing traffic. I only bought from them on the busy days, just in case everyone else knew something I didn't.

My co-worker Pankaj told us that he followed a variation of this rule: he would instantly trust any food vendor if he saw a Sikh man eating there.

The follow-the-crowd rule served us well. One day when I was walking along Chandni Chowk in Old Delhi, I spotted a line at a food stall stretching fifteen feet back into an alley. I instantly joined it, even though I didn't know what I would be buying, and even though it was the kind of line where I was chest-to-back with the person in front of me and all too aware of when the guy behind me spotted a pretty girl walking by. The indignity of the queue paid off in a plate of aloo tikki: fried potato patties stuffed with chickpeas and drowned in yogurt sauce and chutneys. I gobbled it down on the sidewalk while the sweat of the men who bookended me evaporated from my shirt.

Aloo tikki became one of our favorite street foods. Ever paranoid about bacteria as we were, it was soothing to watch the hot oil fry all those nasty pathogens out of the patties (even as we pretended not to notice the distinctly unrefrigerated chutneys in their metal canisters). We also loved chhole bhature, which was a thick gravy of chickpeas topped with ginger slivers and eaten with a fried bread; usually considered a breakfast dish, one plate was sufficient to make us skip lunch. Street vendor selling sprouted lentils would mix them with tomatoes, onions, chillies and cilantro and serve them to us on plates made from dried leaves that, being biodegradable, made us feel less guilty about throwing them in the trash piles that always grew on the ground near vendors' feet. We were told that bhel puri, with puffed rice, nuts and various other dried bits drowned in chutney, always tasted better in Mumbai; but we enjoyed it equally in both cities. The chaiwallah near my office sold samosas that he'd wrap in bags made from old newspapers that turned translucent with grease. Stuffed with potatoes and studded with green peas, the samosas' crust was flaky and sweet and the insides were spicy and succulent, reminiscent only in shape of the frozen versions served at the Indian restaurants back home. The chaiwallahs also sold deep-fried sandwiches with enough grease to eliminate a hangover and induce a heart attack.

We usually avoided street meat. Chicken kebab stands and fried fishwallahs were relatively rare, and while we'd see them in the Old City near the Jama Masjid, our sanitary paranoia was far more pronounced in the face of unrefrigerated chicken than unrefrigerated chickpeas.

The only vegetarian Delhi street food we categorically refused were golgappas. Also called panipuri ("water bread"), golgappas are rigid hollow spheres of fried dough stuffed with potatoes, onions and chickpeas. The vendor hands his customer an empty plate, pokes a hole in a sphere with his thumb, shoves stuffing in with his finger, plunges the sphere into a giant vat of brown-green liquid, and then places it on the waiting plate. The customer grabs it and pops it into his mouth whole, before the water melts through the dough. When bitten, the golgappa explodes. There's far more liquid than we'd have ever imagined the little sphere could contain; it overwhelms the taste buds and fills the mouth and, if our throats aren't ready, makes us choke. We'd chew and fake a smile and try not to let the juice drip down our face, and we'd keep the plate right below our chins just in case it did.

Golgappas seem to occupy a niche in Delhi culture that's similar to Taco Bell in America: both taste best late at night when surrounded by friends. Crowds of men and women congregate around the nearest golgappa vendor in the wee hours, each holding out a plate, their eager faces lit by the white glow of the gas lamp, laughing and chatting and popping their spheres and asking for more.

It wasn't that we didn't like the flavor, although they did tend to be heavy on chaat masala, a spice sprinkled on everything from paneer to lemonade that, to us, tastes vaguely of egg. No, we avoided golgappas for a different reason: the sight of the vendor plunging the spheres into the soup with his bare hand. Over and over again.

Look: we knew that one can't enjoy India if one was constantly paranoid of a few little germs. But the sight of so much unfiltered water coming into contact with so much sweaty skin was too much for our sheltered suburban sensibilities to bear.

That's why we would only relent to eating golgappas at Dilli Haat, the government-run crafts bazaar where it was assured that the vendors cooked with filtered water. A few miles north of Hauz Khas market, Dilli Haat is the exact opposite of what we'd expect from anything that was government-run: it was clean, well-maintained, with a surprising variety of high quality merchandise and, best of all, a few dozen food vendors representing each region in India. In winter, the Kashmir stall serves up a syrupy honey almond chai so delicious that the memory of its warmth stayed with me for a week of frigid nights.

At the Delhi street food stall, we would be heartened to see the golgappa vendor wearing gloves, and heartened further to see him dipping only deep enough to submerge them, as opposed to the street vendors who preferred plunging their hands in up to their wrists. Dilli Haat's vendors, in return, never seemed to tire of the sight of goras trying golgoppas for the first time. They'd giggle as we'd chew and swallow and cough and sputter, and laugh out loud when we'd try to eat it in bites and send juice squirting all over our shirts.

Our Indian friends derided our sanitary paranoia as detracting from the true Indian experience. Filtered water, they'd say, ruins the flavor of the golgappas.

*

The one street food that never triggered our paranoia reflex was chai. We couldn't go more than half a block without passing a chaiwallah seated under a tree or against a wall, selling India's signature brew at four rupees per cup. Chai is milk, tea dust, sugar, and spices boiled to sanitary perfection over a gas flame and then poured through a sieve into a tiny plastic cup. Delhiites' love of chai seemed to transcend culture, class, caste, and weather—a steaming glass somehow cooled us down in summer just as effectively as it warmed us up in winter.

A chai break is a universal and inalienable right. And the laborers who streamed out of the factories drank it side-by-side with the information workers from my office, all of us savoring the fact that for the next five minutes, our bosses were culturally obligated to leave us alone. Similarly, Jenny and I discovered that the aggressive beggars who tailed us through the streets of Jaipur vanished the moment we stepped up to a chai shop. Which means that the chaiwallah is more than a tea maker: he dispenses of an aura of protection that shields his customers from the world beyond his bubble, at least until their cups are empty.

Halfway down the street from my office sat a chaiwallah named Lakshan. When my company first moved to this neighborhood, they paid Lakshan to walk through the office pouring his freshly boiled chai for us four or five times a day. But one awful day, Finance bought a machine that dispensed sweet coffee, tomato soup, and a drink vaguely recognizable as chai. Lakshan's contract was abruptly canceled in favor of lukewarm glop. It was a decision that satisfied nobody except Finance. So instead of Lakshan coming to us, we went to him.

Lakshan sat on the sidewalk under intermittent shade, surrounded by bags of cigarette singles, shiny aluminium packets of mouth freshener, and plates of fried sandwiches and biscuits. He had clearly negotiated some sort of arrangement with the management of the building behind him, because there was a little cement alcove for his stove and he freely went in and out of the building's courtyard to fill his stockpot with water. Lakshan was not a one-man operation: his twelve-year-old son Raju worked with him. One day, as my colleague Dipankar sipped our chai and watched the father and son work, we calculated that Lakshan probably earned around 400 rupees a day after expenses. About $240 a month. With that money, he had to support his wife and at least one child, feed them, clothe them and put a roof over their heads; no wonder he couldn't afford an employee that would allow his son to go to school.

Watching Lakshan make tea cannot be described as watching an artist at work. It was more like watching the practiced hands of a surgeon. Lakshan would perform gestures he'd repeated thousands of times since he presumably apprenticed at his own father's chai stand. His hands moved automatically, measuring tea and sugar in his palms without thought, crunching cardamom and sometimes ginger against the concrete ground with a rock, and pouring the boiling mixture through a sieve into the little plastic cups without spilling a drop. Lakshan would be at his stand before I got to work and would still be pouring when I left. It was possible he lived nearby; more likely, he and his son slept right there on the sidewalk during the week. On Sunday, when the offices in the area were closed, I hope they got to go somewhere else and enjoy their only day of rest.

I loved chai, but it wasn't enough to get me going in the morning. Had I lived in Delhi even ten years earlier, this would have been a big problem; but I was fortunate to arrive just as the city's coffee culture began to truly take off. Delhi hasn't evolved to America's standard of a Starbucks on every corner, but the rapid franchising of Café Coffee Day and Barista (and, to a lesser extent, Costa) means that that day may be close at hand. We'd find at least one representative of these chains in about half the markets we visited in south Delhi. They'd adapted the Starbucks model to local tastes by offering more prepared food than in the US, and by instituting table service for taking orders and delivering lattes. At the time, though, few of them offered wireless Internet, so they weren't yet filled with hipster faces bathed in the holy glow of Apple laptops.

My coffee addiction confounded my co-workers both in how desperately I relied on it to begin my morning and the fact that I prefer my coffee as black as the insides of my ears after a day in Delhi's winter pollution. Murali and Dipankar both argued that black coffee would kill me, although this conversation usually took place as they sucked down cigarettes during chai breaks. They saw the irony.

Because the coffee from the office's cursed tea machine was too sweet for my tastes (yet still not sweet enough to hide the repellent flavor of Nescafé), I scored my fix every morning from the boutique hotel across the street. They didn't have to-go cups, so I would bring an office mug with me and carefully cross back across the street while trying not to spill my seventy rupees' worth of espresso, passing co-workers at the office gate who couldn't understand why I'd spend so much money on such a minuscule amount of coffee. ("Because espresso is concentrated!" I'd tell them, sounding lame even to my own ears.)

While Western-style coffee shops are new to Delhi, coffee itself is not. Coffee is especially popular in south India, where they serve it after meals in a metal cup that overflows into a metal saucer. The customer adds sugar and then pours the coffee back and forth between saucer and cup to mix and cool it. South Indian coffee is cut with chicory, which makes it delicious with milk and sugar but too bitter to drink black. My co-worker Govind once gave me a packet of south Indian coffee to make in my French press (which I employed when I was too lazy to cross the street); I brewed it black, without milk or sugar, and even I couldn't choke it down.

★

At the end of a meal, I like to have coffee. So do south Indians. North Indian meals traditionally culminate with a pinch of anise seeds and sugar crystals from a plate that, along with toothpicks, arrives with the bill. But for many Delhiites, the evening isn't complete until they've had paan.

Paan is one of the most extreme eating experiences we've ever had. It combines a collection of flavors that would each dominate the palate on their own—like cardamom, peppermint, cloves, rose petal preserves and many others—and then wraps them with an aromatic betel leaf into a triangular mass that's almost too big for the mouth. When we'd chew it, our tongue would drown in an eruption of tastes and textures. It would fill our mouths and push out our cheeks and require all our concentration to neither choke nor dribble it down our shirts. There are dozens of varieties of paan, and an entire book could surely be written about its history and variety.

It's nominally intended as an after-dinner digestive, and it was extremely effective in soothing my stomach's angry protests against the quantity of chillies I'd eaten just minutes before. But paan is a social experience as much as a culinary one. While many restaurants sell it, most people seem to prefer buying it from sidewalk vendors who are surrounded by canisters of leaves suspended in water and dozens of jars containing the seeds and pastes and spices that they'll mix together to their own closely guarded proportions. No two paanwallahs make it the same, which is why some of them are putting their kids through college on their earnings and others are so legendary that people drive across the city to partake in their edible artistry.

We first learned the importance of paan as a bonding ritual after a party thrown by Abhishek, the realtor who'd helped us find our apartment. We stayed late enough at the party that we found ourselves helping with the clean-up. (Well, helping Abhishek's wife with the clean-up, anyway. The women had spent the party clustered in the kitchen cooking and watching the children, while the men drank whisky and talked man stuff in the living room. Jenny had refused to toe the gender line, but the men had completely ignored her the entire night.)

Abhishek had chivalrously promised us a lift at the end of the night, and it seemed rude to change our minds. So we waited with him until all the guests had departed. At the end there were Abhishek, his wife and child, his friend Arvind (who was finishing "just one more glass" for the third time as we all sleepily watched him drink) and the two of us. But just as we were finally walking out of the door—and just when we finally began to imagine slipping into bed—Arvind's mouth opened again.

'We must get some paan.'

And so, at two o'clock on a cold Delhi morning, Jenny and I reluctantly piled into Abhishek's car and drove to Nizamuddin Railway Station. Abhishek's fatigue instantly evaporated as he and Arvind piled out of the car, and they laughed and shouted and high-fived and dwelled over their ritualistic bonding. We'd waited in the car because we thought they'd just guzzle the paan and be done with it, and by the time we realized that the paan was so much more than the food itself, we were too tired to get out and join them. We watched through drooping eyelids as

Abhishek and Arvind lived a Mastercard commercial, chatting and carrying on and slapping the backs of the other men who pulled up for the same feeling of kinship. *That* was what paan was all about.

★

Jenny and I rarely ended our meals with paan, and not just because it required a certain gastronomic fortitude to appreciate. It was because we could never choose paan over sweets. Delhi's sweets shops contain a rainbow of variations on the theme of nuts, condensed milk and edible silver foil in glass cases that stretch as far as the competing sweets shops right next door. My favorite was gulab jamun: a ball of dough the size of a donut hole but far denser, rolled in a sugary rose-water syrup. One must be careful with food this sticky, though—I was once three balls into a box of gulab jamuns when I noticed a dead fly embedded in the fourth, its legs spread wide as if run over by a cartoon steamroller. It had gotten stuck, it had gotten squished, and it had nearly gotten ingested.

Some sweets shops also serve food, like Nathu's Sweets in GK-II, where I ate my very first meal in India. In Delhi's restaurant continuum, sweets shops are most comparable to diners in the US: cheap, no-frills, with a counter up front for take-away and tables in the back for eating in. Sweets shops that serve food are often air-conditioned, which sets them higher on Delhi's restaurant continuum than dhabas, a word that technically refers to highway truck stops serving greasy Punjabi fare but is accepted to mean any cheap eatery where price is a bigger concern than comfort or sanitation. A good rule of thumb is this: if the dishes are being washed on the sidewalk, it might be a dhaba; and if it's a twelve-year-old doing the washing, it definitely is.

We rarely ate dinner at sweets shops because we knew we couldn't resist the fatty temptations of dessert. But temptation beckoned even while walking down the street. There's nothing in the world better than hot jalebi—fried batter dipped in inhumanely sweet orange syrup—straight out of the street vendor's oil. Or sweet lassis served in terracotta cups that one smashes to the ground with a satisfying crunch (it's a satisfaction matched in the dessert world only by the act of cracking the charred sugar on a well-made crème brûlée). On the other hand, while we loved kulfi, India's pistachio or saffron-flavored answer to ice cream, any taste of it would only remind us that we weren't eating the kulfi falooda at Roshan Di Kulfi, the landmark Karol Bagh restaurant. On our trips there, we'd begin with chhole bhaturey and raj kachori, a dish that is most accurately described as "a big ball of dough filled with all sorts of stuff and covered in all sorts of sauces." But the main event for us was always the kulfi falooda, in which the ice cream is drowned with sweet rose-water noodles and bits of almond and pistachio.

Roshan Di Kulfi is one of Delhi's more famous food destinations. The crowd spills out of the door and onto the street, and the only way to avoid eating on the sidewalk is to hover over someone's table and snatch it up the moment they stand.

But it is not Delhi's most famous restaurant. That honor belongs to Karim's.

And Karim's reputation perpetuates in the breathless refrain every veteran Delhi expat asks every novice Delhi expat: "You haven't been to Karim's yet?"

Karim's unmarked alley entrance means that one can never stumble upon Karim's. One has to be seeking it out. One has to be in the know. And this defines Karim's allure: the twisting alleys of the Old City hold a million secrets the Western eye will never uncover, but to know about Karim's is to conquer at least one of them.

Some people have told us that Karim's is the oldest restaurant in Delhi. Others have told us that Karim himself invented Mughal-style food. We never really knew, and it never really mattered, because the mystique of Karim's was as satisfying as the food. Ducking our heads to walk through the narrow entrance, we follow the alley just south of Jama Masjid as it opens into a bustling plaza encircled by Karim's multiple dining rooms. Each dining room is overseen by a uniformed head waiter, and each head waiter is beckoning urgently for us to enter as if they're all in competition with each other. But we can't choose one and sit down just yet—we're still coping with the sensory overload. Kebab guys wrap ground meat around skewers that ooze grease into the coals and spew smoke across the plaza. Bread makers sit cross-legged in an alcove, slapping dough into balls and pulling puffy white naan out of the ovens. Busboys balance more dirty dishes on one arm than we'd think a human bicep could manage. And motorcycles honk and weave through what is not just the middle of the restaurant but also an active thoroughfare. We gape until one of the head waiters finally commands our attention again, pulling our sleeves and leading us to the particular dining room over which he stands sentry.

Every time we went to Karim's, we learned a deeper secret. The first visit was one of simple culinary discovery: that chicken curry could be so succulent, that mutton kebabs could be so juicy. In our next visit, we learned that Karim's vegetarian curry, with paneer cubes, dates and a cashew-based gravy, was the stuff of dreams. On one of our last visits, we learned that the quarter-inch of oil puddled atop every bowl of curry wasn't supposed to be eaten. It was there to show that the food was so well cooked that the fat had liquefied; we were supposed to drain it into a separate dish.

And then there was the time we got to the truth about the most tantalizing item on the menu. Its name glistens on the laminated menu cards from the greasy prints of a thousand other patrons who have rested their fingers on it in wonder. It's the tandoori bakra, and it's priced at 4,500 rupees, or ninety dollars. "Please order twenty-four hours in advance," it says.

On a menu where the average dish costs one-fortieth of that price and arrives at the table in five minutes, the name alone had us salivating. With roasted mutton chops this good, what must their tandoori bakra be like? And what the hell's a bakra?

Thanks to EOID, we found out.

The best thing we ever did in India was join a group called Eating Out in Delhi. Founded by one-time Delhi University lecturer Hemanshu Kumar, EOID seeks out local eateries that would never appear in the *Lonely Planet,* usually in neighborhoods the *Lonely Planet* editors had omitted completely. On journeys with EOID, we tried methi chicken in a neighborhood in which every other storefront was selling live chickens. We ate kebabs in the dhabas where Delhi University students hang out. We drank home-made lemon soda from a Chandni Chowk family that's been making it for generations. And we sampled Mallu food in a tiny café so well hidden in a nondescript alley that we'd never noticed it before, even though it was within walking distance of our home.

With EOID, we learned that Indian food really does taste better when eaten with the hands. They taught us how to use bread to grasp each morsel or, for south Indian food, to use our fingers to mix rice and vegetables and chutney together into little mounds before scooping them into our mouths. I never fully mastered either technique, so I'd inevitably smear food all over my lips and cheeks with each bite, going through a dozen napkins during my meal while nobody else needed even one.

We learned about EOID in the very first issue of *Time Out Delhi* we picked up. We decided instantly it was the perfect organization for us, combining as it did our two favorite pastimes: eating and not spending much money. We sent an email asking about their next event and received an immediate response to join them that very night. Go to a certain corner in Connaught Place's Inner Circle, the email told us, and wait.

It was our second Saturday night living in Delhi, and we were still adjusting to being two foreigners in a foreign land. Our parents at home were reading about journalists being kidnapped in Pakistan and Afghanistan, and in their minds the dangers facing those who investigated armed Islamic militancy in failing states were also threatening people who worked in advertising agencies in the world's largest democracy. So they'd made us promise to exercise extreme caution when dealing with strangers, especially strange men. And we abandoned that promise the moment the car pulled up to us as we waited on that corner in Connaught Place.

Three male strangers stared at us. "Are you Dave?" one of them demanded.

I nodded.

"Get in."

Jenny and I looked at each other, thought about our parents' warnings, shrugged, and did as we were told.

No guns were pressed into our sides, fortunately. No hoods were thrown over our heads and no ransom demands were issued. Instead, we were whisked to Gurudwara Bangla Sahib, the most important Sikh temple in Delhi, to meet up with the rest of the EOID gang. Donning scarves to cover our hair in respect, we tasted some of the parshad (the ritual sweet given to anyone coming to pay their respects) and toured the temple grounds, chatting with the friendly people whom we were now pretty sure weren't going to dump our bodies in the Delhi Ridge.

After a leisurely walk around the vast pond, we sat cross-legged on the floor in the Gurudwara kitchen with hundreds of other people to eat the langar, which is the free vegetarian meal given by Sikhs to anybody who wants it, regardless of religion, class or income. With assembly-line efficiency, men spooned hot dal and vegetable mush out of metal buckets, which we mopped up with simple chapattis. It was delicious.

But on an EOID outing, delicious is not enough. The night is not over until at least one person's belt buckle has popped off. So we then went to a dhaba near Connaught Place for tea and pakoras and then, still not satisfied, to Saravana Bhavan for appams drowned in hot coconut milk.

During our time in Delhi, EOID gave us some of our most interesting experiences, favorite memories and closest friends. The EOID event that best combined all three was the evening when Hemanshu decided to solve the mystery of Karim's tandoori bakra. While Jenny stayed home (rightfully anticipating a vegetarian's worst nightmare), thirty-five of my hungriest friends and I descended upon Karim's with our appetites and our orders placed twenty-four hours in advance. There we discovered what tandoori bakra was: a whole goat, stuffed with rice and eggs and almonds, slow-cooked and presented on a silver platter.

As a handful of hurried waiters dropped the two goats we ordered onto our table, my mind and my stomach raced back to the summer of 2000, when my band headlined an outdoor pig roast in the Maine woods. A hundred people, a warm night, and an excess of loud music and cold beer all led up to the main event: the unveiling of the pig, which had been buried in a pit of coals since early that afternoon and was scheduled to rise like a spice-rubbed Lazarus around 10 p.m. But the pig was slow to cook, arriving four beer-soaked hours late to meet a frenzied crowd. We surrounded it, tearing at it with bare hands, stuffing pig flesh into our mouths with one claw while reaching with the other for more. We were men and women reduced to our basest state: grunting, eating, swallowing, slobbering, wiping our hands on our shirts and going back for fourths.

That pig roast was the most delicious meal I've ever had in my life. And this is what I was expecting to waft out of Karim's kitchen: meat that melted off the bone and into my mouth. My heart leapt with the appearance of the men bearing the mutton, followed by other men bearing tiny knives for us to carve with. Hunger and excitement overcame our table manners: ravenous hands sawed and pulled and jerked flesh off the bones and onto our plates. Within moments, we reduced the poor animals to their skeletons.

And that was when my dream of that Maine summer faded. The juicy piece of midsection looked like heaven; but in my mouth, it was tandoori-flavored chewing gum. I worked at it for minutes. The rice, mixed with boiled eggs and spices, was spectacular. The bread melted in our mouths. The side dishes—various curries and kebabs—were as good as ever. But the bakra itself was tragically disappointing.

I was expecting a Maine pig roast. I was expecting Thanksgiving dinner. I was expecting a New York street fair turkey leg. What I got was . . . not.

This was the moment when I realized that life was more interesting when there were mysteries in it. That it was probably better to leave the table before I had eaten my fill. I write these words today with Ganga's food in my heart, with Park Balluchi's paneer on my mind, and with the memory of Sagar Ratna's tomato coconut rava dosa still making my mouth water. But more than all those joys, what makes me wish to return to Delhi is knowing that there are so many aspects of it I have yet to experience.

Which is why, when I do eventually come back, I doubt I'll go to Karim's. Because their menu holds no more question marks for me—except for their "brain curry." Which I'm perfectly content to leave to my imagination.

6

Health: That Which Didn't Kill Us

Both the *Hindustan Times* and the *Times of India* kept a running tally of how many people were killed each year by Delhi's Blueline, the rickety private buses that swept up and spat out and ran over commuters in every corner of the city. Despite the noise with which they prowled the streets—one could hear them coming a quarter-mile away—they still managed to pounce on an astounding number of victims. At least 115 people were killed by Blueline buses in 2008.[1]

The Blueline's grim numbers grew entirely out of two economic incentives: first, because each bus was privately owned, the driver's salary was wholly dependant on how

---

1. http://www.indianexpress.com/news/bluelines-claim-two-lives-in-city-toll-reac/402617

many fares he picked up. And second, because each bus was privately owned, every bus was in direct competition with every other bus on the route. The faster a driver drove, the more competitors he passed, the more passengers he picked up, and the more money he made.

Which is why the last thing a Blueline driver ever wanted to do was come to a stop. Every decision was made with the intent of keeping the bus in motion. He slowed at the bus stop just enough so debarking passengers could jump off, and then picked up speed even while passengers were running alongside the bus, grabbing the iron handholds, and swinging themselves through the door as the conductor screamed at them to hurry. The driver would already have shifted gears by the time the last passenger was dragged inside by his fellow riders; dust would spew at any stragglers running after the bus as he bulldozed back into traffic.

Making the economic incentives worse was the fact that Blueline buses were not typically driven by their owners. Instead, most drivers rented their buses from a small cabal of owners for three or four thousand rupees a day plus the cost of repairs.[2] With passengers usually paying less than fifteen rupees a ride, drivers had to pick up a few hundred people before they could even begin to consider buying lunch, much less investing in upkeep. So their brakes squealed, their headlights didn't work, their tires were balding and patchy, and old vomit stains marred the windowsills where riders couldn't bear the motion or the heat. (With no air-conditioning, Bluelines were only cool

---

2. http://www.rediff.com/news/2007/oct/18spec.htm

when moving fast enough to generate a breeze.) Some Blueline buses were so poorly maintained that their side panels had rusted through. Because of the economics, the driver had no incentive to tell an owner when maintenance was required, lest the owner make him pay for it; and the owner had no idea when the wheels were about to fall off because he was never out driving it. Preventive maintenance was not in either party's economic interest.

So the driver barreled down the street with one hand on the wheel and the other triggering the horn (the one part of the bus that was kept in good repair), invoking Ganesh for luck and Lakshmi for money and every other god in the pantheon for keeping families on scooters out of their way. But with an estimated 2,200[3] Blueline buses careening across Delhi, it's no wonder the newspapers seemed to be printing the same article every couple of days: a bus killed a pedestrian, the driver tried to flee, an angry mob beat him, the police impounded the bus, the driver was jailed, and the owner of the bus bore no responsibility. Or perhaps the driver escaped, in which case the mob found its release in setting fire to the bus.

After the Delhi government pledged to replace the Blueline with modern, city-run buses, the newspapers reported that the cartel of "powerful people" who owned the majority of the Blueline buses weren't going to let the city cut them out of the transit racket quite so easily. Which set the stage for a clash between public interest and

---

3. http://blog.taragana.com/n/delhi-government-to-phase-out-blueline-buses-from-july-70451

private profit, during which time the rupees would keep pouring in, the owners would keep getting their cut, and the newspapers would keep having gruesome subjects to write about.

All of which is to say that we had other threats to worry about in Delhi beyond our fear of being attacked by monkeys.

★

Monkey attacks, incidentally, were a realistic fear. Nine days before we boarded our plane in New York, Delhi's deputy mayor was knocked off his terrace and killed while battling a horde of wild rhesus macaques.[4] Fortunately, we never saw any monkeys in our neighborhood, although there were plenty in other parts of the city. And while we still worried a bit about an out-of-control bus smashing into our third-story living room—with the Blueline, you never know—it quickly became apparent that our biggest concern would be our health.

This went beyond the inevitable cases of Delhi Belly. Jenny and I got sick far more than we had in the US, and we got sick far less once we moved on to Singapore. It's possible that our bodies were particularly weak after a lifetime of American pampering, but it's more likely that Delhi was too extreme an environment for us. The pollution, the dust, the sanitary conditions, the cold, the heat, the exhausting commutes, and the long working hours were

---

4. http://news.bbc.co.uk/2/hi/south_asia/7055625.stm

more than our immune systems could handle. On completion of our first six months in Delhi, we gathered up all the medicine we'd accumulated in the preceding 180 days for a photo shoot. There were seven half-empty bottles of syrup, eighteen packets of pills, a small number of powder sachets and some mosquito cream—and that was just all the medicine we had *left over*. Just before we left Delhi for good, we donated three full plastic bags of surplus medicine to the charity hospital our doctor had opened, which was probably funded by all the consultation fees we'd paid him.

Our ailments were usually minor: colds, coughs, sore throats, headaches, stomach problems. But we also endured worse. Drug-resistant bacteria are a growing problem in India, where antibiotics have been both overprescribed (doctors administer them when they're not needed) and underutilized (patients don't finish the full course of medication). Those two conditions breed bacteria that laugh in the face of ciprofloxacin and eat amoxicillin for breakfast. One newspaper quoted a study estimating that antibiotics accounted for forty to eighty percent of the drugs prescribed in India, "mostly when not required."[5] One day, when I went to work with a sore throat (it was my own fault—I should have known better than to breathe while standing by the side of the road), one colleague suggested I see my doctor. "I had a hoarse throat," he told me, "and my doctor advised me antibiotics for my tummy."

---

5. http://www.dnaindia.com/mumbai/report_antibiotic-misuse-making-bacteria-resistant-to-drugs_1256400

All of which may explain why one infection Jenny suffered was so resistant to oral antibiotics that she ended up requiring three separate cycles of powerful antibiotics that could only be delivered by injection. The poor girl had to go to the emergency room clinic to receive her shots once a day for three sets of five days each. That's *fifteen* total injections.

But doctors alone can't shoulder the blame, because it was extremely easy to get pills without prescription. There were a number of times one of us went to the pharmacy only to realize that we'd left the prescription at home. So we simply told the pharmacist which medication we required, assuring them that we really did have a prescription. Nobody ever questioned us; each time, they happily packed the medication along with their card for future home delivery. The customer is always right, even when the customer is lying to score prescription meds.

This is the exact opposite of the crowded drugstores in New York City, where the customer was the last thing on the employee's mind, and where we considered ourselves lucky to get a scowl out of the cashier because that meant he'd noticed us at all. In a New York City pharmacy, getting medication was often a day-long ordeal: we'd spend twenty minutes waiting in line to drop off the prescription in the morning, knowing that in five or six hours we'd have to stand in line for another twenty minutes to pick up the pills. Delhi was far more efficient. We'd pass our prescription to the pharmacist, who would return a few minutes later with a week's worth of antibiotics, painkillers and vitamins all costing around 150 rupees. Even the prescription paper itself was more user-friendly here—it always had at least six different phone numbers for the doctor on it, giving us the comfort that we could always reach him on his mobile, at his home, at his office, at his other office and, presumably, his two favorite restaurants.

On the off chance that a pharmacy denied our request for prescriptionless medication, we could always just walk to the next one. There were at least four we could choose from in Hauz Khas market. Nearest to our house was one whose red sign read simply "Chemist," along with some Hindi lettering presumably proclaiming the same. It was a dark cave inside, and the long, narrow counter was the only thing preventing the pill packets that were strewn about its shelves from spilling into the aisle, out of the door and drowning all of Hauz Khas market in a flood of Ranbaxy-stamped foil. Just a few doors down was Religare Wellness, a bright and airy pharmacy chain that employed modern inventory control techniques like labeled containers and alphabetical order. We sometimes felt guilty for patronizing a chain store over locally owned shops like Chemist (and its competitor on the other side of Religare, called "Popular Chemist"); but Chemist and Popular Chemist both had doorways that were narrow and forbidding, front windows so cluttered that no light could enter inside, and countermen who would spend minutes hunting up and down their stores to locate the products we asked for. Religare was more organized and more inviting; and in a country called the "capital of counterfeit drugs,"[6] it

---

6. http://www.thehindubusinessline.com/2003/08/03/stories/
2003080301260500.htm

was also much more reassuring that the pills they handed us in the little brown paper bags weren't actually candy-coated rat droppings.

★

Once we realized how often we'd be sick, we prepared ourselves for everything. We never traveled outside of Delhi without a bag full of remedies for headaches, stomach aches, diarrhea, constipation, heartburn, coughs, colds, allergies, sunburns, cuts, blisters, dry eyes and more. We needed to plan ahead because we never knew when we'd be unable to find a pharmacy, or when we'd be unsure of what to do with the medicine once we found one. (We learned the latter lesson on the train back from Jaipur, when Jenny drank an ounce of cough medicine that was meant to be dispensed in millilitres. Her ride home was a hallucinatory experience amplified by windowsill cockroaches and 1970s Hindi music played over the train's loudspeaker that, well, she actually quite enjoyed.)

But despite our preparations, we were still hit by ailments we never anticipated. Like my ear infection, for example, which began as a minor sensitivity to loud noise and conveniently transformed into uncontrollable pain exactly an hour before our plane to Chennai was scheduled to depart. The popping and pressure during the flight was miserable. We landed around 11 p.m. and went straight to one of Chennai's private hospitals, where the emergency room attendant looked at our luggage, listened to my complaint, and coldly informed me that I was suffering from "jet lag." Over the next three weeks in south India, my "jet lag" would force us to supplement the *Lonely Planet*'s suggested itinerary with visits to a second hospital in Chennai, and then other hospitals in Madurai, Kochi and Kovalam.

(Although I must admit that the visit to the doctor in Kovalam was as much to ask about the heat rash I'd developed as it was for my ear pain. We'd been taking cheap local buses all over the south, and the confluence of sweaty skin, vinyl seats, and lack of circulating air were the perfect recipe for heat rash—to say nothing of when the bus would get crowded and my shoulder would be buried six inches deep in the rump of the woman standing in the aisle next to me.)

Our numerous health issues did not go unnoticed by our friends, co-workers and even Ganga, each of whom suggested their own family remedies to supplement our faith in Western medicine. After that so-called single-malt Scotch induced what was diagnosed as "severe food poisoning" (an inadequate label for a stomach that's acting like an industrial-speed blender), it was suggested that I eat nothing but boiled eggs, mashed potatoes and khichri, a bland rice and lentils dish that was meant to be easy for my hyperactive stomach to digest. My mother would have advised bananas, rice, applesauce and toast, which follows on the same principles: for a stomach conducting its own version of the revolt of 1857, bland is good.

Many of the remedies people recommended transcended our two cultures, like that of gargling salt water for a sore throat. Others came as a surprise to us. One day, when complaining of a backache and dreaming of a massage,

Jenny was advised by everyone in her office to simply sit in the sun. That made sense, though she'd never thought of it—after all, heat relaxes muscles—and suddenly Jenny understood why so many old folks in the residential neighborhood where she worked spent their mornings sitting in the sun, reading the newspaper and watching the maids shake out the bed sheets. And while I ignored that one co-worker's suggestion of antibiotics for my sore throat, Ganga alleviated it by brewing up her recipe for ginger tea: she boiled raw ginger for about twenty minutes, then added a teabag and several spoonfuls of sugar. Suddenly, I could talk again, and Ganga's remedy has joined chicken soup in our pantheon of homemade cures.

Some of the remedies we were exposed to totally baffled us. When Jenny fainted at the mehndi ceremony for my co-worker Pankaj's sister—too much heat, not enough food—Pankaj's father rushed over, whipped off Jenny's shoes, and began violently rubbing her feet. We were later assured that rubbing one's feet was supposed to get one's blood circulating, but that's not something we practice in the States. So Jenny, finding herself on the floor with everyone standing above her and staring, was as freaked out by the foot rub as she was about fainting.

★

We attempted to aid our exhausted immune systems by keeping fit. And despite the fact that our blood flowed creamy white with Ganga's raita, we didn't gain any more weight in Delhi once we started using the exercise bike we'd bought. (We'd tried the gyms, but they were too expensive, too inconvenient, and had too many macho men in designer tracksuits puffing their chests while staring at Jenny.) I also supplemented the bike with periodic runs in nearby Gulmohar Park. I'd jog down the dirt path, through the grounds of the centuries-old stone mosque just twenty meters from our flat, past the elderly guard who never returned my smile no matter how many times I gave one to him, and then carefully through the Hauz Khas Apartments and into the park. I'd gasp my way for a couple of laps around the park's perimeter while dodging errant cricket balls, admiring the orchids growing along the path, and waggling my finger at the ten-year-olds sneaking cigarettes near the park's stone ruins.

If it was evening, the park would be filled with people walking: mothers, fathers, children and aunties all trying to reduce their prosperous midsections one slow lap at a time. Many of my colleagues told me to forget running and to forget the exercise bike because morning or evening walks were the sole key to healthy living. And they weren't alone. "In my opinion," wrote Mahatma Gandhi, "a brisk walk in the open is the best form of exercise." A few laps around the local park, Murali assured me, along with some healthy hawking and spitting, were all he needed to make up for all the cigarettes he smoked every day.

We didn't take their advice. And the fact that I gained fifteen pounds after we sold the bike tells me that our exercise routine had been effective. However, their advice did benefit us in one unexpected way: it taught us how to get autorickshaw drivers off our backs.

Jenny and I did enjoy walking, but not for exercise. Rather, we liked to sightsee on foot. But every time we'd walk down the street in a tourist area—the sidewalks near Lodhi Gardens, or anywhere around the Red Fort or India Gate—one auto after another would pull up next to us and demand to take us to our destination. Not a single driver would believe us when we told them we were "just walking"; they'd putter slowly along to match our pace, interpreting our refusals as bargaining ploys.

"Where do you want to go?" They'd always ask, leaning out of their autos and patting the passenger seat behind them.

"Nowhere!" we'd reply cheerfully.

"Where are you going? I'll take you there!"

"That's OK. We're just walking," we'd say, still with a smile.

"Where are you walking? Come with me, very good price."

"No," we'd say, our smiles fading. "We just want to walk!"

"Please, I take you!"

"No! For the love of all that is holy, no!"

It was a terrible nuisance. Nothing worked, not even walking against traffic in hopes that they couldn't sidle along next to us—they'd just park their autos and nag us on foot, or putter alongside us while dodging oncoming cars. We hated getting angry at the drivers, but we'd find ourselves snapping at them the moment they pulled up. It was exactly the kind of loutish tourist behavior we deplore, but there was nothing we could say to them that would communicate our simple desire to walk.

Until we guessed the one phrase that drivers actually took at face value. The words came to us serendipitously one day in Jaipur, where the drivers were even more persistent than in Delhi. "Where do you want to go?" one auto driver after another demanded of us. Our response up until then—"We prefer to walk"—had gotten us nowhere. So this time, I tried something new: "We're just getting exercise."

The auto driver grunted knowingly and drove off. And so did every other driver we tried this line on. Thanks to Gandhi, we finally found a way to walk in peace.

★

My parents were flying back home from their visit to Delhi when the Mumbai terrorists struck. Which was lucky, because if they had opted for their tour company's extended package, they would have been in The Oberoi in Mumbai on the very night the attacks began.

As for us, safe in Delhi, we experienced the Mumbai attacks as two agonizing days and nights of staring at the news, checking the Internet, and watching our colleagues at work grow angrier and angrier—not just at the terrorists, but at the government. They were fed up that the government was unable to protect its people. After all, that year had already seen bombings in Jaipur, Bangalore, Ahmedabad and, a month-and-a-half prior to the Mumbai attacks, in Delhi itself.

The Delhi bombings, which killed thirty people, happened on a Saturday night. We were waiting for our friends Scott and Sally to pick us up for a party when we turned on the TV and learned that five bombs had gone off around the city, including at Connaught Place and GK-I's M-Block market. The media reported that even more bombs had been found and defused, and that security was being bolstered citywide. We wondered if we'd be able to make it to the party at all, or if the security presence would be too tight even to reach our destination just a few miles north of Hauz Khas market.

But we saw no sign of any additional security during the entire ride. If we hadn't turned on the TV, we wouldn't have known anything unusual had happened. It wasn't until the next day, when an auto drove us past the GK-I market, that we saw the police presence: a few yellow barriers had been dragged across the road there, creating a checkpoint that slowed passing cars enough to create a traffic jam but not enough for the two nearby policemen to possibly determine whether the drivers were carrying dynamite on their laps or wearing Al Qaeda lapel pins or whatever other signs they would have been looking for, had they been looking at all, instead of reclining in the shade of a nearby tree.

Before the Mumbai attacks had even ended, my boss Paul (the only other Westerner in my office) decided that if Western hotels could be attacked, Western companies could be as well. So he instituted a new security policy for our office, which was in a detached four-story building in an industrial neighborhood of Gurgaon: the iron gate in front of our office was to be kept closed and padlocked from then on. What's more, our guard Jagdish would henceforth sit in the driveway to challenge visitors before they entered the building, instead of after they'd reached the air-conditioned receptionist's desk.

This new policy was diligently followed for a little more than a week, until the feelings of fear across the country subsided. The office slowly crept back to the old habits: first we stopped padlocking the gate, then we stopped closing it, and then Jagdish returned inside to the air-conditioned reception room. The only tangible effect of our increased security was to deter a roving gang of hijras— eunuchs or transvestites—who, dressed in garish saris, had been bursting into nearby offices to sing and dance until they received payment to leave the premises, threatening to expose their genitals if their demands weren't met. They couldn't get past our padlock, though, so they just shouted at those of us who gathered on the balcony to watch and then continued on to harass the publishing company across the street.

Paul's vigilance for safety at work didn't catch on. But he had also taken measures to protect his family, and he told me I was foolish not to do the same. After all, I was a Westerner. Which meant I was a target. Which meant I should indulge in some common-sense precautions: vary my route, plan for the worst, prepare for self-defense, and trust no one.

Paul's warnings came just as I'd finished reading the hottest book to come out of India at the time we lived there: *The White Tiger*, Aravind Adiga's tale of a poor Delhi driver who kills his rich employer. Taken together with Paul's doomsaying, I started thinking about just how much

Celebrating Holi, the festival of colors, and applauding the foresight we had to wrap our camera in plastic.

At the center of a Holi treat, this pebble of bhang makes the colors extra vibrant.

Hamilton Court rises twenty-six stories above Gurgaon. It was our home for exactly six nights.

Looking west across Old Delhi from the minaret at Jama Masjid, India's largest mosque.

Back at ground level, two boys rush up for an unbidden photo op.

Even if I had bought a motorcycle, I'm sure I would have lost it.

Two of Delhi's 50,000 autorickshaws queue for fuel, wasting not an inch of space.

The Metro is shaping Delhi's future.

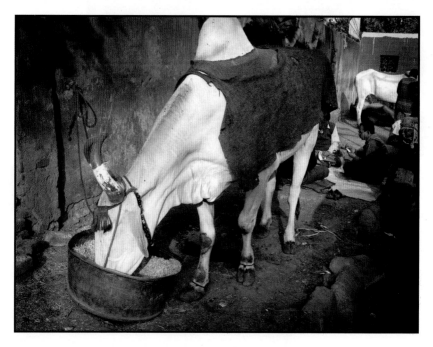

The well-being of livestock often remains the most pressing need of the present.

Curries at Karim's, making me hungry.

Hauz Khas Market tailors humor me as I take yet another picture.

I admired this circus poster almost every morning on my way to the office; with traffic, it generally took fifteen minutes to pass it.

Were it not for the free meals, many of the families supported by the charity Pardada Pardadi could not afford to send their daughters to school.

Looking down from a rooftop bar in Paharganj, Delhi's backpacker hub.

Perched above Delhi's Sunday book market, a worker repairs cables the hard way.

(Below) If asked which books I'd have expected to find in Delhi's Sunday book market, I'd have named none of these.

A letterer paints an ad on an autorickshaw.

Lakshan the chaiwallah and his son Raju, always there to dispense four rupees worth of respite from the office.

A sidewalk barber near Old Delhi.

Riding with my mother among the bicycle rickshaw traffic in Old Delhi.

Caricature artists at a festival in South Delhi's Garden of Five Senses.

A peacock emerges on Jenny's arm after a visit to Hauz Khas Market's sidewalk hennawallah.

A vendor sharpens knives on his cleverly adapted bicycle.

Domestic tourists relaxing inside the Red Fort.

Old Delhi at night. Walk fifty yards and turn left to find Karim's.

The Land Before Trademark.

Nehru Place, Delhi's IT market, where global technology becomes local business.

Shops in Hauz Khas Market, including the store where we bought our mobile phone minutes.

A rainy day in an upscale Delhi market.

Commuters skirt a flooded Aurobindo Marg in the aftermath of a monsoon rain.

An Old Delhi juice vendor preps for the day's customers.

In the southern state of Kerala, Jenny encounters the spirit that defined all of India for us.

Stumbling upon this mosque made me realize that I never knew what I'd find in Old Delhi. I only knew that I'd never probably find it again.

Visit deliriousdelhi.com to see even more pictures.

Birender and his taxi drivers knew about us, our routine, the flimsy deadbolt on our front door, and our total lack of Indian street-smarts. I found myself awake at night mentally mapping escape routes from my office, deciding which kitchen implements would make the best weapons, and realizing that if Al Qaeda had burst into our living room right then, neither Jenny nor I would know what to do beyond locking the bedroom door and hiding in the wardrobe. In New York, we would have called 911. In Delhi, I realized we had no idea how to reach the authorities.

So I queried the online discussion group that Delhi expats normally used to request recommendations for Hindi tutors, ask which stores sold Camembert cheese, and critique the wine selection at the various five-star hotels. To that discourse, I added this question: how do you call the police?

Many people responded to tell me that "100" is the Delhi equivalent of 911. And while there would probably be language challenges, I was told that if I babbled enough keywords ("Hauz Khas" "American" "terrorist with a chainsaw"), I could probably rouse a local cop to saunter over. One person suggested that Jenny and I should be proactive and make friends with the guys at the local police stand, but another advised against it: "We would rather call our embassy or someone known to us who knows someone in police. We don't trust the police in Delhi."

I wasn't sure if I had the answer. So I emailed Lynn, the US embassy employee who was the one who got the call when an American citizen was run over by the Blueline or arrested for stealing the Sankara stones from Mola Ram.

Lynn had spent enough time visiting Americans in Indian jails—and, sadly, Indian morgues—that she could offer reliable advice for those who needed help from the authorities. "The best thing to do, if possible, is file a police complaint or First Information Report. Once you do that, call us and we will follow up with the police to make sure that they do whatever is needed in the situation. The police will not take our call as seriously if the involved party hasn't complained. That being said, we want to hear about whatever is happening regardless of whether a complaint has been lodged. We always want to know if our citizens have emergencies; sometimes we can move things along or make suggestions."

In our eighteen months in Delhi, we never had any reason to contact Lynn in a professional capacity. Nevertheless, though Birender and his team never hatched a plot against us, I'm glad we did the research.

I only wish we had done the same research when it came to medical emergencies. Because had we known whom to call ahead of time, I wouldn't have found myself sprinting up Aurobindo Marg at two o'clock one cold January morning in a desperate search for an autorickshaw while Jenny lay on the sidewalk convulsing with fever.

This story begins with a molar that became sensitive to the cold. Jenny's dentist decided that there was some decay under one of her older fillings, and that a root canal was necessary in a few days' time. To alleviate the pain until that procedure, he yanked out the offending filling, slathered the irritated root with medication, covered it with a temporary filling, and sent her home.

Eight hours later, Jenny was suddenly shivering uncontrollably and burning to the touch. Summoning all my Boy Scout training, I ran around in panicked circles, held my head, and shouted, "Just let me think!"

Finally, despite the fact that it was well after midnight, I decided to call the dentist on each of the six numbers printed on his prescription letterhead until I reached him at home. He told me to take Jenny to Indraprastha Apollo Hospital.

But that was four miles to the east of us. And in my panicked state, that seemed much too far away.

Jenny had found this dentist on a list of recommended medical practitioners published by the US embassy. The same list suggested a hospital much closer to us: Aashlok Hospital in Safdarjung, a private hospital only ten minutes down the road at this time of night. I bundled Jenny in a blanket and helped her down the stairs. With our block's security guard staring at us from beneath his own blanket, we trudged towards Aurobindo Marg to find a ride. Jenny made it about halfway before she needed to rest; I helped her sit on the sidewalk next to the shuttered wooden box where, by day, a paan masala vendor sold shiny foil packets of breath freshener. And then I ran over Aurobindo Marg, deserted at this time of night, and waved like a maniac at passing autos until one stopped for me.

He crossed the U-turn and followed me as I ran back to where Jenny was now lying flat on the dusty sidewalk.

"Aashlok Hospital in Safdarjung!" I told the driver.

"Kya?" he asked me.

I repeated my destination. He repeated his query.

I tried one more time as I glanced towards Aurobindo Marg to see if I could spot another auto. "Aashlok Hospital in Safdarjung! Aashlok! Hospital! *Safdarjung!*"

Finally he clapped in recognition: he'd understood "hospital" and "Safdarjung." Within minutes, we pulled up to a 1970s-style cement building. A few people holding brooms watched from the emergency room entrance as I helped Jenny out of the auto. I handed a hundred rupees to the driver as I gestured to the gawkers to get some help. Though the driver and I hadn't discussed the price, I knew that change should have been forthcoming, even when including his late-night fee; but the driver just shouted, "Thank you, sir!" and drove off before I could argue, guessing correctly that I wouldn't be chasing after him.

I helped Jenny into the building, past a sign displaying the name of the hospital printed in Hindi script as clear as day to anyone who could read Hindi: Safdarjung Hospital.

"Safdarjung Hospital" is not "Aashlok Hospital in Safdarjung."

Once inside, men and women wearing white coats materialized in welcome sanitary contrast to the paan-splattered walls. There was a rush of lights and moans as Jenny's stretcher was wheeled through the halls, up an elevator, and into a room where a young English-speaking doctor queried us about her problems. From the next room over, I heard a whimper and then the sound of liquid splashing on the concrete floor. Some people stopped at the doorway and stared, but most were too wrapped up in their own misery to notice us. A man in a thin hospital gown walked by, pushing an IV stand on wheels.

After a fleeting examination, the doctor decided that Jenny's fever was "just a fever" and gave her a shot of something he said would "make it go away." I have no idea what he injected her with. And while I'm pretty sure I have a memory of the syringe being removed from sanitary wrapping, I'm also pretty sure that my mind would have later invented that memory to save me the horror of imagining otherwise.

"I don't think it's anything to worry about," the doctor said as he pumped Jenny full of who-knows-what. "But there's a chance it could be malaria. Just in case, I want you to take four of these pills tonight, along with half a glass of milk."

The mystery injection did the trick. Jenny's fever went down, her shivering stopped, we returned home, and she slept through the night. We called the dentist first thing in the morning. "You went to Safdarjung Hospital?" he gasped, horrified. "That's a government hospital!"

And then he told us to call Dr. Bhatia. And though we later learned that Jenny's fever had actually been a blood infection caused by a contaminated temporary filling, we are forever grateful to the dentist anyway—because time and again, Dr. Bhatia would be a lifesaver.

We lost count of how many times we subsequently entered the inner sanctum of Dr. Bhatia's Hauz Khas Enclave home office, passing through his immaculately landscaped grounds, feeling intense jealousy towards the German guy who'd been lucky enough to rent the flat in the doctor's guest house, and listening as Dr. Bhatia effortlessly diagnosed our ills while still finding time to recommend tourist sites. He provided curative advice for all our ailments—including my Scotch-induced food poisoning, my laryngitis, my diarrhea, my carpal tunnel syndrome that ended up requiring a month of therapy, the spider bite that caused a quarter-sized patch on my neck to ooze and blister, my nerve hypersensitivity, more diarrhea, and my three-week-long ear infection. ("I strongly recommend that you do not fly!" he told me when I called him about the ear pain I was feeling while sitting at the gate in the airport. When I told him that I intended to fly anyway, he sighed and wished me "All the best" in a tone that could only be interpreted as, "Hey, buddy, it's your funeral.")

So, eight hours after we left that government hospital, Dr. Bhatia appeared at Jenny's bedside—a house call? Only in India!—to listen to her problems, reject the diagnosis of malaria in favor of the blood infection, prescribe antibiotics, and assure us that our problems were over.

Which they were. Until we found out the hard way that chloroquine—malaria medicine—doesn't go down too well on an empty stomach. We hadn't been able to find any milk after leaving the hospital the night before, so Jenny had washed down the pills with a glass of powdered infant formula from an all-night pharmacy. And that hadn't been enough to counterbalance the gastric effects of the chloroquine.

It took the malaria medication about twenty-four hours to do its worst. So by midnight, everything that was inside of Jenny was coming out of her, including her antibiotics.

"I'm afraid," Dr. Bhatia told me, pleasantly unconcerned that I was calling so late, "that you must take her to the hospital."

This time, when he told me which hospital, I listened.

And this time, instead of dashing out to the main road, I called the hospital—Max Hospital in Saket—to request an ambulance. They reached our flat surprisingly fast, and soon Jenny was being ushered across marble floors to a curtained area inside a reassuringly modern emergency room that, aside from three small drops of dried blood on the ceiling, was spotless. Jenny was admitted and examined and given an IV drip to replenish her fluids while I filled out the paperwork and chose between a four-person room, a private room with a couch, and a "luxury suite." My choice became our home for the next two days.

The first day was physically miserable: Jenny's stomach was knotted and cramping, she was weak, her hand was cartoonishly swollen from the IV feeding into her wrist, her bed was uncomfortable, and there was absolutely nothing good on TV. Sleep was impossible, with a constant parade of nurses and doctors and nutritionists and hospitality executives calling on us to explain how Max Hospital gives special attention to its foreign guests. I left the hospital around 2 p.m. to eat a quick gyro sandwich in the Saket PVR market before going home to shower and pick up our books and laptops in the hope of some distraction. I returned to discover the worst of it: the hospital didn't have any Internet.

By the end of the first day, Jenny had physically recovered from the gastroenteritis caused by the malaria medication. But the blood infection still concerned them, so they detained her for another evening of observation. Thus, while the first twenty-four hours had been one of pain and discomfort, the second day consisted of agonizing boredom that almost seemed worse. Still tethered to her IV, Jenny was so determined to be discharged on the second morning that she got herself out of bed and into the shower; she brushed her hair, straightened her clothes, and put on her make-up. Every time a doctor would come in, she'd hide her balloon hand and exuberantly proclaim how ready she was to go home. The doctors would frown, take her temperature, and suggest another night might still be necessary.

In the end, we got out late on the second afternoon with two very valuable lessons learned: first, that the time to find a doctor and hospital is *before* a medical emergency.

And second, that one should never eat gyros at the Saket PVR market. Jenny was the one with gastroenteritis, but I ended up spending just as much time on the toilet.

When I returned to the office a few days later, my co-workers were livid that I'd not asked them for help. "You call to ask how to say 'cauliflower' in Hindi," my colleague Pankaj barked at me, "but not when your wife goes to the hospital?!"

As for Jenny, once she finally got her strength back, she still had to go and get that root canal.

First, though, she found a different dentist.

7

Shopping: Markets, Malls and More For Less

On Sundays, Nehru Place is closed. Its shops are tightly shuttered. And the main plaza is empty except for what appears to be two groups of beggars engaged in a turf war.

While the women slapping each other at the periphery of the plaza first catch our eyes, our attention soon focuses at the center of the otherwise empty expanse, where two stick-thin men writhe and slap and flail in their attempts to pin the other to the ground. They're both oblivious in their efforts to the police officer in his khaki uniform who, with the patience and deliberation of a man who has beaten beggars a hundred times before and will beat beggars a hundred times after, pulls a nice long stick off a nearby tree, saunters casually up to the two struggling men, and whacks them and whacks them and whacks them until Jenny and I decide that maybe it's better if we come back to Nehru Place on any other day.

On any other day, Nehru Place is Delhi's main computer market.

Nehru Place is a collection of concrete 1960s-style skyscrapers clustered around a couple of broad plazas on the eastern side of south Delhi. The buildings themselves contain a number of very established corporations with very attractive offices in which they conduct very legitimate business. But on the ground level, Nehru Place is India's IT boom in populist practice: an explosion of technology brands, a cacophony of shouting vendors, waves of young men in button-down shirts, and ancient diesel generators that rattle into action every time the power goes out. It's a landscape of laptop repair specialists next to competing laptop repair specialists, hardware shops next to competing hardware shops, and printer cartridge vendors as far as the eye can see.

Unlike the handshakes and cappuccino machines in the offices above, everything happening at ground level seems vaguely illegitimate, most likely because of the brazenness in which the unmistakably illegitimate business in conducted. A grinning teenager in a yellow shirt waves a laminated inventory of pirated software at us, promising Microsoft products at McDonald's prices. Though he stands a few deliberate paces away from the nearest shop, his attitude and sales approach are indistinguishable from those of the vendors selling and shouting from inside the establishment, which makes us suspect everything we see on sale: Were the boxes of printer paper yanked off the back of an idling truck? Are the ten-dollar computer speakers built using two-dollar parts? Are the dirt-cheap HP ink cartridges filled with genuine HP ink—or, indeed, any ink at all?

All levels of retail sophistication have a presence at Nehru Place, from mom-and-pop closets stuffed with boxy VGA monitors to gleaming showrooms with spotlit laptops. The shop where I once took my fraying Apple power adapter for repairs was a shadowy explosion of wires and motherboards and empty cases, with a salesman at a desk by the door and the guy who actually did the work hunched in a wooden loft built above the sales floor, surrounded by tools and parts, his head mere inches from the ceiling. His services set me back three dollars, and they extended the life of my power adapter exactly one week before it failed for good.

We can't imagine that Nehru Place once didn't exist. The ancient man screw-driving logic boards must have learned the trade from his grandfather. The overstuffed cubicles must contain computers dating back to the Raj. In Nehru Place, the greatest advances of humankind compete in a shopping environment that feels centuries unchanged. Although there are a few sari houses tucked into far corners of the complex—holdovers from Delhi's 1962 Master Plan, in which Nehru Place was planned as one of fifteen "District Centers" that would usher in a new urban Indian shopping aesthetic[1]—Nehru Place consists almost entirely of IT-related vendors.

---

1. http://www.sarai.net/research/media-city/field-notes/media-markets/nehru-place/

And while we were surprised that so many business owners would choose to locate themselves so close to the competition, Nehru Place isn't unique in being a hub for a particular trade. Delhi's retail topography features many of these trade-specific markets: a spice market, a gold market, a fabric market, an auto parts market, a plant seeds market, a wiring market, a scientific equipment market, a cheap housewares market, an expensive housewares market, a wooden furniture market, a rope market, and a television parts market in which some vendors sell screens, some sell cases, some sell remotes and nobody seems to offer a complete set.

These trade hubs exist in Delhi's economic geography to serve those who prioritize savings over convenience. In these trade-specific markets, the competitive leverage lies with the consumer: when a dozen vendors are selling the same Toshiba laptop, savvy shoppers know they can play each store off the next, bargaining neighbor against neighbor until they arrive at the best deal. If stall number seventeen doesn't offer his absolute lowest price, stall number eighteen will.

Trade hubs like this exist in New York as well. There's the diamond district, the flower district, and there was even an Indian restaurant district on East 6th Street for a while. But what made Delhi's clusters unusual to us was that we had difficulty buying the stuff they sold anywhere else. New York has its trade districts, but it also has jewelry stores and Indian restaurants in every other neighborhood. But in Delhi, we could only find reasonably priced computer parts in Nehru Place. (It's true that I could have ordered

RAM for my laptop from some of the stores in the mall, but the savings I found at Nehru Place far outweighed the hassle incurred by traveling there.)

There was even a trade hub for used books. It was Delhi's Brigadoon: it appeared like a mirage once a week on Sundays to transform the commercial chaos of the Old City into a literary paradise.

The Sunday book market originated near Delhi Gate, an ancient stone arch that stands proud as the high-water point of the British colonial government's urban renewal. (North of Delhi Gate, it's all alleys and shouting and cows and puddles until Old Delhi gives way to the Civil Lines, where the British revved up their well-bred Victorian bulldozers again.) The sidewalk book market stretched westward from Delhi Gate along Asaf Ali Road (the southern border of Old Delhi) and northward on Bahadur Shah Zafar Marg (which bisects Old Delhi and Daryaganj, a neighborhood of art deco architecture that's not on the tourist track but one day will be). The booksellers commandeered the sidewalk every Sunday, spreading their wares before them in neat rows, or in crazy piles, or in towering stacks that threaten to topple and bury unattended children. The selection ranged from the sublime (*The Phantom Tollbooth!*) to the bizarre (Bob Uecker wrote a book?); from the obsolete (manuals for Windows 3.1) to the obscure (guides to indigenous water management techniques in Gujarat). Some books were almost new, some were almost crumbling, and almost all were stepped upon by barefoot salespeople, shouting "dasrupaiyedasrupaiyedasrupaiye" as they took the quickest path between two customers. The ambient pulp smell brought back memories of my dad's childhood books that I found in my grandparents' house when I was a teen, and I always half-expected to stumble upon a red canvas hardcover edition of *Danny Dunn and the Homework Machine* with J-E-F-F P-R-A-G-E-R, G-R-A-D-E F-I-V-E scrawled across the title page.

The Sunday book market showcased the wonders of the global economy: who would have expected the paperback novelization of *The Empire Strikes Back* to make it all the way to India? Who would have thought there was so much demand for romance novels with the covers torn off? And seriously, Bob Uecker wrote a book?

Within the chaos, patterns emerged. One guy sold only hardcover copies of Stephen King, Dean Koontz and Harry Potter, all of them missing their dust jackets. Yet another specialized in 1970s spy novels featuring every James Bond wannabe the world never heard of (Johnny Fedora? Harry Palmer? Duff?). And good news for students of programming languages nobody uses any more: we found more crumbling manuals than we could shake a SPARC station keyboard at.

On one trip, one of the elderly booksellers standing near the Delhi Stock Exchange on Asaf Ali Road overheard me practising my Hindi on a nearby vendor. "You know Hindi?" he demanded, striding across his pile of thin non-fiction paperbacks to look me in the eye.

"Main Hindi sihkraha hai," I agreed eagerly, my accent and conjugation bringing a grimace to his face.

"Then I have something for you." He walked purposefully across his pile and began rummaging, tossing volumes left and right as he burrowed deeper, carving a path this way and that, retracing his steps to toss books he'd tossed once already in case they'd landed on the one he wanted. His purposeful search made me anticipate some enigmatic tome that would unlock the secrets of Hindi to me; I imagined that if I practiced diligently enough he'd invite me to sit at his feet in his family's forgotten haveli where, with dried rose petals fluttering around us, he would teach me mystical practices of meditation and telekinesis and sexual prowess that Westerners expect all Indian wise men to possess.

I stood and waited a few pregnant minutes while he searched, wondering what he'd come up with and hoping that my training would involve fighting monkeys with my bare hands. Then he finally picked up a book of Urdu–English poem translations. He skimmed through it, muttered, scowled, and tossed it aside.

"Sorry," he said. "Can't find it." Then he walked across his books to another customer.

★

If the Sunday book market was Delhi's Brigadoon, Palika Bazaar was Delhi's Biltmore Hotel garage: when it came to a little harmless lawbreaking, Palika Bazaar was the spot.

Palika Bazaar is an underground market located between the inner and outer circles of Connaught Place. Descending down its stairs, we'd enter a strange and fetid labyrinth created by hundreds of vendor stalls and far too many people for such a small space. Palika Bazaar defied every other shopping experience in Delhi. Elsewhere, shopkeepers seemed to have some sort of gentlemanly agreement as to how vigorously they'd solicit passers-by. In Palika, it was a free-for-all. Young men would shout at us and pull at our shirts and follow us around to cajole our patronage, and they'd shoot us looks of disgust when we'd decline. Eternal puddles added to the chaos, as did the stained ceilings and the overwhelming essence of sticky corruption. The layout was a confusion of concentric passages and repetitive storefronts, a muddied echo of Connaught Place's circular layout above, a bewildering maze that seemed purposefully designed to ensure as many people as possible would get trampled should a panicked stampede ever break out.

Palika Bazaar sold, with a thin veneer of subtlety, anything that could be pirated, bootlegged, or frowned upon in the daylight above. This included DVDs, video games, clothes, bags, shoes, electronics and sex toys. We'd walk past T-shirt vendors ("Real Gucci! Real Gucci!") and porn pushers ("You want sexy Indian movie?") before stopping at the DVD guys, who would make a cursory effort to interest us in their handful of legitimate shrink-wrapped discs before pulling out spiral notebooks filled with every title we could imagine watching, both Western and Hindi. We learned the wisdom of checking the quality of the disc before we bought it; the copy of *Nacho Libre* we asked one vendor to test couldn't have been any worse if it had been thrice dubbed off of a decades-old videotape.

The government has its eyes on Palika Bazaar. Not just in the proclamation they made to redevelop it in time for the 2010 Commonwealth Games. (Such proclamations must be taken with an ocean of salt, because the "reparation" of this and the "upgradation" of that were proclaimed a dozen times a week by smiling politicians who never seemed available for comment a year later when the newspapers followed up on the total lack of progress.) More tangible proof of government interest in Palika were the raids that were staged with increasing frequency and consequences. On our final visit to the bazaar, which came after a particularly well-publicized police action, every vendor we spoke to glanced around suspiciously when we asked about "cheaper" DVDs and then denied that they had any idea of what we were talking about.

The fact that the police were doing anything at all about piracy surprised us. Intellectual property enforcement seemed to be lower on the police's priority list than stopping drunk driving. We once bought a bag of mango candies from a sidewalk vendor in the Old City so we had something to hand to beggar children besides money; they'd look at these candies with a kind of suspicion they never showed when we gave them unlabeled bags of leftover food from restaurants. Only when a co-worker burst out laughing upon seeing me eat a piece of my own did we discover why: these candies were bootlegged versions of a popular brand, with the brand name purposefully misspelled and the logo shifted just enough to look completely illegitimate to everybody but us. It's not like we'd bought them from an illicit candy market full of Kat Kits and Cudbary's and Mirs Bars, though—the vendor had just been standing on the street, selling them in the open, seemingly unconcerned about getting caught.

Because he almost certainly wouldn't. Everywhere we turned, we saw violations of all the rules of trademark and copyright I learned at college in my requisite semester of Communications Law 507. Even on TV: one commercial for a line of men's clothing showed a handsome man in a tight button-down shirt walk past a gorgeous lady on the street; the lady, upon seeing his shirt, broke into a sultry dance that sent men all over India rushing to buy his magical sex shirt. The commercial opened with a brief snippet of Frank Sinatra singing "Strangers in the Night"— a song so coveted by advertisers that there's no way this local brand could have afforded the licensing fees, and no way they would have made its use so subtle if they had legally secured the rights. Similarly, our friend Scott spotted an ad for a Gurgaon optician's shop featuring a picture of the famously bespectacled politician Sarah Palin who, for all the twists in her career, probably hadn't cut any endorsement deals with local Indian eyeglasses shops. And a new frozen yogurt shop in Defence Colony called CocoBerry sold fruit-covered desserts that were identical to those sold by PinkBerry, a rapidly growing yogurt chain in the US. The *New York Times* even mentioned CocoBerry in an article about retail knockoffs in India,[2] also pointing to India's *Financial Times* newspaper, which has since 1984 copied London's *Financial Times* down to the pink hue of its newsprint.

---

2. http://www.nytimes.com/2009/07/16/business/global/16brands.html

Not that Sarah Palin's career is necessarily suffering from this unapproved endorsement. There's a broader issue here: if Frank Sinatra and PinkBerry and the *Financial Times* can't get justice, what hope do Delhi's small businessmen have? Every businessman knows he might wake up one morning to discover his carefully built brand pasted onto someone else's letterhead. In Karol Bagh, there's a famous store called Roopak that specializes in spices, nuts and dried fruit. Right next door to it, there's a store that's also called Roopak that also specializes in spices, nuts and dried fruit. We don't know which is the famous Roopak and which is the impostor. Maybe this is nothing more malicious than a family schism, but it could very well be capitalism at its most brazen, with the upstart Roopak calling out the veteran Roopak like two gunslingers facing off in a dusty Western town. Except it turns out that Karol Bagh is big enough for both of them, so every morning the two angry owners must open their shutters with all the ritual stomping, preening and chest puffing of the India–Pakistan flag ceremony at Wagah.

Such tensions must also thicken the air at a set of competing storefront kebab stands near Nizamuddin, where we went with the Eating Out in Delhi crew on one of our last nights in the city. Two sets of grills were assembled in front of two sets of closed metal garage doors, flanked by stacks of tires in front of driveways that were used by day for car repair. (A third garage door was open to reveal someone's living room, with a shirtless man stroking a massive black dog in front of a blaring television and glaring at anyone who stepped over the threshold demarcating where kebab stands ended and his home began.)

Above each of the kebab stands were vinyl signs. The one on the left named the stand below it as "Aap Ki Khatir," with the inexplicable and delightful tagline, "The Musical Drive-Fun." On the right, the identical-looking shop boasted an identical-looking sign that said "Sab Ke Khatir"—an identical-looking name too coincidental to be an accident.

A few months after we visited the stand, our friend Sam Dolnick, a fellow New Yorker working in Delhi for the Associated Press, published a terrific article that got to the bottom of this mystery.[3] He discovered that a former customer of Aap Ki Khatir thought it was such a good idea for a business that, taking advantage of the city's open attitude towards intellectual property, he duplicated its name and menu and opened up right next door.

"He is a friend-enemy," the waiter at Aap Ki Khatir says in Sam's article, describing the owner of Sab Ke Khatir. "We no longer talk. But this is what happens in business."

(On an unrelated note, Sam's article also featured one of the greatest descriptions of love ever put to print. The same waiter went on to tell Sam about his unrequited adoration for a woman in his central Indian village: "When I am with her, I feel like I am in an AC room.")

★

We wasted a significant portion of our first ten days in Delhi searching for a wireless router so we could access

---

3. http://abcnews.go.com/International/wireStory?id=8059804

both the Internet and our couch at the same time. At that point, we hadn't yet learned about the existence of Nehru Place. And the electronics store in Khan Market barely lived up to the name—a keyboard here, a PlayStation there, but apparently wireless routers were too specialized for their inventory. Frustrated with the fruitless search and dreading the possibility of a long Diwali weekend tethered so archaically to a single Ethernet cable, we mentioned our problem to Shankar, our landlord. We knew that his company did something with technology, so maybe he'd know where to go.

Shankar's son Rahul just picked up the phone. Our doorbell rang exactly thirty minutes later with a man bearing a router like he was delivering a pizza.

A love of India flooded our hearts.

New York is a city of two-month waits for a dentist's appointment and cancellation charges if we don't show up. Of surly cashiers who pretend not to notice us standing directly in front of them. Of postal employees hidden behind two-inch-thick bullet-proof glass and even thicker attitudes. Of hospital emergency rooms that are empty of attendants, with nothing but a clipboard for us to put down our names and seats in which to wait while our friend Jeff clutches his burned hand and asks Jenny if she has aspirin in her purse. Of drugstore employees so notoriously unpleasant that our friends Andrew and Heather could dress as them for New York City's Halloween parade and everyone at whom they pretended to yell—of all races, from all neighborhoods, representing all classes—immediately got the joke.

I once watched a customer in line at a Brooklyn supermarket suggest to the cashier that she could "smile a bit more." The cashier immediately began screaming for her manager—and the manager actually took the cashier's side.

But not in Delhi. The Land of Router Delivery! Customer service as we'd only seen on *Leave It to Beaver*! When we needed our teeth cleaned, we could make appointments for that very afternoon. When we bought house-plants, a guy bicycled them to our bungalow and carried them up to our flat. The video rental store would knock on our door to collect overdue movies and then present a binder full of DVDs for subsequent home entertainment. The liquor store would assign someone to carry our beer home. Our accountant would come to meet with us in our living room. The bank representative would promise to call us back with information the next day—and he actually would!

But as deeply as we came to love Delhi's customer service, our first instinct was to resist it. We were both accustomed to New York's style of customer service, in which any drugstore employee asking "May I help you?" was doing so only because her manager was watching. When Jenny and I traveled to friendlier parts of the US, we'd actually be suspicious of employees' sincere offers of assistance. "Why is that guy smiling at us?" I'd whisper to Jenny upon walking into an Albuquerque Walgreens. "Oh my God, why is he actually walking us to the shampoo aisle? And did he just say 'You're welcome'?!"

So the first time Jenny entered a Delhi pharmacy, she had no desire for any interaction with the employees beyond getting a finger pointed towards the shampoo aisle. But instead of giving her directions, the employee she'd queried requested that she wait at the counter. She complied, her initial confusion turning into—yes, anger—as the employee gathered up a single representative of each of the brands on the shelf and then returned to hold them out to her, one by one. And then he did the same thing for hand lotions, and then bath soaps. Later, at the housewares store, a salesman presented her the coffee makers and the kitchen plates in the same sequential manner. Then it happened while buying shirts in the mall. Then while buying pens in the stationery store.

We found ourselves dreading the act of shopping simply because of the attention we knew would be paid to us. Even if we could convince the employee that, no, we needed absolutely no assistance identifying our preferred brand, and that we were perfectly capable of wrapping our fingers around bottles ourselves, the employee still followed two paces behind, ready to spring to assistance. If we picked a bottle of Finesse, he eagerly handed us a bottle of Pantene for comparison.

We fought back. We'd dash into the pharmacy together, split up, and rush around to find the lip balm, never making eye contact with the employees who were chasing after us around the store. We hated the attention, we hated the time that those employees spent helping us, and we hated feeling obligated to buy something because those employees had spent so much time paying attention to us. Why, we'd think, standing outside the pharmacy and plotting our separate routes through the aisles—why can't they just treat us like normal customers?

Finally, we realized what was happening: they were treating us like normal customers.

This is the difference between India's human-scale retail and the corporate-scale retail in the United States. Back home, almost every store we went to for our daily needs was a national chain functioning on a national scale. Individual customers and individual employees were fractions of decimals of cash flow and labor expenditure, which meant that they were insignificant in the macro view of the parent company. Neither the employees' performance nor my satisfaction would impact the company's billions. That's why an employee could roll her eyes at our request for help without getting fired: she has no stake in the company beyond her $7.25 an hour, and she knows her manager would rather lose a customer than fill out the termination paperwork, much less find a new employee who actually has a positive attitude. What's more, every one of us knows that the company sees its employees as trained seals who are pressing buttons, and that their jobs are secure only until the company trains actual seals to do the same thing. The expectations of all parties are lowered accordingly.

But in a Delhi store, the connection between an employee's behavior and the owner's profit is direct. Not only because a mom-and-pop store needs every customer it can get, but because the owner is usually bent over his ledger right there by the cash register, watching the transaction over the rims of his glasses. There's also the pressure of intense competition—for the owner, who knows that any successful company can expect its competitor to open next door and take the same name; and for the employee, who knows that in an economy with such an oversupply of labor, he's lucky to have a job at all.

Most importantly, though, Delhiites simply expect a level of respect New Yorkers have long since given up on.

Our frustration with exuberant customer service faded once we understood its purpose: it was because stores genuinely wanted our business.

*

And once we realized that we were valued as customers, the next logical step was to start taking advantage of our value. And so we learned to bargain.

In the retail environment in which Jenny and I grew up, the price tag is the price tag. Houses and cars are open for negotiation in America, but just about everything else is rung up at cash registers by bored teens who wouldn't have the authority to make a counter-offer even if they knew what one was. This is why Wal-Mart stores are found on every corner not already occupied by Target stores: Americans value convenience over price. We want to buy our clothes, electronics, auto parts, home furnishings and pet food all in the same place. By prioritizing convenience, that means that none of us would ever price a basket of goods at Wal-Mart and then offer the Target manager a few dollars less for the same bundle. Instead, while we accept that Target's margins may be slightly higher on garden hose and Wal-Mart's may be slightly higher on toothpaste, we believe the difference will be worth less than the extra time spent driving to the other store. We have faith that the invisible hand has pushed the price down as far as it can go, and we rarely give it a second thought.

That's why it was so challenging for us to bargain in India. Not just because we didn't know any bargaining techniques, but because we actually discovered in ourselves a culturally imposed taboo against bargaining. To our sensibilities, bargaining felt like we were insulting the seller. Like we were trying to cheat him. We were far more comfortable just asking for the price and paying what we were told.

Then we realized that the salesmen were smirking at our backs every time we accepted their first offer. Bargaining, we finally understood, is built into the price tag. If we accepted the first price, we weren't respecting them—we were just hurting ourselves.

And so we attempted to bargain. It was ungainly at first—laughable, really—but we eventually figured it out. And while the techniques we learned were common sense to anyone who grew up here, they were a revelation to us.

Our most basic tactic was this: whatever it was we wanted, we shouldn't show it. Once the seller knew our intentions, his price would grow remarkably inflexible, and only if he truly thought we'd walk away would his price begin to shrink. We discovered this entirely by accident when I made inadvertent eye contact with a vendor selling poster-sized maps of the city in the Basant Lok market. He held up his wares and quoted 300 rupees. But as soon as we walked past, his price instantly fell by fifty percent. The further we walked away, the lower his price fell, until suddenly he was shouting a number that was a sliver of his original price, and we decided to become owners of the same obligatory wall map that Murali would mock in every expat living room he visited.

The only flaw in this technique is that the seller had to believe we were serious. More often than not, we'd walk out of a shop expecting the salesperson to call after us but hearing only the door clicking shut. We'd look at each other and then sheepishly slink back in to pay his price.

We started supplementing this technique with the good-cop-bad-cop approach, which meant that one of us would eagerly pursue an item while the other would adamantly oppose it. This, too, we learned by accident. Walking through Connaught Place one evening, I spotted a street vendor's bootlegged copy of *Lonely Planet India* just as Jenny spotted something she coveted just as enthusiastically: a McDonalds in which she could use the toilet. As I began expressing interest in the book, she began pulling at my sleeve, and the more urgently she tried to drag me away, the more the vendor improved his price.

I learned our most effective tactic by watching my colleague Dipankar work the guys who sold beanbag chairs in abandoned M.G. Road storefronts. We'd taken the office taxi up the road to make this purchase, knowing that the two beanbags would turn our shared cubicle into the hippest corner of the office. After we picked out the ones we wanted, the vendor named his price. And then Dipankar countered with the five most devastatingly effective words anyone could utter to a Delhi storeowner: 'Can I have a discount?'

Those five words almost unfailingly knocked ten percent off of whatever we were buying. At the vegetable stand, with the custom tailors, buying a stereo system—all we had to do was ask.

Dipankar was a master at this technique. He would apply it in places I'd never imagine, like at a party I threw for my co-workers at a restaurant in GK-II. As soon as Dipankar saw the number of people at the table, he turned to me and said, "Did you ask the owner for a discount?"

"No," I replied. "Why would I do that?"

Dipankar laughed as he got up from the table. "Because that's what you do." He flagged down the manager, pointed out all the people I had gathered in his fine establishment, and asked for a discount on food. Which he received. Just like that.

Jenny and I applied this technique to lower the prices of hotel rooms, guided tours, furniture, and bootleg DVDs in Delhi, south India, Nepal, and even Singapore. All we had to do was ask. The worst they could do was say no; the best they could do was often much better than we expected. I'm pleased to say that the students became the master: at the goodbye party Jenny and I had at a Defence Colony restaurant just before we left Delhi, I flagged down the manager, pointed out all the people I had gathered in his fine establishment, and asked for a discount on booze. And when he only offered two-for-one on hard drinks, I pressed him further and got a thirty percent discount on beer.

In fact, this technique taught us to see the world differently: everything, we suddenly realized, was open for negotiation. When it came time to move out of our Delhi flat, we proposed to our landlord that he halve our final month's rent if we found another foreigner to take our place; he agreed so readily I realized we should have asked for a full month's rent as our fee. When we took our bargaining skills to Singapore, we got twenty-five percent knocked off our monthly rent and a further forty percent off the apartment broker's fee simply by asking: "Can we have a discount?" And when we needed a new computer, we found ourselves walking out of Singapore's Sim Lim Plaza with a free keyboard, a free mouse and free RAM simply because we asked the first vendor for a discount and then played his offer against the other vendors in the complex.

Because Delhiites are such relentless bargainers, business owners have to worry about their margins. This may be why so many of the city's stores and nearly all its markets—even the upscale ones—were generally in need of renovation.

To put it politely.

I don't mean this as a foreigner's clichéd sniff of disdain. Instead, I wonder if in a bargain-obsessed culture, poor lighting or a dirty floor or a dust-covered display might actually give some bargaining leverage back to the business owner.

After all, bargain-minded shoppers would look at a store with mood lighting and waxed counters and calculate how much their purchase price would be marked-up for upkeep. The store next door, with inventory strewn all about and mosquito civilizations evolving in puddles on the sales floor, obviously applies none of its revenue towards aesthetics. Strategic dirt could actually convey the impression of costs cut to the bone, which could then allow the business owner to credibly claim his prices to be as low as he could go. The environment may send goras like me scurrying for the nearest mall, but given the poppadum-thin margins that must exist—especially in the trade-specific markets, where everyone sells the same inventory and the same service—an unkempt environment could actually be a competitive advantage.

★

According to our neighbor Anya, the neighborhood around Hauz Khas market is among the oldest residential developments in south Delhi. It was surrounded by fields and farms when she would visit her grandfather as a child. Back then, Aurobindo Marg was a road to nowhere that bisected nothing. And the homes across the street from our flat—which now house a group of merchant families in circular competition to buy nicer cars and throw louder weddings than the next—are still groves of trees in Anya's memory. Hauz Khas market boasted "a temple, a milk guy, a bread guy, and not much else." When Anya's grandfather first moved there, he could have never expected his quiet exurban neighborhood market to one day boast a store selling three different brands of Swiss muesli, Delhi's "first openly gay-friendly unisex hair salon,"[4] and an America-style coffee lounge in which an upper-class youth in his

---

4. http://thedelhiwalla.blogspot.com/2009/07/city-landmark-nyc-unisex-salon-hauz.html

mid-twenties set up his keyboard every Sunday to serenade patrons with karaoke renditions of "Summer of '69," "Hotel California," and the theme from *Friends*.

These days, Hauz Khas market is typical of many of south Delhi's local markets. We could pick up pomegranates from the fruitwallah, carrots from the veggiewallah, yogurt from the Mother Dairy stall, kitchen sponges from dry goods store, and bread from the guy who sold loaves out of the three-wheeled bread truck that he parked directly across the sidewalk from Prakash General Store, which sold the exact same brands of bread. We could get signs made, keys made, frames made, eyeglasses made and clothes made. We could buy plastic chairs from the guy who sold all forms of plastic furniture except plastic tables, which we had to buy from another guy down the street. There were two butchers to choose from, if we had been at all enticed by the bloody rows of meat on the counter with no refrigerators in sight. Some of the stores in Hauz Khas market were modern and shining, with fluorescent light spilling out of spotless windows onto freshly swept sidewalks. Others were prehistoric and dusty, with inventory sprawled across the floor in piles so ancient that it seemed like the pile had come first and that the store must have been constructed around it.

Hauz Khas market is also typical in its tension between yesterday's India and tomorrow's India. As of 2009, organized retail made up about five percent of India's $450 billion retail industry,[5] with the vast majority of India's

<hr>

5. http://online.wsj.com/article/SB125480846252666899.html

commerce still being conducted by sidewalk vendors on busy streets or at mom-and-pop shops in chaotic local markets. It's mostly still subsidence retail, to coin a phrase: businesses that are making just enough money to survive. But by 2013, organized retail is expected to nearly double in size,[6] and Hauz Khas market demonstrates not only how this change manifests in practice, but where the future is headed.

Let's go for a walk through Hauz Khas market. There's Mayura Clothing ("Tailors of Distinction"), in which wizened men toil behind pedal-powered sewing machines and the owner records his sales in the same ledger book he's used for twenty years. Fifty meters down the road is Freelook, a J.Crew-esque store with a J.Crew-esque logo, air conditioning, plate glass windows, and digital cash registers. (Although Freelook does still employ traditional retail cost-cutting measures: when we open the door, the salesperson rushes to turn on the lights and the music that are kept off to save on electricity.)

We walk further. There's Hans Raj Narang Plastics, which can't be missed thanks to the bare-chested male model on the Amul Macho underwear billboard above its entrance who demonstrates just how snugly Amul Macho underwear fits around a man's most macho protrusions. The inside of this plastics store is lined with ten-foot shelves and lit by a bulb strung over the dusty blade of a motionless ceiling fan. Every item in the store seems twenty years old and deteriorating fast. In fact, roughly one-third of the

---

6. Ibid.

plastic party cups we bought there had degraded so much on the shelves that they dribbled vodka and orange juice onto our guests' shirts. And the plastic forks they sold us had been previously used and half-heartedly washed; we should have known better when we saw that the package was sealed with staples. The proprietor inside scowled at us every time we set foot in his store, as if our desire to exchange money for plastics was some sort of unforgivable imperial arrogance. He'd refuse to help us find any of the items we were looking for, and he'd only grudgingly ring them up if we actually found them. How will he compete when India's version of Bed, Bath & Beyond finally opens?

A few more steps to the north is the dusty electronics shop where we'd refill our mobile phone. I never knew the name of the store because its signboard was completely obscured behind ads for Havells Climate Engineers, Roma Tresa Modular Switches, and vinyl banners for various mobile phone companies. The shop owner, an elderly man with thick glasses and an infectious enthusiasm for both Barack Obama and Manmohan Singh, was a pleasure to talk to. But as nice as he was, his way of business was rapidly becoming extinct. His inventory was stacked chaotically on shelves, stuffed haphazardly in boxes, or hanging unattractively from the ceiling. I have no idea about the extent of his product line because most of it was hidden from view, and certainly not organized in attractive displays to encourage point-of-purchase sales. Low-margin products like light bulbs were the only thing within the customer's reach (covered in dust as they were), while high-ticket items like satellite dishes and cable boxes were in the back, behind the desk that kept out pedestrian traffic, hidden in piles so that customers couldn't pick them up and read the boxes and transform that inventory into cash flow. His transactions were laborious—I once waited twenty minutes while he filled out the forms required to buy a SIM card for my mobile phone. He slowly and agonizingly scrutinized each page as if it was the first time he'd ever conducted this transaction, asking me my information and carefully forming each letter with his pen. A line of customers grew behind me. And then it shrank as people went elsewhere to spend their money.

I loved to chat with him. Behind his thick glasses, his eyes sparkled with vigour and intellect. But with his capital tied up in inventory and his operations running comically inefficient, how much longer can he survive? All around him, the storefronts that were built during Anya's grandfather's day are now filled with boutique clothing stores, a Reebok store, a 7-Eleven-style convenience store called "Big Apple," a modern pharmacy franchisee, and a Café Coffee Day lounge. They all boast computerized tills, barcode scanners and national distribution systems that lower costs and increase efficiency far beyond what this poor old man will ever be able to compete with. His cubbyhole store will inevitably be glommed on to those next door to accommodate some future upscale hair salon.

In fact, outside of the NIIT technical training center just a few doors down, a group of laughing college students are eating momos. They may buy thirty rupees' worth of mobile phone talk time from him today, but in that very building they're learning to network the very computers that will run the very supply chains that will soon drive him out of business.

★

We did most of our shopping for packaged goods at Shri Morning Palace, right in the middle of Hauz Khas market. They specialized in an improbable mix of imported groceries, pet supplies, eyeglasses and underwear. And as is typical in Delhi's hyper-competitive environment, Shri Morning Palace's main competitor in the market—Shri Sant Lal Ramji Dass—was right next door. Shri Sant Lal Ramji Dass's signboard contrasted Shri Morning Palace's emphasis on product breadth ("Hair care / Varieties of Cheese / Confectionaries / Pet food / Undergarments / Skin care") by focusing narrowly on its depth of food offerings, showing a photo of fried vegetables and a bottle of Smith & Jones Tomato Ketchup. Although Shri Sant Lal Ramji Dass had the better selection, its aisles were so narrow as to induce claustrophobia, and the store always smelled unidentifiably but tangibly *wrong*. So we stuck to Shri Morning Palace.

The proprietors at Shri Morning Palace grew familiar with us. Two smiling, soft-spoken men, perhaps brothers, they both had gray hair that they dyed a shocking shade of maroon, as was the style in the city. They were always good for a gentle hello, a friendly smile, and a subtle flick of the hand to order one of their employees to follow us around the store holding our basket for us. The employee would stand patiently by as we scrutinized their selection of Italian pasta or peered into the small mini-fridge that contained the full gamut of their "varieties of cheese." Whenever we'd thank the employee for carrying our purchases, it was one of the proprietors who would say, "You're welcome."

One day I asked them about their store's name. Back in 1956, when the business was founded, they needed a name that reflected the fact they opened up early every morning.

"We chose 'Morning Palace' because we used to open at 5 a.m. and 'Shri' because that's an honorific in our language."

"Why not just 'Morning Palace' on its own?" I asked.

"Because that would have been unlucky."

The very fact that Shri Morning Palace carried so many brands we recognized from the US is apparently a sign of how much Delhi has changed since the early 1990s. That's when India underwent drastic liberalization and deregulation. Even just twenty years prior to our residency, Delhi was a city without the malls and espresso machines and Mexican restaurants we frequented so regularly. ("I remember what this 'city' was like in 1991," wrote a blogger named Tarun Pall. "There were no coffee shops, no Delhi Metro and very little in Gurgaon or Noida, with no toll expressways connecting them to Delhi. There was no such thing as a shopping mall. Khan Market and GK-I were fuddy-duddy markets where women wearing salwar kameezes shopped. There was no Maharaja Mac. There were a total of four ATMs in the city."[7]) And at that time, Shri Morning Palace would have stocked the same inventory found in every

---

7. http://ourdelhistruggle.com/2010/01/21/future-open-question/#comment-2908

other general store in the city—except, like many other general stores, they might have had imported perfume, chocolate and American breakfast cereal hidden under the counter, available only to customers whom they knew and trusted, and then for no less than three times the price.

So we can thank the economic changes of the early 1990s for the fact that Shri Morning Palace legally satisfied our day-to-day cravings for imports. But Shri Morning Palace couldn't satisfy our more obscure desires for, say, canned Lebanese stuffed grape leaves or Smuckers' Goober Peanut Butter and Grape Jelly Stripes. For a broader selection of imports, we had to head elsewhere in the city.

While a number of local markets, like Defence Colony and Basant Lok, catered more specifically to foreign tastes, everyone told us that INA Market had Delhi's best selection of imported goods. But our visits there led us to conclude that INA must have earned its reputation in the days before liberalization. Because the Doritos and Rittersport we found there are now sold all over the city, and the only import we found to be unique to INA Market was an unfamiliar variety of avocado that was too mushy even for guacamole.

The city's most famously foreigner-centric market is Khan Market. This market is also one of the more enduring mysteries we found in Delhi: everyone told us that Khan Market was the most expensive commercial real estate in the world.

Really? *Khan Market?*

Khan Market is a U-shaped collection of buildings, with storefronts lining the perimeter of the U and a semi-developed alley inside of it. The market's main entrance is flanked by magazine vendors, a store selling electronics and music, and a delightfully chaotic bookshop. It attracts a certain class of shoppers: rich foreign mothers wearing jeans and salwar shirts pushing their strollers towards Chokola, young men in pink polo shirts tweaking their collars in the mirrors at the sunglasses stores, and tourists taking photos of the dusty inner alley. It has a McDonald's and a Subway, some coffee shops, and a few upscale home décor boutiques. In the inner alley, clothing boutiques and trendy restaurants compete for attention with dust-covered power cables and open manholes through which the tourists gape at men clearing blocked sewers by hand.

Khan Market does have a number of unique offerings. But many of its tenants—kitchen appliance vendors, butchers, chemists, stationery stores—are indistinguishable from those that are found in every other market in the city. And their prices are only marginally inflated above the rest. Most telling of all, there are very few luxury brands. Delhi's Diors, Guccis and Louis Vuittons are all ten miles down the road at the Emporio Mall in Vasant Kunj.

Khan Market is a nice market, but it's not most-expensive-real-estate-in-the-world nice. And beyond aesthetics, the elite economics aren't there: Khan Market isn't particularly expensive to shop at, its product mix doesn't comprise particularly high-margin goods, and the foot traffic it generates is not that much heavier than other major markets in the city. The differences aren't significant enough to make us believe that its fruit vendors would be paying rent on a Cartier scale.

When we finally decided to research it, we uncovered a truth that was slightly less grandiose but no less implausible:

Khan Market was actually the twenty-first most expensive shopping real estate in the world in 2010,[8] according to a survey by the real estate firm Cushman & Wakefield. (That's down from 2008, when it was sixteenth on their list.) With a reported rental price of $284 per square foot per year, Khan Market was supposedly more expensive than the most expensive shopping districts in Amsterdam, Kuala Lumpur, Brussels, Taipei, Stockholm, Oslo and Tel Aviv, and only around ten percent less expensive than Orchard Road in Singapore.

We don't buy it. We moved to Singapore after we lived in Delhi, and there's no way that Khan Market's square-foot ratios are equal to Orchard Road's billion-dollar malls. Khan Market has neither the foot traffic nor the high-margin products to greatly distinguish it from the inner circle of Connaught Place, much less Orchard Road. Still, bizarrely, another Cushman & Wakefield report says that CP's rents are only around half of what Khan Market's rents supposedly are.[9]

Something doesn't add up. We don't know how Cushman & Wakefield got their numbers, but we can't believe they're correct.

Perhaps Khan Market, like INA Market, is still coasting on a reputation earned before India's liberalization. In the

---

8. http://www.cushwake.com/cwglobal/jsp/kcReportDetail.jsp?
   Country=GLOBAL&Language=EN&catId=100003&pId=
   c31300002p

9. http://www.cushwake.com/cwglobal/jsp/kcReportDetail.jsp?
   Country=GLOBAL&Language=EN&catId=100003&pId=
   c37100002p

'80s and '90s, with its location near many neighborhoods favored by expats, Khan Market was the place where the rich and foreign would spend their time. Now, though, legalized imports have rendered under-the-table cheddar cheese obsolete. And while Khan Market retains its reputation, its revenues are probably a different story because both foreign and domestic wealth alike hang out in the malls.

★

Delhi's malls showcase the divide between the old India we've been told about and the changing India we experienced. We can't imagine Delhi without them. Any time the city threatened to get the best of us—when the heat melted our wills, when the pollution choked our excitement, when the chaos sapped our spirits—the malls were there to revive us. Though we'd left America in part to escape American consumerism, Delhi's malls made us appreciate that there are actually things to appreciate about malls. They were climate-controlled, spotless, and modern: a sanctuary from all the things we needed sanctuary from. Nobody even stared at us in the malls—white people were just as much a part of the mall's scenery as domestic cheese shops and motorcycle showrooms.

Nowhere is the split between Delhi's generations better observed than on a mall's escalators. Teens hop lightly off the escalators, with the girls demonstrating all the good and bad that comes with Western mores and the guys preening in T-shirts printed with phrases they may not fully appreciate.

(We saw one alpha-male-in-training who wore sunglasses, a whisper of a mustache and a stylish shirt that read, "What part of the word 'dyke' don't you understand?") Midway down the escalator, parents hold children who point at what they want to buy next and bored couples laden with shopping bags show dissatisfaction on their faces that all their shopping apparently didn't alleviate. And at the top of the escalator, grandmothers in saris gather their courage and time their leap onto the moving steps; as soon as they make their move, they grip the handrail with both hands and lock their eyes on the sari-gnashing teeth waiting at the escalator's bottom.

It's not just the air conditioning that draws people out of the local markets and into the malls, although that's obviously no small factor. The bigger draw is that malls do everything they can to attract customers, whereas local markets do the bare minimum to avoid completely driving customers away. Malls are clean, well maintained and safe for kids to run around without falling into festering ditches. What's more, malls go out of their way to create an environment that makes people want to return. Saket Citywalk Mall, for instance, hosts everything from flea markets to yoga camps.

The majority of local markets, meanwhile, are nice to visit only within the threshold of any individual shop. With very few exceptions (the two markets in GK-I come to mind), the local markets pay lip service to beautification with a sweeper here or central park there, but little is done to make the experience of walking between the shops as pleasant as being inside of one. The state of the markets may provide business owners a competitive advantage in day-to-day bargaining (the shoddier the market, the cheaper the perceived prices), but that race to the bottom won't sustain them in Delhi's evolving retail environment.

I don't think that the local markets are run by profiteers who revel in decay. Rather, I think they've just never felt any competitive pressure that would force them to put their customers' needs above their own. ("Khan Market has enough parking for about 500 cars," reports the *Times of India*. "About 300 of them belong to the shopkeepers themselves."[10]) The markets have been protected from competition by Delhi's street grid, which makes it so difficult to travel between neighborhoods that, for staples like food and household goods, the local markets had a monopoly.

But the malls' amenities are more powerful than the markets' geographic monopolies. They provide clean and safe public spaces where families can stroll without SUVs running them down from behind. They sell everything from consumer electronics to furniture to vegetables, and in a climate-controlled environment with nice bathrooms to boot. They're worth traveling for, in other words. And until the markets improve, the malls will continue to siphon their business.

I'm torn by this. On the one hand, I'm a progressive American who is repulsed by the rampant consumerism back home. I hate to see Western-style shopping assimilate yet another culture, creating one more link in the global

---

10. http://timesofindia.indiatimes.com/Delhi/Glitzy_makeover_for_posh_Khan_Market/articleshow/3888181.cms

chain of Wal-Marts and Ikeas that will one day stretch unbroken across the world and ensure that all of humanity is never more than ten minutes' drive from a Starbucks latte and a President's Day sale.

On the other hand, the spread of malls could actually *help* the local markets by sparking a customer-centric arms race in Delhi. Local markets will finally feel competitive pressures, which will make them desperate to re-attract the people who have abandoned them for the comfort of the malls. And because they'll still retain the powerful advantage of location, they'll just need to improve the infrastructure and environment.

I foresee a coming boom in market beautification. And if I squint into the future, I can imagine this beautification extending to the surrounding neighborhoods and then across the city as businesses realize that when they invest in the collective good, the collective responds by spending more money.

Khan Market is already leading this charge. At the time we were leaving Delhi, it had pledged to modernize its inner lane, to bury the high-voltage canopy of overhead wires, to install a functional drainage system, and to replace the gray tile sidewalk with attractive red anti-skid granite stone.[11] Other markets are sure to follow its lead. Perhaps one day we'll return to a Delhi in which Defence Colony market has replaced its chaotic parking lot with a lush pedestrian garden, Nehru Place has evolved into a cultural hub complete with loft apartments and outdoor theater

---

11. Ibid.

performances, and Hauz Khas market is now the world headquarters for a vast electronics retail empire headed by that elderly shop owner with the thick glasses who sold us our mobile phone top-ups. He'd read this book, considered our suggestions, and hired those NIIT students to take his own business into the next century.

8

Working (Late, Again)

The eighteen months during which I was employed in Delhi were defined by my commute. I don't diminish the experiences I had on the job, where my responsibilities far exceeded those I'd had in New York and extended to teaching everyone in the office how to throw a Nerf football. But when I look back on it, the commute that bookended each workday weighs more significantly in my mind. And I believe that I derived more important lessons about life in India from my time sitting in my taxi than that spent sitting at my desk.

Jenny's time working in Delhi was defined by something more agreeable: a feeling of fulfilment. Jenny experienced job satisfaction of the sort she'd never imagined possible at any of her other jobs. She was employed by a charity called the Pardada Pardadi Educational Society, and she spent each day improving the lives of a thousand poor girls who were enrolled in the organization's school out in rural Uttar Pradesh.

Pardada Pardadi was Jenny's second job in Delhi. It was far more rewarding than her first one, which was a brief stint at an advertising agency. During her interview, the boss had said he wanted to hire her because "as a foreigner, you would have a lot of insights and unique suggestions that would help us increase our professionalism." Left unsaid was what turned out to be a more accurate reason: as a blond, female American, her presence alone would give the agency some clout with the client. Still, she enjoyed her brief time there, where she was inspired by the number of women in positions of responsibility and entertained by the office boys who would spy on her throughout the day, peeking at her from around corners and softly singing love songs to each other. And she was engrossed—in both senses of the word—by the smell from the basement.

The smell would billow up the office stairwell every two or three weeks. Each time it made Jenny think something had gone terribly wrong and that evacuation of the office was imminent. It was a terrible odor for which she had no frame of reference within an office environment. It was far worse than a refrigerator opened after weeks of forgotten festering lunches, and it saturated all four floors of the building, crawled underneath the closed office door, and made it impossible for Jenny to work.

But only Jenny was bothered by it. While she coughed and choked, everyone else just went stoically about their business, enduring without complaint something that would drive every American office worker out of their minds.

One day, fed up with mouth breathing, Jenny made some inquiries. While the aboveground floors of the building were home to one of India's best-known new media companies, its basement housed a distributor of raw and processed meat products. Among their clients, one co-worker reported, were many of the Subway franchises that had sprung up all around Delhi.

Whether the smell was meat being cooked, strips of flesh curing in the basement heat, or blood being burned off a killing floor, nobody knew; all anybody knew was that it was meat. Which made it all the more surprising that an office half-full of vegetarian Hindus would be so silent about the awful airborne particles polluting their bodies by way of their nasal passages.

And there is a lesson in this: that discomfort does not supersede responsibility. This lesson mirrors the lesson that I learned during my commute: no matter how tough a workplace may be, and no matter how heavily the work environment might bear upon those toiling in it, the only ones who complained were the ones who were ignorant about how bad things could otherwise be.

Or, to be more direct: we foreigners had no idea what "hard work" actually meant.

★

My company worked out of three different office buildings during my time in Delhi. For my first month, we were located in the collection of low-rise offices known as Okhla Industrial Estates Phase III. Although there were a few

dozen buildings in the complex, there was just a single
entrance, and it was accessible to southbound commuters
only by taking a U-turn under a major flyover. So every
morning, four lanes of cars jammed up as they fought to
funnel into a two-lane entrance. I couldn't believe that the
businesses paying rent in Okhla hadn't agitated for a
widening of this entrance, because it essentially functioned
as a fifteen-minute tax levied against every single worker in
the complex.

But I soon found out that traffic at Okhla was nothing to
complain about. Because then our office shifted to Gurgaon.

Delhi's great corporate exodus to Gurgaon seemed to
reach critical mass during our stay in the city. The rents
were cheaper in Gurgaon; but more importantly, business
after business watched their clients move there, saw their
competitors follow, and realized that they had no other
choice. Sometimes it seemed like every professional I met
either worked in Gurgaon or was preparing for an imminent
move. And usually it seemed like every single one was
driving on M.G. Road at the exact same time.

There was nothing I hated worse than Mehrauli–Gurgaon
Road. It was a six-mile stretch of pain upon which I would
stop-and-go and stop-and-go for three hours of every
working day. M.G. Road was one of only two routes that
led from Delhi to Gurgaon, and this bottleneck was just the
first of many failures of urban planning that should have
deterred companies from moving to Gurgaon, but didn't.

The other road was NH-8, the national highway, which
fully opened two months after we arrived in Delhi. For
weeks prior to the scheduled December 31 inauguration,

my co-workers and I eagerly anticipated completion of the final flyovers that would let cars zip from Haryana's border straight to Delhi's Ring Roads and take the pressure off of M.G. Road. But December 31 came and went, and the road remained closed—even though, as the newspapers reported, construction was completely finished.

As the days turned into weeks with no green light, the newspapers grew increasingly agitated. Their populist indignation decried two conspiracies that were denying the people their improved commute: first, that the corporation running the toll plaza wasn't yet prepared to charge tolls but wouldn't allow the road to be opened for free; and second, that the area's politicians and dignitaries were mired in a squabble about the road's inaugural photo-op, agreeing only that it should remain closed until they decided who should hold the giant ribbon-cutting scissors or whatever it was they were arguing about. By the third week of January, the newspapers were publicly calling for a commuter revolution. This inspired a number of people to ignore the "road closed" signs and drive along the overpass anyway, which in turn inspired the newspapers to publicly congratulate themselves for single-handedly kick-starting the grand bourgeoisie revolution. The newspapers also gleefully gossiped about the political scuffles that followed as ministers and muckety-mucks jostled over the details of the increasingly unnecessary inaugural celebration until, finally, nearly four weeks after the road was ready for cars, the people in power gathered and posed and elbowed each other out of the pictures, and the road was officially open.

At that point, NH-8 became a high-speed gateway between Delhi and Gurgaon. And it was a genuine showpiece of modern infrastructure. It was rarely jammed except for near the airport runways, where the slow lanes were often blocked by parked cars watching the planes land. But for the first six months, any time one gained on the highway was immediately snatched back by the bureaucracy at the toll plaza on the Haryana state border, where twenty-minute queues generated scores of angry editorials for months until the toll plaza management finally added the signs, lane markers and staff they should have had from the opening day.

(Growing pains. By the time we moved out of Delhi, the toll plaza was far more impressive to behold. Its collectors would snatch outstretched money and return exact change in a single swipe, screaming "Jaldi, bhai, jaldi!" to any driver who might try to count his change or ask the time or dawdle in any way. The plaza soon shrunk to the status of minor inconvenience for everyone except those poor drivers who invested in automated toll tags—because their lines were always longer and slower than the lines for those who were paying cash.)

But NH-8 didn't improve my commute. Even after they got the toll plaza functional, any time I gained on the highway was lost once I exited on to the Outer Ring Road, where construction on a series of flyovers remained stalled for almost our entire duration in Delhi. The first half-mile after the highway was lined by massive steel support beams that had been placed on the sidewalk in preparation for construction that only finally started in our last month in the city. For a few miles beyond that, the center lanes had been closed off to accommodate the frozen worksite. Commuters had been routed on to now-crumbling dirt shoulders that were creating jams so miserable that M.G. Road actually became the better choice.

Still, for those continuing on NH-8 directly into central or north Delhi, the highway was a godsend. And while it reduced the pressure on M.G. Road, it did so just as M.G. Road itself narrowed like a bacon lover's arteries. Giant cement pylons began sprouting in the center of the road, protected on either side by metal dividers that lopped off three of the road's six lanes. This was construction for the southern portion of the Delhi Metro.

At least these jams represented progress. They had a purpose. It was still miserable to be stuck in traffic, but it was genuinely satisfying to watch the pylons sprout and then see the massive launching machine hang cement track segments between them, creating an elegantly modern sculpture that now stretches from Qutub Minar onwards until it and M.G. Road part ways in Gurgaon.

The Metro is now the pride of Delhi, and justifiably so. In its massive spotless stations, polite riders queue patiently and give ample space for departing passengers to exit. Its cars are air-conditioned and their windows are wide enough to admire the 108-foot tall statue of the monkey god Hanuman that we'd pass on our way to Roshan Di Kulfi in Karol Bagh. Each time we rode the Metro, I felt a nostalgia for a Delhi that did not yet exist, the Delhi-to-come in which the aboveground city is as modern and functional as the one below.

But to prepare M.G. Road for Delhi's most conspicuous symbol of modernity, the government besmirched M.G. Road with an equally conspicuous symbol of incompetence. Before we'd moved to Delhi, M.G. Road had apparently bustled with fashion malls and furniture stores. But in 2006, the government decided that almost all of them were "illegal constructions" that needed to be "sealed."[1] And "sealing," as it turned out, is a bureaucratic term for a practice that is better defined as half-hearted bulldozing: the city sent in a fleet of wreckers to knock down just enough ground-level columns on the condemned buildings that their facades would collapse. It was destruction on a level sufficient to discourage retail inhabitation but not enough to incur municipal responsibility for cleaning up the buildings.

And it transformed M.G. Road into a post-apocalyptic commute, like driving to Gurgaon by way of Baghdad. Shattered and deserted buildings lined the road in long stretches, empty but for the cows and ragpickers who wandered the broken windows and strewn cement. On some buildings, four floors of bare concrete rested precariously on columns that had been chewed by jackhammers down to the bare rebar, just a minor earthquake away from collapsing into traffic. On one building, a two-hundred-square-foot chunk of roof dangled over three collapsed floors below, held in place only by a few bent strands of steel. For the first months of my commute, the only sign of life was a hundred-meter stretch of singlestory

---

1. http://www.thehindu.com/2006/02/24/stories/2006022413780100.htm%E2%80%9C

ruins where a few brave vendors had built a thriving beanbag chair market.

But one day I realized that commerce had begun to trickle back. My workward slogs began revealing new sights: first, men with sledgehammers gnawing at the piles of concrete; and then men shoring up supports, laying new marble, and fitting plate glass over the freshly rebuilt interiors; and finally, bored salesgirls from northeast India staring glumly out of brightly lit showrooms, surrounded by lamps and couches and shoes and upscale religious handicrafts and no customers at all. Wicker World and Twinkle Sofa Mall had returned to M.G. Road, but their customers had not. That's because the Metro construction had shifted traffic on top of the sidewalks; there was nowhere to park.

I don't think these shops were there to make immediate sales. They were claims being staked on the future of M.G. Road: a day when the Metro was complete, the traffic was reduced, the government was supportive, the shops were legal, and the customers existed once again. And when this day arrives, the M.G. Road of the past will re-emerge as one of Future Delhi's showcase boulevards.

★

My commute, unfortunately, took place on the M.G. Road of the present. Stuck in the queue of cars merging with the overhead tracks at the vanishing point, watching the minutes tick down on my life, my cab felt like a jail cell. I was trapped in a private hell.

But in this, I soon grew to realize, I was lucky. For at least my hell was private.

As with most of the miseries I experienced in India, I only needed to stop wallowing for a moment to realize how good I actually had it. I'd sit there in M.G. Road's traffic, wondering why God would curse me with such suffering without providing any good movies to watch on my laptop. And then I'd look to the car next to me and see a five-seat Tata Indica identical to my own with six guys in the back seat and three more in the front.

With the Metro a distant future gleam, the state of public transit between Delhi and Gurgaon was dismal. The Haryana bureaucracy put incentives in place that deterred most mass transportation, such as tolls for taxis but not private cars and, until about halfway through our stay in Delhi, prohibitions against autorickshaws from crossing state boundaries altogether. The market response to this shortfall was an informal fleet of private cars that would pick up young men at various points along M.G. Road. A crowd would rush to squeeze into any car that stopped near them, each person eager to pay a handful of rupees for a ride into the Millennium City. On the days when I'd give Dipankar a lift to work, I'd pick him up at one of those corners where everyone gathered, and he'd have to swat the other commuters away from the door and gesture at my foreign skin as proof that this car wasn't for hire. They'd stare in bald envy as he slammed the door behind him.

I don't believe that the fleet of private cars was organized. Rather, I think it was made up of individual entrepreneurs who each spotted the same profit potential. These were car owners, taxi drivers making a few rupees when the boss thought they were on a call, or salaried drivers making illicit runs while their employers sipped lattes at the mall. Regardless of their provenance, each driver's goal was the same: to maximize profit by squeezing in as many passengers as possible.

The lucky passengers were the two or sometimes three guys in the front seat, because at least the air conditioning there would blow on them directly; in the back, four guys would sit on the seat and two more would sit on their laps—on *strangers'* laps—with their necks crooked uncomfortably against the roof of the car and their faces pressing grease stains against the windows. They'd stare without expression at me in all my air-conditioned misery, with my feet stretched glumly across the length of my car, my bag wretchedly strewn on one of my three empty seats, my face a grimace of unhappiness wholly at odds with my luxurious surroundings.

And yet nobody in these cars ever looked as miserable as I felt. It's just as one of the characters in *Shantaram* says about the capacity of Indians to cope: "If there were a billion Frenchmen living in such a crowded space, there would be rivers of blood."

I was spoiled. I knew it. And I was reminded how spoiled I was every time I'd whine about how hot the office was, or every time I'd lose my concentration because I was hungry for lunch, or every time I'd walk out of the office to escape the generator exhaust that was saturating our floor. Because I'd be the only one without the will to endure. When I'd be stuck in traffic because some stupid truck had spilled stupid cattle fodder all over stupid M.G. Road, I'd scream and holler and shake my fist when we finally passed the accident that had stolen an hour of my life—and then I'd notice my driver staring at me in the mirror, clearly wondering why I was so upset when I was stuck so much more comfortably than everyone else.

This was the thing: I had no perspective. I was unable to imagine anything worse than how uncomfortable my knees were pressed into the seat in front of me. But the guys in the identical Indica a few feet over knew they had it better than anyone riding the bus, which would have a hundred men packed armpit-to-armpit in a vehicle that had no air conditioning because it had no windows. Traffic jams were as hot as they were long in those buses, and it was not uncommon to see riders vomiting out of the windows. Still, every guy in the bus showed the same patience on their faces as the guys in the cars, because each of them knew they had it better than the flatbed trucks that carried dozens of villagers to their construction site for the day, the sun beating down on them as they crouched on the hot corrugated metal, knowing they'd soon be stacking bricks on their head and carrying them up a ten-story ramp to the top of Gurgaon's next skyscraper. The women in the flatbed were grateful for their jobs, the guys in the bus were grateful for the roof, the guys in the Indica were grateful for its air conditioning, and the guy writing this book was whining because the road was too bouncy for him to read the Batman comic he'd downloaded to his laptop.

Who is throwing up their hands and cursing the gods? Only I, the one without perspective. The only one who has no real problems anyway.

I believe that Delhiites' dignity in hardship stems from their understanding that the universe can change any circumstance at any time. A traffic jam can pop up on even the quietest road. Power can fail on even the coolest afternoon. One day the finance director quits after a week on the job. The next day the new copywriter quits after just a few hours. One day a steam shovel pulls up to your paan stand and destroys it while a crowd watches and the American who catches a drive-by glimpse is emotional only because he wishes he had his camera. One day you're suddenly getting married to someone you've never met. One day your country is partitioned and you're on the wrong side of the new border. Life should be expected to throw anything at you at any time. Joy. Misery. An out-of-control bull.

Maybe this explains why so many foreigners complain about a lack of long-term planning in Indian culture. They don't realize that Indians know better than anyone that by the time the long-term rolls around, everything will have changed anyway.

For Americans like me, all suffering is eternal; all happiness, meanwhile, is forgotten even before I've finished experiencing it.

Eventually, I learned from those around me. When stuck in traffic, I no longer gave in to my anger. I adopted the patience of everyone else trapped in the jam. Traffic, I grew to understand, like the sun, can only be silently endured. Fate should not be bemoaned, because what is the point? Like weather, it either passes, or it doesn't.

★

But all jams eventually loosen, and at some point in the morning my taxi would cross into Gurgaon, make a right, pass the dead crow, pass the gorgeous kingfishers, and open up to a straightaway where, looming in the distance before me, was the second office building in which I worked. Part of a development called DLF Cyber City (which was named after the corporation responsible for much of the way Gurgaon is today), it was sixteen massive stories tall, with aqua-green windows and a giant architectural flourish that ran diagonally up the side of the structure and cantilevered out five stories above and beyond the building itself.

This pompadour was little more than a steel skeleton when we moved in. In fact, for the first couple of months, this building was like the second Death Star: what appeared to be an active construction site was actually . . . well, certainly not *fully* operational, but operational enough that our business could function, although not without certain hardships. Though we'd moved in late October, it wasn't until February when there were enough operative elevators to accommodate the building's workers. Until then, only four elevators served sixteen floors, with each one assigned a separate call button. If I wanted to ride one up, I'd have to press 'down' on four different panels and then ride the elevator down the third basement—because it would invariably be too full to enter by the time it returned to the ground floor. Most days I just walked up the four paan-stained flights of stairs and through the unfinished hallway, admiring how my co-workers' fresh footprints stood out so starkly against the sawdust-covered slate tiles.

The first time they switched on the air conditioning in our office, clouds of construction dust billowed out of the vents. This surely shortened the lifespans of both the computer equipment and of most of my co-workers, who sat at their desks and covered their mouths and worked anyway while the office boys ran around with futile dust rags. (The expats in the office were the only ones who abandoned ship, sprinting for the food court.) After the dust stopped billowing, we discovered that the air conditioner was apparently unable to operate at anything less than arctic capacity. It blasted icy air with such intensity that everyone wore scarves and hats for weeks until they got it fixed.

In spite of these initial difficulties (and others: there was nowhere to wash dishes but the men's room sink; all the office taxi drivers had to wait for our calls in the third basement parking garage, about two levels lower than mobile phone signals could reach; and clear glass had been installed as urinal barriers, which made for some awkward male moments), it was eventually a well-built and modern office. My favorite aspect of it, though, had nothing to do with its construction. It was the fact that our finance head, Sudhakaran, insisted that the "Gayatri mantra" be repeated over the loudspeakers for at least an hour every morning. Even though the tape was so old that it would speed up and slow down with alien vibrato, I found it soothing and comforting. It was the ideal soundtrack to put the traffic stress behind me so I could focus on the day ahead. Jenny and I would hear this mantra all over India, emanating from market stalls as vendors prepared for the work stress, drifting through bicycle rickshaw stands as drivers bathed on the sidewalk, and accompanying the hiss of the chaiwallah's propane stove as the morning crowd gathered around for a quick hit before work began. Each time I heard it, it made me happy for the day ahead.

The ground floor of our building was given over to expensive restaurants, pompous nightclubs and arrogantly upscale furniture stores. A few other buildings in the area boasted food courts for common workers that—joy of joys!—even had coffee shops. I'd often jump out of my taxi before reaching my office, Frogger across the road, get my coffee, and then walk down the sandy shoulder towards my building, weaving around parked bicycle rickshaw drivers who'd pat their seat to entice my patronage, vendors selling nimbu pani or raw cucumbers, and boys washing dishes for sidewalk dhabas. After climbing the stairs or shoving into the elevators, I'd reach my desk in the corner of our open office, sip my coffee, and behold our spectacular bird's-eye view of the shamelessly inadequate four-lane road that serviced this and the dozen other buildings in the area.

I was mesmerised by the way the traffic patterns shifted and danced. The morning rush would loosen around 11 a.m., transforming the tightly packed chaos into loosely packed chaos, which would by four o'clock loosen further still into something that nearly approximated flowing traffic. That four o'clock road would beckon to me with its seductive promise of a swift journey home, if only I could escape the office before the sun went down, the traffic came out, and the air polluted up. But I was never able to answer the call of the momentarily open road, and the transformation of the road home into the parking lot to nowhere cranked my blood pressure each time. (The stoic outlook I eventually adopted towards traffic only calmed me when I was actually in my car.)

In those pre-commute moments, when the chorus of honking would penetrate the plate glass windows, the only thing worse than seeing the endless line of headlights awaiting me was not seeing it: a road completely empty in one direction meant some catastrophic accident had occurred somewhere down the line, and the unexpected backup on top of the regular backup would ensure that my driver would be at least an hour late. I'd find myself yelling at any co-worker responsible in any way for the fact that I was still in the office after 7.30 p.m.—anyone whose work I had to approve, or whose meeting I had to attend, or whose input I needed to finish a task.

But working late was ingrained in my office's culture for two reasons: first was Murali's management style, which decreed that no team could leave the office until each team member had finished their work and every other member had approved it. As frustrating as this was, I have to admit it was also the only way we could ensure quality control. But the second reason drove me crazy: no one but I actually seemed to be in any hurry to get home.

Most of my team members, including the married ones, had far more space and freedom at the office. So many of them actually preferred to be at work. Even after their work obligations were fulfilled, and even after all their teammates were ready to go, people would still happily dawdle.

This theory was bolstered one Friday night when I chose to take the office taxi home. Our office had contracted a fleet of Indicas and Innovas to criss-cross the city transporting employees who didn't own cars or who didn't want to depreciate them by bouncing down to Gurgaon every day. I saw Friday night as the beginning of the weekend, so I longed to be home in time to take advantage of it. But I guess most of my co-workers saw Friday night as an opportunity to have fun with office friends without the burden of getting up early the next day. It took forty-five minutes from the time everyone in my cab said they were ready to leave until the time everyone actually got into the cab. The decision was immediately made that we should stop for booze (which I was in favor of), but only I seemed frustrated when the booze quest stretched into a bathroom stop, a cigarette break, and a gossip session at the side of the road. After the vodka, Limca and bags of roasted dal were finally purchased, and once drinks were poured and passed around to everyone (including the driver), we slowly wound our way up the back roads of Vasant Kunj, stopping for at least one more bathroom break before finally reaching the Outer Ring Road in twice the time it would have taken me in my own cab.

When the group voted to stop for kebabs somewhere near Safdarjung, I gave up. I said my goodbyes to their furrowed brows, flagged an auto and zipped home. It's true that they wanted to enjoy their Friday night as much as I did—but whereas my Friday night began the moment I stepped through the door of my flat, that's when their Friday night was over.

★

In the spring, my company split into two parts, and half of us moved to a new office. (Sudhakaran's morning mantra, alas, didn't join us.) Though the split had officially taken place at the start of the new year, our half of the company had been allowed to stay put while our new office was being renovated. This created some uncomfortable corporate tension during the subsequent months of cohabitation that included delayed pay checks, parties to which only half the office was invited, and awkward carrom games between the principals of the two companies in which their friendly banter was belied by steely-eyed concentration that made it clear both men were staking their manhood on its outcome. And in one infamous incident, one of my team members was accused of stealing paper towels from the bathroom for "personal use." Outraged by the accusation, this co-worker responded by stealing the office phone from the security guard's desk (which was an act that seemed logical to him at the time). The head of our now-former company, who was nominally in charge of this office, responded by banning this employee from the premises.

The bosses then spent two days yelling at each other. Finally, the other boss agreed to let our employee back on condition that Jagdish, the office security guard, would henceforth search all our bags as each of us left for the day.

Jagdish, who along with half of the office peons defected to our company when we finally moved out, was always very apologetic as he went through our bags. Fortunately, no more paper towels were ever reported missing.

Now, readers of this book who have never worked in India may have done a double take at a word I used in the last paragraph: "peon." In the West, that word holds connotations of economic oppression. But in Delhi, "peon" was actually the official job title for the lowliest workers in our office, as printed in my company's employee handbook, which also explained that while regular employees could be reimbursed for taxis on nights they worked late, peons could only be reimbursed for bus fare. Peons were responsible for an office's manual labor, no matter how menial—and it could be extremely menial, as I discovered during one of my first days in the office, when one of my new co-workers hollered across the room: "Harish! Pani!"

It wasn't an unfriendly shout. It was the same tone of voice I'd use to holler across our flat to ask Jenny if she'd seen my iPod. From across the office, Harish looked up, his face neither surprised nor perturbed by the request. And though the person shouting was closer to the kitchen than Harish was, Harish nevertheless walked past him and emerged holding a glass of water on a tray. He waited patiently at the shouter's side while the shouter ignored him for a moment, for two moments, for one more moment, and then took the glass from the tray.

Every business has peons, or office boys, as they're also called. Uneducated and unskilled as compared to the rest of the employees, they're hired to do whatever is required so that the skilled workers can maximize the time spent using their brains. They wash dishes, fetch tea, make copies, move tables, empty trash bins, clean desks, courier documents, hand out cake and pour soda during office birthday celebrations, mop up any cake that spilled as it was ceremoniously smeared on the birthday person's face, go down to the chaiwallah to pick up cigarettes for anyone who runs out, and journey to Café Coffee Day to bring back cappuccinos for everyone in the office except themselves. When my colleague Bharat bought a new motorcycle and when my colleague Tapan had a child, they both brought sweets to celebrate their fortune with the office; but it was the peons who took them from person to person, offering the box and telling us whom they were from and why. One day Bharat brought in a lassi as a gift for me, and he had the peon carry it over—even though Bharat sat only fifteen feet away.

Peons exist because of India's glut of unskilled labor. The excess labor supply pushes wages down to the point where it's cheaper to hire someone to fetch water for employees than it is for employees to spend thirty seconds getting it themselves.

At first, I was horrified by the existence of peons. And I was shocked by what I viewed as my co-workers' exploitation of them. One late night, we ordered McDonald's for dinner and left the conference table strewn with wrappers. But when I grabbed a trash can and started clearing the table, my co-workers restrained me: cleaning was the peons' job, they said, and the mess should wait for them until the morning. This was common practice: I'd often arrive early in the morning to find the office strewn with dirty plates bearing piles of last night's chicken bones. Even though the basement had a rat problem and this mess might bring them sniffing around upstairs, it was the peons' job to clean, so the employees left the plates for them. "Please don't do this, Dave," Bharat said, laying his hand on my arm as I swept up the McDonald's wrappers anyway.

Because how could I demean a fellow human being by making him do something I was perfectly capable of doing myself? When I needed a drink, or a pen, or a photocopy of my passport, I would get up and get it myself—not just because I was uncomfortable with asking someone to do something so trivial, but because I wanted to make a statement: that I was enlightened. That I was everyone's equal. That I didn't believe in class or caste or hierarchy. That I didn't think my relative wealth made me too good for a little manual labor.

But the peons didn't like it. They'd eyeball me suspiciously as I'd wave them away from the copier, staring with distrust at my broadest and most egalitarian of smiles. They'd hover as I'd press the green button, clearly unhappy that I was encroaching on their domain. I couldn't understand why. Couldn't they see that I was the only one treating them with respect?

Eventually, I saw things from the peons' point of view: that this strange gora had flown all the way from America to make them redundant.

What if everyone in the office adopted my misguided enlightenment? An office in which everyone microwaved their own lunches and straightened their own papers wouldn't need to employ peons at all. And what then? Their jobs were demeaning, no doubt about that, but at least they were being demeaned indoors, in air conditioning, during normal business hours. Refilling staplers and clearing McDonald's wrappers is a hell of a lot better than guarding a cold ATM vestibule or walking up a ten-story ramp with a load of bricks balanced on their heads.

With this perspective, I realized that the more I asked the peons to do, the more job security I gave them. I wouldn't be demeaning them by giving them work—I'd be supporting their families. So when I arrived in the morning, I'd seek out the peon sweeping the office, hand him my dirty coffee mug, and tell him "Saff karo." I'd give another peon a prescription and 200 rupees and instruct him to go pick up the medicine at the pharmacy (although "instructing him" usually entailed asking my co-worker Anurag to translate). When I needed a pen or a paper clip, I knew whom to call: the supply closet wasn't my domain, it was theirs. More than that, it was their livelihood.

★

My company's third office was in Udyog Vihar, which is an industrial neighborhood a highway across and a generation removed from DLF Cyber City. The fact that we shifted here, instead of into another of DLF's sparkling high-rise buildings, was striking testament to the divergence between Western and Indian perceptions of status. Paul, the French-American who headed up our office, probably selected this former manufacturing space with our company's Paris office in mind. That office was a spectacularly converted factory full of exposed wood, brushed metal and old equipment repurposed as modern art. It had artistic cachet as a rejection of the standard twentieth-century office milieu; Paul obviously wanted that image here in Udyog Vihar.

But Paul didn't consider it from the Indian standpoint. Westerners have been desensitized to the office aesthetic by decades of mind-numbing meetings in high-rise conference rooms. In Delhi, though, so few people have had the opportunity to work in skyscrapers that there was no cultural currency in rejecting them. It's far more desirable to work in a brand-new high-rise than a twenty-year-old gray cement box in an industrial neighborhood, no matter how fluorescent green and pink the walls were painted.

Just like nobody understood why Jenny and I wouldn't want to live in a 4,500-square-foot penthouse on the twenty-third floor of Hamilton Court, nobody understood why Paul would force our company to endure such a huge step-down. But it was his decision, so we all glumly said goodbye to our former co-workers in Cyber City, packed up our computers and the shoddier of the two carrom boards, and moved ten more minutes down the road. My route to work shifted slightly: instead of driving the packed stretch through Cyber City's skyscrapers, I'd now turn right at the urology hospital and cut through the residential neighborhoods to the northeast, lurching over a dozen speed bumps until we reached the point at which we'd meet NH-8's massive twin flyovers.

To enter Udyog Vihar from that point, we had to follow a four-lane-wide turn-off for a quarter of a mile in the shadow of the flyover. Because the city hadn't installed traffic lights despite the four lanes of traffic, our passage was regulated by traffic police who would let each direction flow for five-minute bursts. Between bursts, paused in the welcome shade, I could hear the traffic atop the cantilevered concrete behemoth flowing smoothly above towards points deeper in Gurgaon. The price of their swift passage was paid by those of us down here: a restless mass of cars and cycle rickshaws and motorcycles all jostling for advantage, Udyog Vihar beckoning from the sunlight beyond, everyone but the beggars impatient for the policeman to blow his whistle and let us through to our offices.

In the cumulative hours I sat at this eternal intersection, I memorized the scene. I knew the ripped circus posters. I knew the cops with Rajasthani mustaches curled up the sides of their cheeks. And I knew the people who called the weedy median home: the withered men with faces wrinkled from a lifetime spent staring into the sun, the exhausted migrant women, the undiscourageable children, the little girl whose full-length skirt was smeared with dirt but not enough to hide the vibrant mustard yellow of the material. We all shared the same daily ritual: I sat in my car, the cops whistled at us to wait or waved at us to go, the engines idled, the exhaust pipes coughed, the cycle rickshaws wove through the cars, and the migrants sat and stared or walked through traffic and begged.

Then one day, a new sight broke the monotony of the ritual: a woman, her two-year-old son and her battered suitcase.

She had the look of a person in transit. Her pale-blue outfit was powdered with dust. Squatting on the cement wall of the median, she was clearly waiting for someone, and her face spoke of anticipation and excitement that even her son, young as he was, seemed to share. His posture was stunning: naked but for a string around his waist, he sat straight upright, attentive, patient—a two-year-old with the manner of a Buckingham Palace guard. They were so striking that I thought about them the whole morning. What was she waiting for—a bus? a rickshaw? her taxi-driving son, making it big in the big city?—and how long would she be waiting? I imagined what it would be like to wait at a prearranged corner on a prearranged date, far from home, with no magazine to kill the time, with no way to know if my ride would be late, with nowhere to go if my ride didn't show up. What was life like before mobile phones? I realized I'd forgotten.

Seven hours later, she was still there.

I was returning from a late meal with Murali and Dipankar. It had been a celebratory lunch, and our bellies were full of what had been their first taste of sushi. (Despite our distance from the ocean, a sushi place had opened up on M.G. Road, and I had been ranting for weeks about the incomparable joys of uncooked fish.) On our way back to the office, we passed through the same intersection, and the woman and the child were still sitting there.

As we passed by, I saw her face.

It was the face of a person who'd been squatting in dust and exhaust for seven straight hours. She looked defeated. Her son drooped next to her, like leaves on a plant that hadn't been watered. In the preceding seven hours, I don't think they'd moved. How could they have? If they'd moved, she'd always wonder: had her ride come while she was gone?

I didn't pass by her corner when I left that night. But the next morning, my heart tore: the woman and her son remained. Had they eaten? Did they have any water? Did they sleep right there? Did they sleep at all?

The morning after that, they were gone.

★

Once the traffic police granted my car permission to enter Udyog Vihar, it was just a short drive past the Trident Hotel to the office, an uninspiring three-story building with a generator as tall as a bus parked in our driveway to facilitate our uninterrupted computing and air-conditioning needs. Jagdish would turn the generator on when the first employee arrived at the office, flipping a switch and shattering the morning's calm. Unlike our Okhla office, in which the power only failed periodically and our backup needs were less complex, generators were obligatory in Gurgaon to supplement its wholly unreliable municipal supply. (One day back in Okhla, I'd asked Deep, the office IT guy—who, incidentally, was the exact opposite of American IT guys in that he was always the best-dressed person in the office—to show me where our backup power came from. He opened a door to reveal a few dozen car batteries wired together in a closet.)

Our Udyog Vihar office boasted four full floors dedicated to making our client happy. In the basement was the canteen and social area, where lunchtime found all the employees but me sharing meals, playing carrom on a board that was a pale reminder of the frictionless masterpiece the old office got to keep, and cheering each other as they played a modified indoor version of cricket. Every other time of the day, the basement was used primarily for catnaps on the padded benches. The ground floor had one large conference room and four small ones that had been intended as ad hoc meeting rooms; but because this was the only quiet spot in the building, a few senior staff members commandeered them as semi-permanent offices. The creative teams sat on the second floor, and the account servicing and finance teams sat on the third.

When Paul commissioned the office's remodeling, he'd given the architects a bold vision of an office filled with "fun" and "mystery." He imagined an office so comfortable and so vibrant that our clients would gladly descend from their glass tower and catered lunches to hang out in our cubicles, jam with office musicians, paint office murals, and discuss philosophy over late night tea and hookah. But the budget for "fun" and "mystery" only extended so far as to install circular windows in the conference room. Which is too bad, because Paul actually had the right idea: if we were going to succeed, we had to get the client to love us.

This wasn't supposed to be necessary. At the global level, we were this client's Direct Marketing Agency of Record. But that was only on paper. While the corporate honchos in New York shared cigars and handshakes over lobster dinners they expensed to the company, their broad vision didn't map to the reality of New Delhi's advertising industry, in which ad agencies are seen as vendors to be squeezed.

The competitive environment was as fierce for Delhi's ad industry as it was for laptop repairmen in Nehru Place. There were hordes of agencies promising to do the same work we did twice as fast and half as expensive, and our client knew it. So while our relationship was officially a long-term partnership focused on long-term results, our client in India was feeling the pressures of the global recession, and short-term budget pains are hard to ignore especially when there was a queue of competing yes-men elbowing each other aside with promises of cut-rate work at breakneck speed. Making matters worse, our branch of the company existed only to serve this single client. They couldn't officially fire us, but they could certainly stop giving us work. If they weren't happy, we were all out of luck.

Which is why it's commendable that Paul took a big risk with our office. He had to do *something* to secure our relationship and our jobs. So to appreciate Paul's effort to save our company from the circling vultures, I tried to overlook the office's physical failures—of which there were many. We had no microwave, no refrigerator, and nowhere more appropriate to wash our dishes than the spigot in the driveway. Worst of all, the improperly installed urinals emptied into the same line that drained the floor, which essentially created a stagnant open-air sewer that filled the stairwell with the stench of urine.

Nasal comfort, sanitary adequacy, visual appeal: we had none, but we made do. We made it work with what we had.

And this is the single most important concept we learned during our time in India: jugaad.

Making do.

The nearest English equivalent to "jugaad" is "jury-rigging," but that translation doesn't do jugaad justice. Artist Sanjeev Shankar describes it as "attaining any objective with the available resources at hand." My colleague Anurag translates it as "a duct-tape arrangement." Either way, jugaad is about making do. Improvising a solution. Creating options where there are none.

Many of our friends said that the concept of jugaad was best illustrated by a common rural vehicle that people actually call a 'jugaad': a homemade truck made by cobbling together a wooden cart with a diesel irrigation pump. After being fitted with makeshift steering and braking mechanisms, the pump becomes an engine that enables the vehicle to transport people from one village to another, with dozens of riders crammed onto the back as tightly as the bundles of sugarcane it can also transport. More significantly, this setup enables the pump to actually move itself to the next field in which it's needed for irrigation duties. No two jugaads are the same, because each one is an improvised solution using unlikely parts. But they're all pure representations of this spirit of ingenuity.

Indians swell with pride at their capacity for jugaad. "We are like that only," Murali would tell me when describing solutions to situations that would have made most goras thankful they had the embassy on speed dial. The variety of solutions they'd create for seemingly intractable problems proved this pride was well founded: the way motorcycles were chopped in half and welded to carts to create centaur goods haulers; the way mother, father and three kids could fit themselves onto a single scooter; the repurposing of used water bottles as cooking oil containers; rope spun from discarded foil packets; and cricket wickets made from balanced stacks of rocks.

Humble Indian villagers are idealized by Delhiites much in the same way that small-town America is idealized in American politics. And what makes the villagers so noble are their MacGyveresque abilities to adapt available materials to solve problems that would confound sophisticated city dwellers. As one blogger put it when describing those water pump trucks, "These vehicles reflect the true spirit of innovation in rural India."[2]

But we think that the spirit of jugaad is actually broader than clever mechanics. Jugaad is the philosophical outlook necessary to make it work, regardless of what "it" is. It's about solving problems with what you have, not what you wish you had. Jugaad is the human Tetris that fits nine people into a car built for five. And it's also the patience that total strangers require to sit on each other's laps and breathe each other's sweat for a ninety-minute sauna down M.G. Road. Jugaad is the ability to endure thirty-two hours on the train from Mumbai to Amritsar, when the mere three-hour stretch of that route that Jenny and I rode from Bharatpur to Delhi left us exhausted and claustrophobic. Jugaad is the hope for the future that lets a woman and her son spend two days waiting on a median for someone to pick them up.

Jugaad is how everyone gets by.

Jenny and I come from a tool-addicted culture. Before we came to Delhi, we couldn't function without a certain baseline of modern conveniences: we needed adequate light, temperate air, comfortable chairs, personal space and no meaty smells rolling up from the basement. And if any of those aren't in place, we're unable to do our jobs. But the jugaad philosophy suggests a different approach: that while modern tools and technology should be appreciated when they're there, they are not cardinal requirements.

2. http://www.hokindia.com/2009/03/who-needs-a-nano-when-you-can-have-your-own-jugaad.html

Technology is a comfort, but not a necessity. And a lack of technology doesn't change the fact that the job's got to get done.

Under the jugaad philosophy, only we Americans whine that the air conditioning has gone out. Everyone else reflects in the good fortune of having had air conditioning at all, and gets their work done anyway.

★

One reason jugaad might be so idealized is because so many elements of the culture seem to emphasize the exact opposite. The government adheres to stifling bureaucracy, the schools fixate on memorization, and the chain stores that represent India's growing organized retail sector direct their employees to follow rigid processes and forbid any deviation.

We're thinking of Barista and Café Coffee Day specifically. For example: we didn't like Barista's iced coffee because it came from a powdered mix that was too sweet for our tastes. But numerous waiters and waitresses at numerous branches all refused to indulge any requests for brewed coffee on the rocks, or for a small-sized coffee served in a glass large enough to add ice cubes, or for any other deviation from the menu. Our only solution was to request a cup of ice without mentioning our intention to mix it with the coffee, and then make sure the waiter was far away when we'd combine the two.

Similarly, when my parents ordered toast at the Café Coffee Day lounge in Hauz Khas market, they were told it wasn't on the menu. After fruitless debate, they finally resorted to ordering a toasted corn-and-spinach sandwich with crumbled paneer—hold the corn, hold the spinach, hold the paneer.

The management of these chains seemed to prize process over everything else. This must create a problem for employees who hope to advance: if they're forbidden from showing creativity or initiative, how do they distinguish themselves? How does an employee impress management when management doesn't want its employees to stand out?

This may explain why employees were always so enthusiastic for us to fill out comment cards. They'd press them into our hands long before our food had arrived at our table. At one Domino's pizza counter, we were given the comment card not only before we'd eaten our pizza, not only before we'd received our pizza, but before we'd even been handed our change. Employees would hover over our table with hopeful looks, pouncing the moment we'd put down our pen and then dashing behind the counter to read the card with the other employees reading over their shoulder. It was their best and only hope, we realized, of proving their worth to their employers.

So we always left glowing comments, even when service wasn't out of the ordinary. If we had any complaints about service, the worst we'd do is refuse to fill out a comment card.

The Delhiites around us, on the other hand, never hesitated to make it clear when they didn't get their money's worth. They'd say exactly what they meant—on comment cards and in any other instance when an opinion was offered. We'd exalt in watching an incompetent co-worker get a dressing-down from the client. We'd revel in time saved when the boss cut off a bad idea with a dismissive bark. We'd laugh in surprise when club patrons would shout at the DJ to change a song they didn't like. We'd gasp at our neighbor Mr. M.'s unadulterated opinions on politics, his countrymen, or us ("You look very sick—your eye has all those red veins!"). We'd be shocked when politicians would speak of vast swaths of Indians as "backward castes"— such a term would be politically explosive if applied to underdeveloped parts of the US.

But of all the unadulterated honesty we saw in Delhi, we were most shocked by how bluntly people discussed each other's weight. On that day when I was on the company terrace watching the cross-dressed hijras torment the company across the street, with their security guard vainly trying to push them out while Jagdish double-checked the lock on our gate, my co-worker Tapan gave me a sidelong glance.

"Dave," he said, "you're looking fatter and fatter every day."

My jaw dropped so far that a hijra picked it up and demanded payment for its return.

In America, few subjects are more sensitive than someone's weight. Had I made a comment like Tapan's to a co-worker in New York, I'd have become the office pariah when word got around about what I'd said. But in Delhi, my weight was open for comment. And so was everyone else's. Even a woman's weight—and if weight is a sensitive issue in America, a woman's weight is doubly so. If the subject of a woman's weight had come up in the New York office, the only acceptable response on any man's part would have been positive reassurance ("No . . . you look great!") followed by a rapid change in subject.

But not here. I remember one co-worker, a twenty-something guy, telling another co-worker, a twenty-something girl, "You need to lose weight." There were six of us chatting in my hip beanbag corner of the office: five guys and that girl. When the pronouncement was made, I gasped and got ready for her to smack him; but instead, as all the other guys looked at her midsection and nodded in agreement, so did she. I couldn't believe what I'd just witnessed. But I was the only one who'd thought it was extraordinary.

After Tapan shattered my self-confidence, I wandered through the office to find someone who could commiserate. Coming across Sonia in the conference room that she'd commandeered as her office, I told her what Tapan had said. "Oh," she laughed, "he's only saying that because I told him a few days ago that his belly had gotten huge."

★

Such are the hardships I faced in India: worrying that my belly looked too big in a country where, if someone was thin, it wasn't because they spent their days at the gym.

From that perspective, Jenny's employment at Pardada Pardadi was good for me, too: it helped emancipate me from my American-style ennui as much as it helped her accomplish something more meaningful than impressing clients with the color of her hair.

Pardada Pardadi was founded by Sam Singh, an Uttar Pradesh native who returned to his home village after decades climbing the corporate ladder at DuPont. Sam has dedicated his life and his fortune to eradicating poverty in the villages around his childhood home, and his organization is transforming traditionally oppressive gender roles to help girls lift their families out of poverty. The school he founded, which now has well over 1,000 students, educates its girls in both academic and vocational matters. It also deposits ten rupees into their account for every day they attend, payable upon graduation. Taken together, this means that a fresh graduate is one of the richest and most educated women in her region. She has the power and means to make revolutionary decisions for herself and her family, and the education to pursue a future beyond the farm.

Across a handful of rural villages surrounding Anupshahr, a small city four hours east of Delhi, Sam's students are learning to reject the patriarchy and shift themselves from third-class citizens (girls there are valued less than sons and less than the family water buffalo, in that order; when parents are asked how many children they have, they only count the boys) into community leaders who can derail the poverty cycle. As the *Wall Street Journal* affiliate *Live Mint* put it in their profile of Sam, Pardada Pardadi is building "a generation of women that won't silently acquiesce to being nameless entries in countless family trees."[3]

---

3. http://www.livemint.com/2007/12/30230813/Virendra-Sam-Singh—Turning.html

Because Jenny worked for the school's administrative office in Delhi, we were able to visit the school and see for ourselves the striking difference it made in its students' lives. Sam took us to a tiny farming village, where two girls, both students at the school, led us on a tour. They showed us their small brick homes, their immaculate pounded dirt yards, and their family goats, talking to us with poise and confidence despite the fact that we were both foreign and I am male. As we were walking around, we realized we were being followed: behind us were two girls who weren't students at the school, wearing dirty clothes and peeking at us from around corners. Whenever we turned towards them, they ducked their heads and hid. It was clear to us which of the girls in this village would have the self-confidence to convince their parents that a marriage at age fourteen was a bad idea, that a girl should be seen as more than a crippling dowry waiting to be paid, and that the best thing any family could do is educate both male and female children.

Soon after we left the village, Sam abruptly asked his driver to slow the car. He pointed to a family walking down the road: the man was sauntering casually along the roadside, his hands clasped behind his back and a carefree look on his face. His wife was a dozen paces behind him, leading a tired child with one hand and balancing a great bale of cattle fodder on her head with the other.

The tour resumed. We stopped by an open-air factory where farmers were boiling sugarcane. We toured 'downtown Anupshahr', as Sam called it. We took a boat ride along the Ganges, during which a single raftsman gently poled our boat up and down the shallow banks, the sun casting golden light on the farms to the east while bells and chants drifted from the ghats to the west. And then we stopped at a local lawyer's house to meet a former Pardada Pardadi student named Rukhsana. Rukhsana was not a graduate. She'd quit school at the age of thirteen, when her grandmother forced her to marry.

Sam had begun telling Rukhsana's story on the drive to Anupshahr. Rukhsana had been one of hundreds of Sam's students at the time, just one anonymous girl in her green-and-yellow school uniform, until the morning the halls began buzzing with rumor: just four hours east of New Delhi's tree-lined boulevards and Gurgaon's shining skyscrapers, thirteen-year-old Rukhsana was getting married.

Sam called Rukhsana into his office and learned that the rumors were true. In one week, she would quit school to become wife to a forty-year-old street barber from a neighboring village. Her grandmother had arranged everything.

Rukhsana was her grandmother's ward. Rukhsana's mother was mentally handicapped and fully unreliable as a parent ("She runs around the village naked," as Sam put it). Her father was an unknown rapist.

So Sam immediately went to see her grandmother. "Why are you marrying off such a young girl?" he demanded. "Why are you throwing her future away? What can we do to prevent this?"

Nothing. The grandmother was in ill health and had nothing to leave her granddaughter. She feared that the moment she died, Rukhsana would be forced into prostitution. To the grandmother's way of thinking, marriage—even to such an undesirable partner as a barber three times older—was the best choice for her granddaughter's future.

Sam's protests were futile. "You want to help her?" the grandmother demanded. "You adopt her or you marry her."

Sam could do neither.

As Sam told this story, Jenny found herself thinking about when she was thirteen. She was an eighth-grader at Madison Middle School in Albuquerque. She had a swimming pool in her backyard and a black poodle named Gypsy. She was on the yearbook committee. She was reading *Roots*. To amuse her friends, she'd smash packages of crackers from the cafeteria, pour the crumbs into her mouth, and then shower her friends with cracker dust when she talked. She loved how they always hid Wilson's face on *Home Improvement*.

When Rukhsana was thirteen, she had her first child.

After telling us Rukhsana's story, Sam confided that he hadn't thought about her in a long time. As sad as her story was, it was just one of many sad stories in this part of his country. Spurred by our questions, though, he arranged for us to meet Rukhsana in the home of this prominent village lawyer. And there we all learned that things hadn't gotten much better for Rukhsana in the four intervening years. Though she now had an adorable son, her husband had left her. Rukhsana's grandmother was still alive, but she was even more frail and even more terrified for her granddaughter's future—and, now, for her three-year-old great-grandson's future as well. Against all odds, she'd somehow arranged another marriage for Rukhsana.

This time, Sam was able to present Rukhsana's grandmother with another option. His connections in India's charity world had grown in the intervening years, and he now knew of an organization that taught vocational skills to young Muslim girls. It was located in Goa, unfortunately, which was inconceivably distant to a woman who had probably never been west of Delhi. Sam could arrange for them to take care of Rukhsana, to teach her the skills she'd require to earn a brighter future for herself and her son, if only her grandmother could bear the humiliation of canceling the marriage and the possibility of never seeing her granddaughter and great-grandson again. It was an unimaginable future, but it was certainly brighter than the imaginable one.

Rukhsana cast her eyes downward and smiled bashfully as the adults discussed her fate. Her son sat quietly on her lap for a time; when he squirmed too much, she put him down and he stood patiently at her feet. Jenny and I watched in silence as well while the two prominent men—one dressed in Western clothes and another in fine white robes—berated and pleaded and cajoled the grandmother, explaining the possibilities that awaited Rukhsana if she left, and the misery that was sure to find her if she stayed. Finally, Sam turned to Rukhsana and asked her what she wanted to do.

Rukhsana glanced at her grandmother. A negative twitch of her grandmother's head sealed Rukhsana's fate: she would stay, and she would get married, for the second time, at seventeen years of age.

We left the lawyer's house after the sun began to set, anxious to get off the roads before the drunken truck drivers took to them. We were silent as we drove down the narrow road to Bichola, the tiny village where Sam's family lived for centuries in a mansion befitting their status as the area's historic zamindars—feudal landlords, or tax collectors. The road was bumpy, but we didn't complain. After all, the car was air-conditioned, and a comfortable sofa and a well-stocked bar awaited us. This brief moment of hardship, we knew, we could endure.

9

Challenges of a Megacity

Delhi is a tough city. No doubt about it. The traffic is tough, the weather is tough, the pollution is tough, and even going out to eat is tough by virtue of the fact that any given meal might be garnished with E. coli.

In fact, there were times when dining out in Delhi required us to steel ourselves against sights that should have made us run with waving hands for the first flight to Paris. There were times we'd see a cook's sweat dripping into his mixing bowl, or when we'd enter restaurant bathrooms so dirty that we'd curse our bladders for lacking the fortitude to wait until we got home. There was even a time at a trendy restaurant in Basant Lok when a mouse ran across the feet of the four ladies seated across from me. The impromptu chorus line that occurred as they all kicked would have been funny if I hadn't been so busy jumping up on my own seat as well. But a cook's special seasoning or a four-legged foot massage would not deter us from enjoying our meals. Because through the moistest of alleyways and upon the greasiest of tabletops awaited some of the most unforgettable meals we've ever had.

And this describes life in Delhi in a nutshell: every reward has an equal and opposite challenge necessary to redeem it.

It's an infinite loop. It's a downward spiral. The challenges that shape the city's environment exist *because of* the city's environment. Extreme reactions intensify already extreme problems, and they catalyse more extreme reactions in response.

Our bungalow provided a microcosm of this cause-and-effect-and-cause. For eighteen months, we watched how our neighbors responded to a tough city by making sure they were tougher than it—no matter what effect it had on neighborly relations.

Our neighbors were always friendly to Jenny and me, of course. Dr. T. on the ground floor, our landlord Shankar, our friend and oracle Anya, eccentric Mr. M., frail Mrs. M., and the various maids, office employees, deliverymen and underlings who flowed up and down the arterial stairwell all day long—they were all perfectly pleasant to the two of us. (In fact, it turns out that they were all looking forward to our presence even before we'd seen the flat. As Anya told it, the moment Shankar had learned that foreigners were coming to view his empty flat, he threw the whole bungalow into a tizzy. His main office boy raced around to make sure everything was in perfect order, even telling Anya to remove her sheets from the clothesline on the terrace in case the sight of bedding proved unacceptable to foreign sensibilities. Even Shilpa the garbage maid ran up and down the stairs shouting, "Foreigners coming! Foreigners coming!" Her excitement was understandable—just as Shankar was anticipating inflated monthly rent from foreigners who were ignorant of market rates, Shilpa might have been hoping for an equally rich stream of garbage she could recycle for profit. They both got what they hoped for.)

We'd read some books about life in India before we made the move, and they told us to expect a hyper-efficient neighborhood grapevine in which gossip traveled faster than events themselves. Guards that spoke to drivers who listened to their passengers told what they heard to maids who repeated everything to their mistresses, and anyone's business was everyone's knowledge. If that was true, and if the entire bungalow did actually know that we were coming, then everyone in the neighborhood must have as well. So our actual arrival—the sunny morning when we pulled our oversized bags out of the trunk of the taxi and beamed at our new surroundings—was probably a surprise only to the stray dogs that stirred sleepily as we stepped gingerly around them.

We were far too ignorant of language and culture at this point to interpret the gossip around us. So we have no idea how people reacted to our strange foreign behavior. What did our new neighbors say that first morning when we dismissed our driver and carried our heavy bags up to our flat all by ourselves? Or later on, when we'd stumble home after midnight? Or when Jenny would leave for a night on the town without me? What did they think when three young American ladies spent the night in our flat? What did they think about the visit by our friend Trevor, a tall, flamboyant black man with long dreadlocks and a penchant for sunbathing on the roof in his underwear? Or when an unknown American male arrived one morning, shook my hand outside our flat, watched me get into a cab of my own, and then spent the next week in my house with my wife while I was nowhere to be seen?

(The truth of that last tale is far less titillating than the gossips probably speculated: a few days before Tony's visit, my visa problems came to a head and I had to fly all the way back to the US—seriously! Thanks, Indian bureaucracy!—to get them sorted out. No sooner had I left than Tony promptly fell ill, which explains why he looked so exhausted—and why Jenny was holding his elbow—the few times he actually did emerge.)

But our neighbors weren't the only ones exchanging gossip. Jenny and I kept our mouths shut and our eyes open, and we shared with each other what we saw. And we realized that life within our bungalow—which should have been a collective stronghold against the challenges of the city beyond—was not one in which the residents always appreciated the pleasure of each other's company.

The residents of the bungalow were all men and women of strong wills, inflexible opinions and, in certain cases, over-abundant amounts of leisure time. History was never relegated to the past among these folks. Every slight was remembered, every insult was internalized, and every offense was spitefully repaid. Though shared real estate forced them into a coincidental partnership, the stairwell that bound them all nevertheless beat with tension that even Jenny and I, in our ignorance of pretty much everything, noticed.

Intrigue and politics throbbed in the bungalow. This one hated that one because of a misdiagnosis of a family member's illness. That one hated this one because their dogs didn't get along. And on and on, a string of misunderstandings and retributions magnified by time and proximity: issues of construction noise, unpaid common-area painting bills, stolen scrap metal, ruptured garbage bags, ant infestations, dog noise, dog damage, dog stains. Jenny and I were the only neutral parties, and we remained that way because we feigned ignorance of everyone's grievances and pretended not to understand when one party wanted to use us for strategic maneuvers against another.

This wasn't a cage match, though. This was Royal Rumble politics, which meant that alliances formed and collapsed in response to an ever-shifting battlefield. Every opportunity to save money, save time, or transfer responsibility changed the political calculus, creating and destroying coalitions on the fly. Shankar and Mr. and Mrs. M. would team up against Anya's dogs; Anya and Shankar would team up against the construction noise coming from the empty flat; Shankar would ask us to tell Shilpa to clean up the grease spots Anya's dogs left. Sometimes it seemed like they went after each other simply for the joy of the combat.

Like when the hole appeared in the driveway. The driveway hole used to be an access hatch for the sewer pipes that serviced the empty flat on the second landing. Normally, it was covered by a cement slab that kept stench in and tender ankles out. But one day, that slab crumbled under the weight of Dr. T.'s beastly Tata Sumo DC (a vehicle with all the immensity of an SUV but none of the grace). Although Dr. T. was able to extract the Sumo's wheel by shifting into reverse, the shattered cover was a total loss.

As common property, the responsibility for the driveway was nominally shared among the five owners of the six units. But it was Dr. T.'s car that broke the cover, and it was the empty flat's pipes that were now exposed.

And so the dispute was gleefully on. Shankar, Anya and Mr. and Mrs. M. insisted together that the empty flat should pay for a new iron cover. The empty flat's owner, presumably reached by telephone wherever he or she was, wanted the doctor to pay. And Dr. T. wanted all parties to share the cost equally. As the only uninterested people in the bungalow, Jenny and I were the only ones not exchanging cold silences, wordless recriminations and averted eyes as we passed on the stairs.

When no one gave ground, temporary solutions were attempted. Twice Mr. M. told Anya to tell Shankar to order his main office boy to do something about the driveway. Twice, a new concrete slab was laid over the hole. And twice that new concrete slab was transformed by a car wheel into dust and chunks at the bottom of the hatch. As the stalemate continued, my taxi drivers must have driven into the open hole a half-dozen times, cursing with each jarring thud and thanking their good fortune that an Indica's wheels are slightly larger than the width of the missing lid.

We don't know who gave in first. The hole was still there when we moved out.

But don't think that our bungalow's politics were so divisive as to prevent household unity when an outside threat demanded it. In extraordinary circumstances, our bungalow could stand together against the best of them. Like when they presented a unified front in collective refusal to contribute to the salary of the neighborhood guard. Although Jenny and I had only ever known the guard to sit just beyond our bungalow, he apparently used to sit at the mouth of our block, protecting every bungalow including ours from the criminals of the night. But when our entire bungalow decided not to pay—for reasons not made clear when we were told this story—the neighborhood association retaliated by shifting the guard and his barricade twenty feet down the road, to a spot just after our bungalow.

That would show us, right? We were now wounded prey without a protector. The guard, presumably, was instructed to give criminals free reign to walk in to the stairwell and steal our light bulbs.

The neighborhood association must have been dismayed that our bungalow was not robbed. And the fact that we weren't robbed means one of two things: either Delhi's evil underbelly wasn't connected to our local gossip grapevine and thus remained unaware of our bungalow's exclusion from the neighborhood defense pact; or that the guard's presence was enough to deter crime even if he wasn't actively protecting us. I imagine our bungalow, united, had counted on the latter. And their gamble paid off: our bungalow escaped their contribution to his 4,000 rupees-a-month salary with no detrimental effect to their lives or property. I can picture everyone in our bungalow nodding and smiling at each other as they came to this agreement over tea in one of their flats. And I can imagine the afterglow of their victory must have surely meant shared smiles and exchanged greetings on the stairwell for a few days after the triumph, before the squabbles began anew.

★

Presumably, the same sort of politics and pressures that our neighbors used to make each others' lives more difficult were playing out in all the bungalows in our neighborhood. And presumably, there were even more entrenched feuds beyond borders: bungalow versus bungalow, neighborhood association versus neighborhood association. We imagine it mirroring the battles of the neighborhood's stray dogs, except where dogs snarl and bark to assert their territory, civilized human beings channel their disagreements into passive-aggressive parking, enforced servant-on-servant snobbery and anonymous calls to the police.

Unfortunately, while our bungalow's residents could still ally with each other when extraordinary circumstances demanded, the inter-bungalow feuds must have been so entrenched as to be beyond repair even when faced with the darkest of challenges. Why else wouldn't the whole neighborhood have immediately come together to stop ICICI Bank's assault on our slumber?

The disturbance manifested one morning around 3 a.m. with what sounded like pieces of sheet metal being hit with sledgehammers just outside our window. Our first thought was that the very worst had happened: our air conditioner must be malfunctioning. I dragged myself to the window and raised the heavy fabric shade, expecting to see smoke belching from the unit or a monkey tearing it apart with its bare hands. That's when I saw the armored cars, the armed men, and the laborers removing metal boxes from the armored cars and tossing them on the ground with sleep-shattering crashes. Still other men picked up the heavy boxes and lugged them into a bungalow that was otherwise unremarkable but for the small ICICI Bank logo above the doorway.

That doorway that had, until 3 a.m. on this night, always been covered by a metal shutter. A few weeks before that colossal racket, we'd spotted some renovation work in the upper floors of the building. This building was located a few dozen meters down the main road between our flat and Hauz Khas market, and although the potted plants on the building's windowsills had always been kept trimmed and watered, the building had never before shown any signs of life. The workers had been given the privilege of living on-site for the duration of the job, and what had drawn our attention was their shadows being thrown against the upper-floor walls as they bent over their indoor—indoor!—cooking fires.

Now there was this colossal 3 a.m. racket, which lasted until 5 a.m. The racket began again the next day at a slightly more reasonable 6 a.m., and repeated itself two or three times a week thereafter for the duration of our stay in India.

Until we learned to sleep through it, this wake-up call often forced us out of bed at ungodly hours. I'd walk out on the balcony and study these men while sipping my coffee, slowly assigning them "mortal enemy" status in my sleep-deprived brain. Their operation involved a disproportionate number of thin older men standing around the armored cars, holding ancient rifles with worn wooden stocks that wouldn't have looked out of place firing on the British in Meerut. They were doing their best to look intimidating and alert, but they were casting longing glances at the chaiwallah setting up for the day in the shade of the nearby tree. Beyond establishing their security perimeter, the older men did nothing more than watch the younger men in the trucks throw the boxes. The boxes would land with spectacular thuds, making the kind of sound that metal boxes dropped from a truck make when they're full of thick, juicy stacks of rupees.

Once the trucks were empty, the young men would re-emerge from the building carrying multiple metal boxes with an ease that implied that their contents had been emptied, presumably into a big pool of money in which ICICI executives would bathe. They'd toss the empties lackadaisically into the trucks, and then the guards and the men would stand around and scratch themselves for a few minutes before hitching up their pants, spitting one last time, and piling into the trucks to drive away.

Everyone in the neighborhood surely hated the ICICI guys as much as we did. (Except perhaps the rich merchants across the street, whose houses were next door to the ICICI building—it may have been the sound of their money echoing around the neighborhood.) We couldn't believe a corporation could inflict such misery upon a neighborhood with no concern over publicity repercussions or lost customers. Especially since the noise wasn't their only transgression: the men also blocked traffic and spat and urinated all over the place. Anya told us that she'd berate them every time she walked by, saying things like, "If you do it in the road, what is the difference between you and a stray dog?" The men would hang their heads and avoid her gaze, but their stream of bodily fluids would renew as soon as she passed.

★

Anya wasn't alone in her anti-urination campaign. In fact, the urinary habits of Delhi men are legendary across India.

"When it comes to answering the call of nature, the Delhi male does not look very far and relieves himself as soon as he finds a wall, corner or crevice," the *Hindustan Times* reported in a 2006 exposé on the urinary habits of the male of the Delhi species.[1]

Three years later, another campaign intended to shame city men into zipping up their pants[2] may well have been a direct reprint of the last. "Practically every large wall in Delhi bears a warning against urinating upon it and below are telltale wet patches left behind by men who don't care two hoots."

---

1. http://www.hindustantimes.com/news/specials/toilet/
    index291006.shtml
2. http://www.irishtimes.com/newspaper/world/2009/0929/
    1224255438055.html

Jenny and I would spot urinating men everywhere we went in Delhi, and we'd smell everywhere they'd been. No journey down a Delhi street was complete until we'd both smelled humid urine and passed someone unloading a fresh addition into a bush, onto a wall, next to a public urinal, or wherever else they could let loose with their back to passing traffic so nobody could see too much of their willy.

The media, in their constant clamor against the urinary scourge, blamed two municipal conditions: Delhi's lack of public facilities and Delhiites' lack of civic sense. The *Hindustan Times* points out that the only place that's truly urine-free is the Metro—because, as their commentator put it, it's one of the few points of pride for the city.[3] Because Delhiites don't feel a sense of ownership of the city, the papers said, they don't mind urinating all over it. Journalist Manoj Joshi elaborated on this point in *Time* magazine. "If you ask anyone in Delhi where they come from, they don't say Delhi, they name their native city or village. No one knows anyone else, so people behave very differently from how they would where they come from. They have no affiliation with the city."[4] Many of our friends and co-workers echoed this, telling us that the bulk of their fellow residents feel no kinship towards Delhi.

But in terms of public facilities, we don't think it's their absence that causes the problems so much as their inaccessibility. In south Delhi, public urinals are situated

---

3. http://www.hindustantimes.com/News/columnsothers/
   People-don-t-feel-they-have-a-stake-in-the-city/458704/
   Article1-458701.aspx

4. http://www.time.com/time/printout/0,8816,1926146,00.html

most prominently in neighborhood markets that are tucked at the center of Delhi's island neighborhoods, far away from the urgent urges of the men traveling the main city streets. The bulk of the peeing we spotted took place on Delhi's broad boulevards, with men aimed against the cement walls that segregated those who live inside from those they want to keep out. These roads are plied by men who travel long distances; when nature calls, they have neither the time nor the inclination to leave the stream of traffic and negotiate unfamiliar neighborhoods in search of public toilets. It's far easier to just pull over, jump out and let loose. Thus, with the sheer volume of men on the roads, our journeys from any point A to any point B would inevitably pass dozens of point Ps along the way: men silhouetted against the sun, a golden stream twinkling, our eyes turning away but not before—despite the man's best efforts at shielding himself—alighting on the tip of a disgorging member or on one shaking out those last few drops.

I'm a critic of street-side peeing—as are most men, if you ask them. And like most men, I suspect, I'm also a practitioner, having peed on the side of a Delhi road exactly once, in the wilds south of Vasant Kunj, on that eternal Friday night ride home in my co-workers' cab, when our booze and our bouncing got the best of all of us. Someone called the driver to a halt, and we men all spilled out of the cab and onto the ground.

Assuming my experience is not unique, it seems possible that Delhi's urine challenge is a problem of numbers, not manners. What if the male half of Delhi's sixteen million citizens pee on the street no more than once a year? That's still 21,918 men peeing on the road any given day. And if the problem is even slightly more habitual, with each man averaging ten times a year, then we've suddenly got 219,180 men urinating on just 25,000 kilometers of road[5] daily. That's one man for every 114 meters.

That's why Jenny and I think this repugnant fixture of the urban landscape is less about the lack of public facilities than it is about their inaccessibly—which, in south Delhi, is caused by inward-focused urban planning that makes street-sides featureless and anonymous, good for nothing but passing by and peeing on.

The newspapers' quality-of-life campaigns, regular though they have been, haven't seemed to change much. We admire the approach taken by the Sulabh International Social Service Organization, which helps entrepreneurs build spotless for-profit toilet blocks that convert swollen bladders into steaming rupees.[6] It solves two problems at once, and we wish they'd build more of them. Otherwise, we know of only two techniques successful in dissuading men from peeing on walls: using shame, and using divinity. Mr. M. and Anya both made liberal use of the former, shouting at men until they'd pinch off, zip up and move on. But that technique relied on spotting a man in the act. For deterrence, the only way to stop urinators was to plaster tile portraits of Lord Hanuman or Lord Krishna or

---

5. http://www.delhitrafficpolice.nic.in/articles/cops-moot-rs-1000-as-minimum-challan.htm

6. http://www.rediff.com/money/2008/may/16ft.htm

Lord Jesus into the wall. No man will pee on another man's god.

It goes without saying that we never saw any women peeing on the street. Modesty forbids it: no matter how bad a woman has to go, she has to hold it until she is somewhere decent. As always, life in Delhi is much harder for women.

★

Urination is just one of the problems that the newspapers regularly criticized Delhiites for inflicting upon their own city. There's also spitting at red lights, for instance, in which drivers open their car doors and spit upon the pavement—not a hawking, forceful phwat with the goal of distance, but a weak-lipped sputter that drips big red gobs of paan down to the street below. And spitting isn't confined to the roads, either: red stains also ran up and down the under-construction stairwells of my Gurgaon office building, speaking either of a downpour of spat paan or of repeated ritual sacrifice of tiny leprechauns on each and every landing.

The newspapers also criticized the city's littering, a practice to which I never saw anyone give a second thought other than my co-worker Govind, whom I once saw groan in protest when someone tossed some paper out of the window of our car; the man doing the tossing was genuinely confused as to what Govind was unhappy about. Litter is generally dropped wherever it is convenient, as attested by the mountains of used cups that grow at the feet of every chaiwallah. Jenny and I could never bring ourselves to follow suit, which meant we'd carry empty cups for hours while looking in vain for a trash can. We'd usually arrive home before we found one.

The newspapers also regularly targeted the state of food sanitation in the city. When the Confederation of Indian Industry surveyed 1,000 restaurants and eateries to see which ones qualified for a sanitary stamp of approval, the newspapers led the chorus of shock at the results: not a single one did.[7] Given those dismal statistics, we learned to follow the reaction of people around us when eating out: if nobody else seemed bothered by what was revealed when the kitchen door swung open, why should we worry?

Still, as much as we trusted the collective wisdom, sometimes our eyes beheld sights that were too much even for our hungry stomachs to bear. Our last trip with the Eating Out in Delhi crew took us to that set of competing storefront kebab stands near Nizamuddin, where grease from daytime auto repair mingled on the cement with that of nightly mutton burra. This was our fourth eatery of the night but the first to really give us pause. We'd started at a paratha stand across from the *Times of India* building, which had been built on the kind of cracked pavement that vermin love; but although cockroaches did dart about, they were far enough away that we could pretend they always kept their distance from where food was stored. The second stop was a perfectly hygienic restaurant in Old Delhi. The third stop—a paratha vendor outside the Nizamuddin Railway Station—would have been far too

7. http://www.indianexpress.com/news/first-thousand-eateries-get-thumbs-down-in-quality-survey/530375/

close to the public urinal for nasal comfort had the breeze not been so favorable.

So far, so good. But at this final stop of the night, Jenny and I watched an employee stomp through black puddles on his way to a basin of steaming brown water into which he dunked an armful of dirty plates. As our group stood around in a circle waiting for the employees to hose off a table for us (they did, in fact, use a hose), our friend Supratim idly rocked back and forth on a poorly fitted manhole; though he didn't notice it, his absent shifts on the unbalanced lid caused bubbles of black liquid to gurgle forth from the loose seal. We could smell the kebabs cooking, but we could also smell something else.

We had full trust in EOID. And we reminded ourselves over and over that they'd never steered us wrong before. But we couldn't do it. Suddenly, I loudly realized that that very last bite of the very last paratha we'd eaten at the previous stop had, amazingly enough, been exactly what it took to make me completely full. Jenny then took the opportunity to remind everyone that she was a vegetarian but no, she didn't want any paneer tikka because she wasn't hungry anyway.

★

Urination, spitting, unsanitary food stalls—in Delhi, filth begets filth. But it goes the other way, too. And this is why I have full faith in Delhi's ultimate redemption: because in Delhi, clean also begets clean.

Take the Metro, for example. It's spotless and it's shining. Nobody litters in it. Nobody pees in it. The Metro proves that Delhiites are neither barbarians nor sophisticates at their core—instead, like citizens of every other city, they simply act in accordance with the influence of their surroundings. In dirty areas, they feel no injunction against being dirty. In clean areas, they keep things clean. It's like the 'broken windows theory' of crime, which suggests that graffiti and vandalism create a sense of decline that leads to further criminal activity.

Call it the "spotless Metro theory": cleanliness creates a sense of responsibility that leads to further conscientiousness.

Proof of this theory lies in the orderliness of the queues in the Metro. In most other parts of the city, a queue is chest-to-back whether there are two hundred people in line or only two. And if there's even an inch of space between two people in a queue, they can rest assured that a third person will slip into it. My boss Murali explained to me that these queues became part of the culture because of economics. Until the 1990s, he told me, India was a country of shortages. It lacked food, water, and power, but it also lacked motor-scooters and air conditioners and other consumer goods. Queues and waiting lists were the norm. Journalist Amit Varma had a similar recollection. "When I was growing up in the 1980s, getting a telephone was difficult. The state had a monopoly over the telecom industry, and one could be on a waiting list for a telephone for years. (Yes, years.)"[8]

So Indians learned to jump queues, to jam into elevators, to ride on the roofs of the trains—not because they were

---

8. http://www.econlib.org/library/Columns/y2008/Varmaprofit.html

impolite or impatient or insane, but because there was never a guarantee that another train would arrive, that the elevator would return any emptier, or that whatever they were queuing for wouldn't abruptly run out. In a country of a billion, opportunities were fleeting and must be instantly seized.

In the Metro, Murali told me, expectations are different: if people miss one train, they have full confidence another is right behind it. Confidence begets respect, and respect begets cleanliness.

We believe that the underground expectations of Delhi's citizens will eventually be replicated above. Scourges like urination—which are failures of infrastructure, not culture—will be fairly easy to solve.

And because the newspapers will need to find new moral outrages, I'm hopeful they'll turn their attention to what will probably be a much more challenging problem to solve: Delhiites' penchant for drunk driving.

We were introduced to the casualness with which Delhiites drive drunk in our first month in Delhi following that party thrown by Abhishek, the realtor who'd found our flat for us. As Abhishek wound down his 2 a.m. paan detour with his friend Arvind at Nizamuddin Railway Station, we finally thought our night was concluding. But though Abhishek had been the one to drive us all to Nizamuddin, it was Arvind—the same Arvind who had been prolonging the party with 'just one more scotch' for hours—who collapsed into the driver's seat.

Arvind fumbled the key into the ignition. Then he turned to the radio and commenced an intense minutes-long search for the perfect song. Abhishek, meanwhile, got in on the passenger's side, laughing as he wiped the last of the paan juice from his mouth. He twisted around to talk to us. "Arvind's going to drop me and then take you home," he said amicably. Then, seeing the horror cross our faces, he added, "Don't worry! He's the best drunk driver in Delhi."

Abhishek faced forward and focused on the music as Arvind sloppily rejected one station after another. A moment later, a thought crossed his mind. He turned to look at us again. "But he's not drunk."

Arvind did indeed get us home safe and sound. However, we aren't ready to bestow the mantle of Delhi's Best Drunk Driver upon him, because he has a lot of competition. Drunk driving may rival golgappas as Delhi's favorite nightcap. It's a practice enjoyed by the richest BMW-driving trust-funder and the poorest autowallah. Hardly a week went by when we didn't hear some terrible story about a family of pavement dwellers crushed beneath an inebriated driver's wheels. On winter nights, auto drivers would pull quick sips from small bottles. Sometimes it was hard to know what was scarier: the daytime traffic, when no Blueline bus could be counted on to have functional brakes; or nighttime, when no driver could be counted on to actually be awake. We once rode in a taxi with a driver so drunk that he wouldn't pull over no matter how much we shouted at him. He finally agreed to stop his vehicle only because we convinced him that the side of the Ring Road was actually the GK-II main market.

★

But of all the problems we read about, the one the papers covered above all others was crime.

Every city has crime, of course, and every newspaper in the world relies on breathless crime reporting to boost circulation. Even in Singapore, where crime is famously low, the papers give ink to it whenever they can. (Although theirs is a lower threshold: while we lived there, the *Straits Times* devoted space on its front page to a crime spree in which vandals broke into a total of seven parked cars.[9]) But we'd moved to India thinking that all its crime was concentrated in Mumbai. That's because we'd read Suketu Mehta's book *Maximum City*, which presented a Mumbai so terrifying and violent that when Murali and I were asked to fly out for a twelve-hour focus group, I initially refused to go. My colleagues were surprised that I was more worried about Mumbai than Delhi, because Delhi is considered to be the most dangerous city in the country.

Especially for women. Our friend Tarn, who grew up in Mumbai, had been warned by her female friends before moving to Delhi that "for women, Delhi was different." Delhi was reputed to be much more conservative, which meant that single women who lived by free-wheeling Mumbai mores were in constant danger, and that it simply wouldn't be safe for her to be out after 9 p.m. Tarn told us that she didn't believe it when she first moved to Delhi, until the night she and her friends were followed around Saket PVR market (an upscale, youth-friendly market) by a

---

9. http://motoring.asiaone.com/Motoring/News/Story/
A1Story20090831-164485.html

group of thuggish men who grew increasingly threatening and refused to relent until Tarn called some male friends to rush to the market and chase them away.

Journalist Ketaki Gokhale argued in the *Wall Street Journal* that Delhi's women were suffering deeply because of the cultural acceptability of "eve-teasing." "That's a benign-sounding term for the catcalls, groping and other forms of abuse that women here endure daily. It forces us to modify our behavior—from walking a longer route home to wearing thick scarves in the dead of summer—in ways in which men are never troubled."[10]

Our neighbors and our co-workers all echoed the newspapers in their belief that Delhi was India's Mos Eisley. We were taking our life into our hands, they'd tell us, every time we rode in an auto, walked through the Old City, or generally left our house after sundown. But despite everyone's insistence that it was always open season on law-abiding citizens, we were only confronted with crime once in our eighteen months in Delhi.

On Saturdays, some beggars carry buckets filled with mustard oil. People can wash away their sins by dropping coins into the oil as an offering to the god Shani. That's why, when the bucket-bearing foursome first approached us on this Saturday, we didn't take notice. Until their attack began.

"Money!" the thieves screamed, surrounding us as we stepped out of our auto. "Please, sir! Money! Chapatti!"

---

10. http://online.wsj.com/article/SB125291645948508175. html?mod=googlenews_wsj

One of the thieves backed into Jenny with his arms spread wide, forcing her backwards as the remaining three danced around me, screaming and swiping at my pockets.

"Watch your bag, Jenny!" I hollered, jamming my hands into my pockets, wrapping my left hand around my cheap Nokia mobile and my right hand around my wallet. My image of myself as my wife's able protector evaporated as my voice cracked in a way Jean-Claude Van Damme's never has. "Let's get out of here!"

Saket Citywalk Mall was just six busy lanes of traffic away: a gleaming refuge of air-conditioned marble whose security perimeter would save us, if only we could reach it. But that street is hard enough to cross without getting killed even when we're not dodging the sticky fingers of four master criminals.

Somehow, we made it to the concrete median. But the thugs had followed us. Traffic raced by on both sides of the street. We were trapped.

And the bandits had discovered that there was *something* in my unguarded back pocket. I had to alternate between covering my phone and swatting at their grasping hands. It was just my Moleskine notebook—hardly worth stealing, but how could I explain that to them? The bad guys were to my right, but traffic was coming from my left; my head jerked back and forth, searching for a break in the cars while keeping an eye on my assailants, unable to concentrate successfully on either one.

Across the road, I glimpsed salvation: crowds, open space and security guards whose dominion of protection didn't seem to extend across the street.

"Hut!" I shouted in my most commanding Hindi. "Away!" All four of the thieves jumped. I shoved the nearest one in his chest. He began flailing wildly at me, screaming, pumping his fists. Fortunately, I was much taller than he was; I kept him at arm's length, his fists landing on my arms but causing no pain. The traffic finally cleared, and we dashed across the street and past the guards who hadn't noticed our plight. Our attackers shouted after us from the median, but they came no closer. Our belongings were accounted for. We were safe.

And those four six-year-olds were the biggest threat we encountered in Delhi.

In fact, we were more comfortable walking around Delhi than the downtown Denver neighborhood to which we moved upon our return to the States. Certainly, a considerable portion of our comfort can be attributed to our skin color (nobody is going to victimize the one couple on the street whom everyone is looking at). But even accounting for that, we actually felt safer in Delhi than in New York.

Consider this: on my first day in the Okhla office, the first thing I did was lock my laptop to the table. After all, that's what I did at every office in New York. But my co-workers teased me about that act for the next eighteen months. "Is there that much crime in America," Murali tittered, "that you can't even trust your own co-workers?"

The answer is yes. At my second job in New York City, a dozen computers were stolen one night. There were no signs of a break-in, which meant that the thief had a key. A few weeks later, our IT guy spotted a bundle of equipment on eBay that matched what had been taken from us. It was being sold by a username that was suspiciously similar to one of our co-worker's. The police weren't interested, so we had to settle for the lesson that laptops should always be locked up.

I believe that if 16 million New Yorkers magically traded places with 16 million Delhiites, Delhi would explode. I often wonder why there wasn't *more* crime in Delhi.

After all, demographics and economics suggest that Delhiites should be perpetuating far more violence on each other. The city skews young and male: fifty-five percent of Delhi is male,[11] as compared to fifty-two percent across India and a global average of slightly more than fifty percent.[12] Over fifty-three percent of the city is under the age of twenty-five,[13] compared to about thirty-four percent in New York City.[14] Young males in America turn to sex and violence to vent their energy and aggression, but Delhi is so conservative that it's much harder for young men to engage in the former. The city's economic gulf is incredibly wide and incredibly visible (I'm talking Ferraris-driving-past-pavement dwellers wide and visible). And the hardships of the city—heat, cold, traffic, pollution, water shortages, high population density, minimal personal space, insults

11. http://delhigovt.nic.in/dept/economic/populationdetail.asp
12. http://censusindia.gov.in/Census_And_You/gender_composition.aspx
13. http://delhigovt.nic.in/dept/economic/populationdetail.asp
14. http://www.nyc.gov/html/dcp/pdf/census/projections_report.pdf, appendix table 1

and indignities—are overwhelming even to people who can afford to overcome them.

Any American city would surely be torn apart by these social forces.

The official crime statistics show that while Delhi is dangerous by Indian standards (the *Times of India* calls it India's "crime capital"[15]), it's positively tranquil as compared to American cities. The Delhi region had 495 murders in 2007,[16] or 2.95 murders for every 100,000 people as calculated against the National Crime Records Bureau's population estimates.[17] In that same year, however, New York City had 5.94 murders per 100,000 people[18]—and that was a year in which New York City was named "the safest big city in the United States."[19] There's a similar story for forcible rape in 2007: 3.57 per 100,000 in New Delhi,[20] 10.48 per 100,000 in New York.[21]

Side-by-side, the statistics are clearly in Delhi's favor. So the question is this: are the statistics accurate? Our friend Sachin, an editor at one of the city's major newspapers, emphatically believes that they're not. The police often refuse to file complaints or First Information Reports, he wrote to us, for two reasons. "One, if an FIR is lodged, the

15. http://timesofindia.indiatimes.com/india/Delhi-tops-crime-charts-for-fifth-year-in-a-row/articleshow/2665983.cms
16. http://ncrb.nic.in/cii2007/cii-2007/Table%203.1.pdf
17. http://ncrb.nic.in/cii2007/cii-2007/Table%201.6.pdf
18. http://www.fbi.gov/ucr/08aprelim/table_4mt-oh.html
19. http://www.govtech.com/gt/370385
20. http://ncrb.nic.in/cii2007/cii-2007/Table%203.1.pdf
21. http://www.fbi.gov/ucr/08aprelim/table_4mt-oh.html

police are obliged to investigate the case, which they certainly don't want to as it may intrude upon their extortion time; and two, the chief inspector of a police station wants his jurisdiction to be the 'most crime-free' so that his area or police station is rewarded by the state government."

In a patriarchal society in which rape victims are often stagmatized, most rapes go unreported. And while it's hard to believe that three murders per 100,000 are swept so easily under the official radar, Sachin thinks that's the case. "A government report published earlier this year supplied statistics of how Delhi Police are the most corrupt government servants in the country," he wrote. "I believe Delhi is a far more dangerous place than Mumbai (or New York), not only because I hear about the multitude and the variety of crimes in our daily editorial meetings, but also because the law and order machinery is so inept and corrupt, it has compromised the safety of the city's residents."

We'd certainly heard enough rumors of India's corruption to enter the country with wariness of anyone wearing a uniform. The few interactions we did have with the police were merely minor abuses of power, like when cops would briefly commandeer our autorickshaws. They'd wave us down from the side of the road, hop in the front seat, and give our driver directions with no regard to the whims of the paying customers. The officer would wrap his arm around the driver as if they were good friends, as if this was just a polite autowallah doing his friendly neighborhood constable a favor; but the moment the officer jumped out, the driver would sag in his seat with relief. I also had an experience in which an officer arbitrarily singled out my taxi driver one night on my commute home, planting himself in front of the bumper and pointing and screaming at him. He advanced menacingly, fingering his beating stick in preparation for unleashing noble justice. And then he noticed my pasty white face cowering in the back seat and suddenly decided we weren't doing anything wrong after all.

Our only full taste of the corruption Sachin describes came in the Jahanpanah City Forest, a protected wilderness area near GK-II. An oasis of scrub brush, trees and fresh air along its 800 acres of meandering paths, the Jahanpanah City Forest should have provided us with regular escape from the heat and pollution of the cemented-over parts of the city. But we never returned there—not after the experience we had on Jenny's first day in India, which was just the first day of my second week. I'd been telling Jenny all I'd learned about India—how to hail an autorickshaw, how to spot suspicious bottled water, how to order lunch at a restaurant—but I obviously hadn't learned enough, because I decided to take us on a hike at 2 p.m. on a scorching August Saturday. The blazing sun was high overhead and sweat had been pouring down my back even before we reached the gate to the park. It didn't improve things that we had no water. It made things worse when we got lost. And just when we were at our most miserable, a policeman appeared on his motorcycle and began to blackmail us.

We'd heard his bike puttering around the corner of the path, so we knew someone was coming. He was surprised to see us, but he'd regained his composure as soon as he pulled to a halt, and he'd clearly formulated a strategy by the time he dismounted his bike. "Park closed," he told us, advancing menacingly. "Park closed!" From there he launched into a string of Hindi, miming that he didn't understand English every time we spoke but somehow managing to summon enough vocabulary to demand that we come to the station and pay a 30,000-rupee fine for being in the park during closing time.

Or, you know, we could pay him 5,000 rupees right then and there.

Panicking, terrified, and soaked after fifteen sweaty minutes spent trying to figure out what he wanted, I finally called my landlord who was one of only two people in the country whose phone number I had, and the only one of the two who spoke Hindi. I explained that I urgently needed him to translate, and then I handed the phone to the cop.

They spoke briefly, and then the cop returned the phone. I put it to my ear and asked my landlord what he'd learned.

He began by apologizing to me on behalf of his country. "This man is only trying to extort a bribe," he told me. "I suggest you give him nothing."

With our understanding of the situation now clarified, Jenny and I started shuffling our feet and edging away. Suddenly, the policeman's demeanour changed. His glowering was replaced by pleading. His shoulders sagged. His eyes welled with actual fake tears.

"Gift for policeman!" he begged, blocking our way. "Please, sir! Gift for policeman!"

What now? Could we ignore him and move on? Or was not bribing a policeman an arrestable offense? And what was the going rate for a bribe, anyway?

I opened my wallet and tentatively handed him 400 rupees.

Suddenly his English improved dramatically. "Please, ma'am," he asked Jenny as the money disappeared into his pocket. "I beg of you. Double that!"

Jenny shook her head cautiously. And then the officer's demeanor changed again. He grinned broadly. He gave first Jenny and then me a tremendous handshake. He pointed us down the path that would return us to GK-II. He even watched us walk away to make sure we took the correct fork in the road, and then he waved at us happily as we did so.

Of all the photo opportunities we missed in India, the moment we most deeply regret not capturing was when Jenny saw an elephant get pulled over by the traffic police. But this encounter ranks as our second-most lamented missed photo opportunity. Because I'm sure that policeman would have eagerly posed with us.

10

Cheap Labor: Their Delhi Struggle

At the conclusion of my first week in New Delhi, I crafted an email to my colleagues back in the New York office. I had worked harder in that single week in Delhi than I ever had in my New York career, and I wanted my soon-to-be-ex-colleagues to know it for two reasons. The first was to demonstrate that the company's investment in me was paying off—given that I was plucked from corporate obscurity just one week before I was shipped off to New Delhi, I felt pressure to show them I was worth it.

The second reason for my email was that I'd had a genuine epiphany: I'd realized that Americans were far luckier than we appreciate. An obvious realization, I know, and one that seems absurdly naïve when put in print. But it's one thing to learn about the world's inequities from newspapers and quite another to see it with my own eyes.

And that's what had happened: the full weight of America's good fortune was suddenly clear from just a week of watching my co-workers do their jobs.

We were doing the same tasks for the same high-tech client in New Delhi that I had been doing in New York. But the workload in Delhi was twice what I was accustomed to, and the deadlines were half of what I'd have expected, which meant that any given day in Delhi required four times the amount of work as in New York. I didn't leave the office before 8 p.m. those first couple of weeks, and I was still leaving hours earlier than almost everyone else. And while there are obviously plenty of companies in America in which people work just as hard, what struck me wasn't as much the effort that my Indian colleagues put in as it was how work was prioritized in the hierarchy of their lives: work came above *everything* else.

I asked a co-worker why they all worked so intensely, with the obvious toll it took on friends, family and life. This co-worker responded by telling me of the weight of history. When India and Pakistan were partitioned by the British in 1947, millions of Hindus were forced to abandon prosperity in Lahore and other cities and to move to Delhi with nothing at all. Meanwhile, millions of Muslims living in Indian cities were forced on the opposite journey. By some estimates, a half-million people were killed as ten to twelve million refugees crossed the new border, with Muslims going northwest and Hindus going southeast.[1] Many of my colleagues' grandparents had arrived in the

---

1. http://www.globalsecurity.org/military/world/war/indo-pak-partition2.htm

city with nothing; for them, absolute poverty is less than two generations removed.

I clumsily articulated this attitude and its ramifications in my email to New York ("So they all work like crazy, and their economy grows like crazy, and while the country clearly has its problems, they will surely be addressed with the same drive"), along with some more mundane thoughts ("Haven't gotten sick yet, although my co-workers took me to a really dodgy tea stand for samosas yesterday, so my stomach may yet have something in store for me."). And while so many of my first impressions of India were reversed as I learned more about it, this one—of the omnipresent specter of Partition—never lost its significance.

But there is another layer to it. The pain of absolute poverty is not just prominent in recent history. It's also showcased on every street corner.

In America, poverty is sanitized, ghettoized and even romanticized by the more fortunate classes. But in India, it's impossible to look out of a window without seeing economic reality. For every street lined with nice houses, there's a family picking scraps in the alley behind it. For every parking lot full of nice cars, there's a thin man in thin clothes guarding it. Maids live in slums just beyond the high-rise apartment buildings in which they serve; ice cream vendors sleep atop the carts they push around all day long.

Compare our commutes to work. In New York, Jenny and I would stare glumly at the other sleepy faces on the subway and wonder what the point was. In Delhi, we'd gape out of the taxi window at faces that made the point perfectly clear. On the other side of any window were people coping with an economy shaped entirely by its massive oversupply of labor. Everyone—up to and including my co-workers—toiled with the awareness that someone else would eagerly take their job for half the pay. The scenes my colleagues saw on their commutes were daily reminders of stories they'd heard from their grandparents. And they were proof that there were worse things in life than being at the office when your daughter said her first words.

Like most expats, we were shocked by some of the sights we saw. And like most expats, we quickly grew desensitized. (Quicker than we're comfortable admitting.) But then we read Edward Luce's book *In Spite of the Gods*, and a phrase that one of his colleagues said to him stuck with us: 'In India, things are never as good or as bad as they seem.' And that inspired us to look closer at sights from which we'd normally turn away.

And what we saw surprised us. This, too, sounds callous to put into print, but we realized that even the beggars are economic actors. Even within desperate situations, there are patterns of commerce. There is ingenuity. There is profit. We learned that people with no other choice are often amazingly creative: anywhere a rupee could be made, three people were competing to make that rupee. We discovered that there is such a thing as economic jugaad: improvising a livelihood out of the most unlikely opportunities.

Like the simple intersection of two streets. What could be a more unlikely location for opportunity to manifest?

But this was the case: anywhere anyone was forced to wait, an economy would spring up. Where auto drivers waited for fares, where private drivers waited for bosses, where passengers waited for trains or buses, but especially where cars revved their engines in front of eternal red lights—in all these places, a tide of entrepreneurs rose to transform the transient needs of the impatient into a trickle of rupees that provided a meal for a day, a livelihood for a family, or more: a career, a path out of poverty, a citywide merchandising empire.

Some red-light economies were small. A minor intersection would be operated upon by a family of beggars or by men selling snacks. They'd wander through the idling cars offering their indulgences or their misfortunes for a few rupees each. But some red-light economies had evolved complex ebbs and flows of commerce that were timed to the fractional duration of the delay. When the light was green, the players in this economy were regrouping, replenishing their stock, readying themselves to wade into the islands of rattling tailpipes the moment the light turned red and the cars begin to pile up. And when the first car rocked to a halt, the well-rehearsed red-light economy churned forth. First came the adult vendors, surging through to offer both practical goods and impulse buys: masala peanuts, belts, model airplanes, mobile phone chargers, orange towels. On some days, every major red light in the city might have someone selling the same suction-cup window shades or sheets of glow-in-the-dark ceiling stickers, making it clear that each red light was connected to a massive underground distribution chain. Jenny and I would watch them pass, tempted by the coconut slices but wary of the water sprinkled to keep them moist, curious about the electric mosquito swatters but unwilling to hold up traffic to complete a negotiation.

Once the adult vendors had crested, the children began to swell. They'd lean stacks of books against their chests, their chins pressed down against the top one to secure the pile as they speed-waddled over, holding up the covers one by one. These were pirated books—photocopied reproductions of *City of Djinns*, *The White Tiger*, *The Inscrutable Americans*, self-help guides, biographies of prominent businessmen, and various Ghosh and Rushdie titles with the pages pasted out of order and maybe missing whole chapters. A survey of the titles being pirated functioned as a barometer of Delhi's literary interests in any given month. (If you bought this book off the street, that means it's a success! Except that bootleggers don't pay royalties, so we hope the cheap ink rubs off on your cheap fingers.)

If the children were selling magazines, they were often wearing shirts emblazoned with the logo of the title employing them. It was initially horrifying to see twelve-year-olds working under the hot sun for global brands in an official capacity, but we soon realized that at least they're earning a living. They should be in school, yes, of course, they should have caring parents who feed them and clothe them and love them and give them a proper childhood. But if they don't have parents, or homes, or love, at least they have jobs. Because they could have it much worse.

And in the most highly evolved red-light economies, the next wave makes it clear how much worse it could be.

Sometimes the beggars were elderly men or women, hobbling over on crutches to stand motionless by our auto with their hands clasped together in that namaste pose westerners learn in yoga class; they'd close their eyes and look serene for a moment before hobbling on to the next one. Sometimes the beggars were dirty young women with hair matted in accidental dreadlocks and unconscious babies flopping like rag dolls; they reached into our auto to touch our feet and gesture at the flies landing on the babies' leaky noses. Sometimes the beggars were deformed men dangling boneless limbs or walking on all fours like dogs, wearing flip-flops to protect their hands from gravel. Sometimes the beggars were children, pointing to their mouths and their stomachs, crying fake tears that carved real valleys through the dust on their cheeks.

The children always came last. The order of the red-light economy was probably determined by a number of factors (agreements, bribes, threats, seniority and beatings surely figured in determinations of hierarchy), but it generally resulted in businessmen before beggars, and adults before children. Sometimes the children were actually enjoying themselves, pretending misery but peering at us as they wiped their eyes to see if we were buying it, and then bounding joyfully to the next car if we weren't. Other times they were genuinely, wretchedly miserable, crying with exhaustion because whoever put them on the street wouldn't let them quit for the night until they'd earned a certain amount. Sometimes they worked in teams, with a boy beating a drum while a girl, with a black mustache painted on her face, turned a few cartwheels on the pavement before clasping her hands together and bringing them in a full circle around her body (a trick that requires dislocating her shoulders to perform).

The red-light economy, heart-wrenching and terrible as it can be, was designed that way. Every component was strategically implemented to maximize someone's profit. This knowledge helped us learn to say "no" to people whose lives we could conceivably change with what we'd spend on dinner that night. Because even the beggars are economic actors, and giving to them only boosts their profitability.

Still, such knowledge did nothing to make us feel better about it. Children would rush to us barefoot over the hot pavement and pull at our pants legs, sobbing and begging for chapatti and touching our feet and pointing at their empty mouths. And we'd sadly shake our heads and purse our lips in sympathy; or, as difficult as it was, we'd stare in the other direction and pretend not to notice at all. We felt terrible every time, but we knew that any money we gave would just be passed up to whomever forced them onto the street in the first place. A terrible choice that made us hate this country, hate this universe, hate ourselves.

Every so often, though, a child gave us hope: maybe, just maybe, things weren't as bad as they appeared. These glimmers came in the moments a child decided our alms were a lost cause. Usually, she would just move on to the next vehicle. But sometimes—and these are the moments we'd cling to—she would straighten up off the auto floor where she'd dramatically collapsed, cease her sobs, and dash merrily back to her siblings who were chasing crows on the traffic island, running that determined gait universal to happy children. Sometimes she'd even run alongside our auto as we accelerated, smiling and waving at the foreigners and charming us into smiling and waving back. Sometimes we could get her to break character as she howled on our auto floor by practising our Hindi on her; she'd snap off a false sob, break into delighted laughter, and wave some other children over to hear us talk. How bad could things be, we'd think—we'd hope, we'd pray—if a beggar child can still show such genuine happiness?

More of these moments: one little boy used this break to play, taking an object from his pocket and prancing it up and down my leg like a toy dinosaur. One little girl laid her head on Jenny's leg and looked up at us with big brown eyes, perhaps imagining that she was part of the billboard family smiling over the intersection, or maybe just appreciating this respite from the sun. One time, as we were in a taxi waiting out a light, Jenny opened her window and handed a boy a ten-rupee note. He took it, studied it, studied us, and then stuck his hand in for more. Jenny started to gently roll up the window: sorry, kid, that's all you get. But the boy called her bluff, keeping his hand in the gap with the full knowledge that she would never close it on him. He spent the duration of the light making the saddest faces he could at his captive audience: he stuck out his lower lip and made it quiver, he squinted his eyes to make them water, he uttered mewing noises. But when the light changed, the driver revved the engine, and the little boy knew we'd won the stand-off. His face erupted into the most adorable grin we'd ever seen, and he pulled his hand out and ran alongside the car as we picked up speed, shouting and waving and laughing as we did the same.

In times like these, we'd return to Edward Luce's *In Spite of the Gods*. "In India, things are never as good or as bad as they seem." We highlighted that quote in our copy of his book. We desperately needed to believe that it was true.

★

The profit potential of any red-light economy was limited to the duration of its delay. If Delhi's vendors and beggars had their way, every red light's duration would be like the one we had the misfortune to encounter a few hours east of New Delhi. Because at this railroad crossing, the economy had control of the red light.

We were in Sam Singh's car, on the way to Anupshahr in Uttar Pradesh, to visit Pardada Pardadi's school. Sam drives this road two or three times a week, so he knew exactly what's made this particular railroad crossing so miserable: a cabal of vendors and beggars had collectively bribed some Indian Railways employees to lower the crossing guard far earlier than the passing train required, creating a captive audience of cars that would sit there for twenty minutes out of every hour. On our trip, Sam groaned as he saw the gate begin its descent—had we been two minutes earlier, we would have been spared the next twenty minutes we instead spent staring despairingly down the empty tracks as the tide surged around our car.

It was orderly in the beginning, with snack vendors tapping politely on our windows, followed by guys selling idols, mobile phone protectors, and other knick-knacks, and then the beggars spilling over us. But as the minutes ticked away and the rumbling of the train grew audible in the distance, the entrepreneurs abandoned decorum to close any last-second sales. Old men on crutches slapped the car doors to get our attention, roasted channa vendors shoved their wares through the cracked windows, and children mashed their faces into the windshield and hollered. When the gate lifted, the vendors and beggars scrambled away, and both directions of traffic surged. In their haste to cross, the lanes were blurred, which created instant head-to-head gridlock that nearly trapped us in another cycle.

When we made the trip to the school again a few months later, the jam stretched into the hours. We would have expected authorities to take action as the jams grew more and more significant, but the opposite had apparently happened: the longer the jam grew, the more money was being made, and the more the men profiting from it were able to bribe anyone trying to shut it down. We assume that increasing amounts of money were required as increasingly higher authorities became aware of the situation.

Which provides a good illustration of how we imagine illegal businesses to be operating in Delhi: it's trickle-up economics. Beggars and belt sellers and sidewalk barbers may not be licensed, but they're still taxed—first by the police, who demand payment not to enforce the licensing laws; and then by the neighborhood mobsters, who place their hands in the pockets of anyone operating in their territory. Based on what we've seen, what we've read, and what we've been told, we speculate that any space from which someone can sell or beg is controlled by both the police and the local strongmen, and any vendor or beggar who wants to operate there has to come to an agreement with both.

By this reckoning, money earned by Delhi's poorest moves inexorably upward into the pockets of those who have power over them. The more money any one person is earning, the higher up the food chain people take notice, and the more he has to pay just to stay in business. Small payments to local thugs aggregate into bigger payments to neighborhood bosses. Small bribes to local cops aggregate into bigger payments to neighborhood constables. At the bottom, the poor struggle to get by; at the top, the rich make enough to become politicians.

What happens when someone crosses the system? Well, for as long as we lived in Hauz Khas, there was always a guy selling omelettes from a folding table set up between our bungalow and the market. Except, one day, there were suddenly two. Two guys, both selling omelettes from folding tables set up immediately adjacent to each other, both with crates of eggs, gas burners and small plastic containers of pre-diced chillies and herbs. From behind both tables, both men stared directly ahead, neither acknowledging the other even when I attempted to amuse them by rubbing my eyes and miming exaggerated double takes.

What was happening here? Was this pure ugly capitalism like at those competing kebab stands, or the dueling Roopaks in Karol Bagh? Had the new guy simply seen all the money to be made selling omelettes from this spot and decided he wanted a piece of the action?

Or—was this how the trickle-up economy enforced compliance? Had the invading egg man been sent by a local mobster to provoke a protection payment, or to drive a too-honest vendor out of business?

A few days later, one of the two omelette vendors disappeared. Unfortunately, we don't know if the new guy drove the original out of his livelihood, or if the original egg man got the message and paid his dues. We'd never looked at the original vendor closely enough to recognize which one was the last egg man standing.

★

Not every poor person is a beggar, a vendor, or a cog in Delhi's vast orange towel distribution network. Many people earn their livelihoods using the most basic gifts their gods gave them: backs that can support weight, arms that can operate shovels, wrists that can move in the back-and-forth motion necessary to wield a paintbrush, mouths that can tell someone where an entrance to a mall is along with fingers that can point appropriately, or bodies that merely exist in three-dimensional space and thus can be positioned anywhere there's something worth guarding. If there's a pattern, it's this: anything a machine can do, a person can almost always do cheaper.

We were inevitably surprised to see new examples of things being done by hand that we'd intrinsically assumed were done by machines. On the roads along which the Metro was being constructed, for instance, miles of seven-foot-tall metal barriers protected the worksite and discouraged adventurous drivers against shortcuts through active construction zones. Each pale blue barrier segment sported Metro logos, matching stripes and bold warnings in large red letters. Exposed as they were to the erosive effects of passing traffic—caustic pollution, scouring dirt kicked up by passing cars, periodic Blueline sideswipes—they'd quickly become scratched and faded. Thus teams of painters were regularly unleashed to touch them up, reforming the logos and letters with the same precision, we realized, that had formed them to begin with. Every single letter of every single one of these thousands of barriers was hand-painted.

In the United States, if these barriers weren't machine-painted in the factory, they would have had printed decals affixed to them. The very last method any American factory would have engaged is hand-painting. The labor costs are far too expensive. But here in Delhi, labor was so cheap that most signage was still done by hand, from the placard on our block advertising Dr. T.'s medical practice to the post office marquee in Hauz Khas market. In a market oversupplied by labor, a squadron of sign painters is cheaper than a machine that prints decals. An old man with a bicycle cart is cheaper than a van for transporting the heavy potted plants we bought at a nursery near Okhla to our house four miles away. And an army of village women is cheaper than a crane for bringing building materials up to the tenth floor of a Gurgaon construction site, which is why single-file chains of women could always be seen marching up the steep ramps affixed to the sides of skyscrapers-to-be with piles of bricks balanced on their heads. These are terrible jobs, dangerous jobs, jobs with no career path that teach no marketable skills. But they're jobs nonetheless, and those people filling them are probably grateful to have them at all.

The low price of labor was made even lower by the fact that forty percent of Delhi's workforce are migrants.[2] These poor villagers spend every last rupee to reach Delhi in hopes of a better life, even though they know they'll have to sleep on the sidewalk on their way to achieving it. Delhi's *First City* magazine ran a monthly feature called "Minute-Old Migrant" that put stories to the faces we saw every day: following failed rains or health crises, these migrants often arrived in Delhi bearing nothing but the hopes of the family relying on them. This total blank slate allows employers to lower wages even further by including food and accommodation as part of an employment package.

That was clearly the situation at a construction site near our first flat in GK-II: during the day, we'd see an entire family filling pans from a giant dirt pile and carrying them on their heads into the building. At night, we'd see the whole family—men, women and children—sleeping atop the same pile of dirt. We also saw this across the street in Hauz Khas, where two families were rebuilding a sidewalk during the day and sleeping on it at night. We even saw this after late-night milkshakes at the Café Coffee Day lounge. We emerged from our dessert to discover that Hauz Khas market had closed up for the night, and as we walked home we saw the fruit vendors and the newspaperwallahs dragging cots and spreading bedrolls along the ground in front of

---

2. http://www.time.com/time/printout/0,8816,1926146,00.html

their stands. One cot outside a flower stand already had two people fast asleep in it.

Similarly, the grounds of Gurgaon's biggest construction projects would have corrugated shanty towns to house workers and their families. And while the city is making slow progress in assuring that the most conspicuous construction sites provide sanitary facilities and childcare services,[3] even those who get a cot to sleep on and nothing else know it's probably better than the alternative. The same goes for the people sleeping on the sidewalk across from us: it beats sleeping on the side of the Ring Road. At least they're in a safe neighborhood with night watchmen, and at least they don't have to worry about being kicked awake by a police officer demanding payment lest he run them in for vagrancy.

One of my taxi drivers told me that room and board are not necessarily employee perks, like the Friday morning bagels in my New York office. At Birender's stand, half of this driver's 200-rupee-per-day salary was deducted for the food he ate and the canvas tent he slept in. This seemed to be a common arrangement between employee and employer; and while it made sense from the perspectives of both bosses and employees, it also created some perverse incentives on either side. For the bosses, every rupee they skimp on accommodations is multiplied by the quantity of their workforce into pure profit. And for the employees who might face both joblessness and homelessness once the

---

3. http://www.indianexpress.com/news/delhi-govt-to-build-shelters-for-migrant-workforce/489417/0

task is finished, their only incentive is to make each job last as long as possible. Which is why we came home at two o'clock one very late night to find an exhausted Anya feeding her dogs in the driveway. She'd just finished spending her third full day managing the laborers painting her apartment, and this was the first moment she'd had to do the rest of her household chores.

"Three days to paint a two-bedroom apartment?" we'd scoffed. "How can it possibly take so long?"

It took so long because the laborers had every incentive to work as slow as possible. If Anya hadn't been hovering over them all day long, it would have probably taken them even longer. After all, it took three days for the painters Shankar hired simply to paint our spare bedroom. While Anya had had to pester her painters all day to achieve her level of productivity, the painters in our flat were managed by Shankar's main office boy, who spent three days running up and down the stairs between Shankar's office and our flat in his attempt to do two full-time jobs at once. The moment he'd step out of our door, the painters' pace would slacken noticeably.

When we first got to Delhi, it was the beggars who broke our hearts. But as we grew to better understand the city, we began to feel worse for the laborers. Those who suffer the most, we realized, are not the ones making drama (and profit) of it.

This revelation came on a frigid night a few days before our first Christmas: as I was escorting the last of our holiday party guests to their cars, the neighborhood guard rushed up to me and began pleading for something in Hindi. I

couldn't understand what he wanted, of course, but one of
my guests could. "He's asking if you have any paper to
burn. He's cold."

I was staggered. While Jenny and I had spent the last few
weeks whining because our electric heaters weren't as
powerful as the steam radiators back in Brooklyn, this
sixteen-year-old guard had been burning empty plastic chai
cups to keep warm, just three stories below our bedroom. I
quickly ran upstairs and gathered all the paper I could find
for him. And then, after I locked the bungalow's front gate
and returned back upstairs, I stepped on to our terrace to
look at him. Warm in my heavy winter jacket, I watched
him rub his hands together above a fire he wouldn't have
had if I hadn't happened to walk my party guests to
their car.

I realized why his plight moved me so much: because the
people whose misfortunes have become their livelihoods—
the dislocated children, the crippled men, the withered
mothers—aren't the poorest people in this city. The poorest
are all those who endure inhuman professions because they
have no other choice.

Like this guard. As in many Delhi neighborhoods of a
certain class, our front doors were watched over by private
guards while we sat on our sofas and slept in our beds. Our
daytime guard was a smiling, round-faced fellow who
looked around forty-five and shared his name with India's
fourth-richest man. His days were spent chatting with
passing servants, raising the simple metal arm that blocked
the road whenever a vehicle needed to pass, and sitting on
the plastic bus-station-style chairs that, along with a simple

open-air shelter and a single light bulb hanging from the tree, were the only comforts the neighborhood association provided for him and his night-time counterpart. The changing of the guard happened sometime after sunset, when the night-time guard—we cycled through a few, most of them teenagers—would take over. The flow of traffic would cease by midnight, at which point he'd slam shut the iron gate that closed off our street. And from then until sunrise, his job was to sit next to the gate and open it for any vehicle that honked to pass through.

That was his whole job: sit, wait, and snap to attention when honked at.

In winter, we'd see him shivering or dozing fitfully when we'd come home late. We'd open the human-sized door built into the gate as quietly as we could so as not to wake him. We pitied him for being cold, but we also pitied him for being bored: his whole livelihood was to act as a human motion detector. A simple machine could have done his job just as well, but he was far cheaper than a simple machine. Economics gave him no choice but to accept a job sitting in the cold from an employer who provided no jacket and no firewood, and who didn't pay enough that he could afford protection against the chill beyond the ratty blanket he'd wrapped around himself.

Human motion detectors are everywhere in Delhi. In the third basement of my company's DLF Cyber City building, a young woman was employed to stand near the elevators and direct anyone unclear as to how to get to the lobby above. All I ever saw her do was stand and stare at cement walls while businesspeople conversant in the way elevators worked pressed the button without assistance. In my office a few floors above, our guard Jagdish would staff the reception desk from before the first person arrived until after the very last person left, sometimes pacing the reception area in his efforts to stay awake. Outside a trendy bar in GK-II, we saw the same bushy-mustached guard each and every time we passed by for eighteen full months; the entirety of the professional existence of this fifty-year-old man was to open the door for anyone coming in.

To us, this is true suffering: enduring physical misery and abject boredom because, in an economy so tragically oversupplied by labor, there is no other choice. Being trapped in all-consuming circumstances that exhaust the body or destroy the soul yet teach no useful skills, contain no possibility of advancement and provide no trajectory out. True suffering is endured by a sixteen-year-old guard who sees stretched out before him a lifetime of huddling in the cold, opening the gate and not much else.

★

The same economic structure that has peons making copies and children washing dishes for sidewalk dhabas is the reason Ganga was part of our household. Growing up middle class in the US, maids were something Jenny and I saw only on sitcoms or in movies like *Mary Poppins*, in which silent servants attended caricatures of the disgustingly wealthy who'd complain about "the help" even while taking crystal glasses off silver trays being held by them.

Nobody we knew had any "help." Our parents taught us both that everyone was equal and that nobody was above manual labor, which is why my siblings Eric and Susan and I were responsible for a roster of household chores that increased as we grew older: cleaning the dishes, making our beds, folding the laundry, mowing the lawn, taking out the garbage, and doing whatever else our parents could find for us to do when *Married With Children* was on and they didn't want us to watch it. The closest we came to having a maid was the cleaning service my mom hired twice a month to scrub the bathtubs, wax the floors, and do the other jobs that were worth paying someone else to do. But even that somehow increased our workload: on the evenings before the service was scheduled to come, my mom would run around the house ordering all of us to "Clean up!" because "The cleaning lady is coming tomorrow!"

Aside from that indulgence, both Jenny and I were raised to believe that it was both extravagant and exploitative to hire someone to do what we were perfectly capable of doing ourselves. And just as I was uncomfortable telling a peon to make a photocopy, neither could I imagine telling a maid to peel my orange and butter my toast. But two things changed our outlook on maids: first, we saw that in this vast oversupply of labor, it's almost a social imperative for wealthier people to provide livelihoods for those who would otherwise have none. That's why Shankar would pay someone just to change a light bulb or tighten a screw. Because whole families were supported by the meager earnings such labor provided.

The second thing that changed our opinion of maids was realizing how wonderful it was to have one.

It was terrific. Once Ganga came into our lives, dirty dishes would just disappear from the sink. The toilet would suddenly be disinfected and shining. Clothes that might have languished at the bottom of the laundry basket instead appeared pressed and folded on our bed. Dust that had been building up in the corners when we left for work would be gone when we returned. Food would magically appear in the refrigerator. Sheets and towels would magically freshen. Toilet paper rolls would magically replenish. And all this with a maid only three days a week!

We originally hired Ganga solely because we'd read that it was the obligation of rich foreigners to do so; her cooking had been an unexpected windfall. We were initially quite uncomfortable telling her what to do, and our discomfort was exacerbated by the fact that a woman our age was calling us "sir" and "ma'am." (Such a difference the accident of geography makes: but for the country of our birth, Jenny and I were living the glamorous life of expat travel while Ganga had two kids and managed rich people's households for a living.) But as the benefits of having a maid revealed themselves, and we realized the relative lightness of Ganga's responsibilities as compared to most maids in the neighborhood, we grew at ease with our decision to employ her. I even began fantasizing about life with full-time help—or better yet, with the full complement of household staff that the folks living the lucky expat life in Lutyens's Delhi were surely enjoying. I imagined my staff lined up in the foyer at 6:01 p.m., when I'd march through my door. "Good evening, sir," they'd say in unison, knowing that my slippers, sherry, and pipe would be due at 6:02.

But Ganga made life pleasant enough, and that Mary Poppins lifestyle comes at a cost: we'd overhear the exhausted housewives—expat *and* local—commiserating over Khan Market coffees about their difficulties commanding platoons of maids, cooks, gardeners, drivers, guards, garbage collectors and toilet cleaners. Not only were there the challenges of making sure they were all doing their jobs properly—had the closet been dusted? was the toilet cleaned *below* the rim? did they put too much salt in the food again? my god, did they look through our underwear drawer?—but there was also the internal politics: this one refuses to take orders from that one, that one refuses to share food with this one, and all sorts of servant-on-servant power struggles.

Ganga's impact on our lives went beyond her dal makhani, though. She taught us about the responsibilities of those who are fortunate (even as we enjoyed the benefits that came with it). Ganga considered herself lucky in life, and her self-image manifested in the concern she showed not just for her family, and not just for Jenny and me, but for everyone less fortunate than her. She imparted her outlook to us, training us in recycling habits that far surpassed the mandates of the Bloomberg administration. Our copies of *The New Yorker* were saved for her children's English lessons. Our old clothes were given to her neighbors. Glass jars, torn purses, inside-out umbrellas—anything that could be reused, repaired, or repurposed was to be put aside for her thoughtful redistribution.

Especially food. This was, to her, a household's most valuable resource. When Jenny threw away a gallon-sized container of granola because she found a mouse dropping in it, Ganga took it out of our bin and gently chastened her, tactfully explaining that our view of spoiled food was not a universal one: "People still want it."

Shilpa, the bungalow's garbage maid, shared a similar outlook. One morning she rang our doorbell and, holding up a week-old container of yogurt she'd pulled from our trash, began shouting at us in Hindi. We couldn't understand her words, but we certainly got the gist.

We tried to be receptive to their training. Our challenge was with food that we were sure had spoiled in our refrigerator. Even though we knew people were hungry, we didn't want anyone getting sick from our moldy mangoes or the jar of liver pâté that I left mostly uneaten in the refrigerator for months because it was so incredibly gross. In these cases, we couldn't take the shame of Ganga or Shilpa's disapproval; we'd walk up Aurobindo Marg to throw it away ourselves, tossing our anonymous plastic bags and disappearing before anyone could connect us with such ostentatious waste, hoping that the cows would get to it before the ragpickers did.

★

Ragpickers are yet another manifestation of Delhi's labor situation. If there are rupees to be found in garbage bags, there are people whose livelihoods were structured around finding them. "Ragpickers" is a catch-all term for anyone who makes their living as a scavenger, whether they recover vegetable scraps to feed their goat or metal bits to sell to recyclers. As economic actors, ragpickers ensure that very little waste in Delhi is truly wasted—anything that can be broken down into component parts and sold for profit is done so by garbage maids like Shilpa, by kabadiwallahs who cycle around the neighborhoods, and even, as Sam Miller recounts in his book *Delhi: Adventures in a Megacity*, by the hordes of adults and children who pick over Delhi's massive landfills.

Unfortunately for all those actors, though, the cheap labor situation keeps a great deal of what Americans would consider trash from entering the waste stream at all. This is more than just Ganga's redistribution of our old socks; in a culture in which every rupee is considered against the potential recurrence of historic ruin, repairmen of all levels of cost and expertise exist to ensure anything short of a melted tiffin box can be repaired instead of thrown away. (And even my melted tiffin box was probably resurrected somewhere along the line.)

America has repairmen, of course. But our cost of labor drastically raises the price-point at which goods become candidates for repair: in the US, anything cheaper than a mid-range DVD player or a window air-conditioning unit doesn't make much sense to get fixed. This is obvious when walking down a Brooklyn sidewalk on trash pickup day: lining the streets are stereo speakers, blenders and old televisions that would mean business for any Delhi repairman but just aren't worth it in our economy. (It does create opportunities for creativity, though, like when I picked an old Macintosh computer out of the garbage, gutted it, filled it with dirt, planted flowers in it, and entered it into a local decorating competition. It was a finalist!) The same goes for clothes that don't fit: we'd stuff them into neighborhood charity boxes, despite knowing that the so-called charities were just selling them to Africa by the ton. Even furniture would just be put to the curb for the city to deal with, or for neighbors to collect before the city could get to it.

(I saw nothing wrong with this practice, but my grandparents certainly did. For years after they learned that the sofas in my college apartment had been scavenged from the sidewalk, they entertained themselves by sarcastically admiring every piece of discarded furniture we'd pass in their car. "Look at that one, Dave! No banana peels on it or anything. Want us to stop?" There were times when an item they'd point out would actually pique my interest, but even if I could have gotten it on the train back to the city, I knew they'd never let me hear the end of it; so I'd just laugh with them and gaze wistfully as we drove by.)

We never found any "good trash" in Delhi. Nothing good ever made it as far as the curb. If it was recyclable, someone would scavenge it. And if it was fixable, it would certainly be fixed. That goes for furniture and for computers, but it also goes for far cheaper items. I'd pass a half-dozen tailors in the market, each one of them capable of and eager to take my measurements, pop the seams on the too-big Indiana Jones T-shirt I'd bought in Thailand, and reassemble it to fit my figure for the cost of a spool of thread back home. I'd also pass by at least three electricians sitting in closet-sized shops overflowing with spools of wire and dusty motors from appliances long since disassembled. After just 150 rupees and two days, our toaster would be toasting again.

Of course, repairmen in Delhi have the same incentives as anyone else in the low end of the economy. So a month later, my T-shirt's stitches would fray, our toaster would short out once more, our water tank would stop automatically refilling, our air conditioner would break down, our backup power supply would fail, and each repairman would have another customer.

★

So why doesn't America have sidewalk tailors, human motion detectors and maids for the middle class? It's not because we're any more enlightened, egalitarian and morally superior. It's because in our economy, mechanical motion detectors are cheaper than human ones. Simple as that.

Which is why we think that India's days of cheap repairmen, red-light economies, child labor, and office peons are numbered. Because as India's economy grows, its middle class will swell, its supply of labor will equalize, and two things will happen: labor will command more money for menial jobs, and the market for menial employment will shrink as people find it more economical to do things for themselves. India's economy will feel more like America's.

It will take time, of course, and it will require staunching the flow of migrants to the city (240,000 people a year, by the city's estimates),[4] which will in turn require economic growth in other parts of the country to reduce migratory incentives. But we believe this will happen, and that much of what we wrote about in this chapter will cease to exist. This is the future we see for India: a far more prosperous

---

4. http://timesofindia.indiatimes.com/Cities/Delhi/Truth-behind-rising-infant-deaths-in-city/articleshow/4694480.cms

society in which more children have to do their own household chores but far fewer children live on the street.

We think that future generations of Indians will experience childhoods that mirror ours, including career paths that begin with lousy teenage jobs. I remember my colleague Anurag's reaction when I told him I'd spent the summer of my sixteenth year picking up discarded cups of tobacco spit at the movie theater: he angrily told me to stop lying, except he used words he wouldn't want me to put into print. "My grandmother would roll over in her grave," he told me, "if I had to sweep a movie theater." But this was the case: between the ages of sixteen and eighteen, I was employed to sweep movie theater floors, mop restaurants after closing time, and dig up weedy gardens in the hot sun. (I was also hired for a few wonderful months to sort old comic books at the local collectables shop. I worked alone in the back room with no supervision for a few hours after school each day, happily reading what Superman had been up to in the early 1980s before putting his bygone adventure in the appropriate box and moving on to Green Lantern.) Jenny followed a similarly mundane career path in her teens: she took telephone orders at a fast food pizza place, straightened hangers at a discount clothing shop, and cleared dirty dishes from tables in an Italian restaurant.

From Anurag's perspective, having grown up in an economy shaped by such a substantial surplus of labor, nobody with a future as a knowledge worker would have a past as a sweeper. Even the fact that I'd mow my neighbors' lawns for baseball card money was beyond his experience—not when there were so many people who'd do the same task to feed their family.

(Incidentally, Anurag was also horrified that I used to play in the sandbox as a child. "Indian mothers," he told me, "would never allow their kids to play in the dirt.")

Such is the middle-class lifestyle in the US. But this is a relatively recent phenomenon. Just a few generations ago, America's economic structure looked different. My dad's father was a dry goods peddler, and my mom's father was a bartender. Jenny's grandfather on her mother's side was a poorly educated forester and part-time deputy sheriff who immigrated from Italy. Jenny's dad never knew his own father, but the family that adopted him after his mother passed away was of equally modest means. None of our grandparents would have been surprised by the intensity with which my Delhi co-workers approached their jobs—because for them, the memory of war and migration and calamity was fresh in their minds as well, and the consequences of failure were also perfectly clear.

Two generations removed from our grandparents' suffering, the trajectory of the US economy has shifted to where Jenny and I are today: complacent enough to sacrifice our incomes in New York for lower-paying jobs overseas, and complacent enough still that I could quit working for a few months altogether to write this book.

We're sure that India will see a similar evolution.

With India's middle class growing so rapidly—the McKinsey Global Institute expects another 290 million of them by 2025[5]—Anurag's children will surely be the last generation to rise to prosperity without having to endure

---

5. http://www.atimes.com/atimes/South_Asia/IF01Df04.html

the indignities of working in fast food. And they may also be the last to see men supporting families by selling coconut slices at traffic signals. Even today, a generation of young, educated, English-speaking twenty-somethings are tearing movie tickets or taking popcorn orders in Delhi theaters. They will rise the corporate ladder in the next decades, and their career paths will mean the end of the taboo against lousy teenage jobs even as more of the poorest Indians are absorbed into the formal economy. Their children will be spending their teenage years flipping dosas, making cappuccinos, and cleaning their own rooms just like we did.

11

Expat Issues: We'll Complain Anyway

Back when we were still surrounded by supermarkets that spanned acres and a Starbucks on every corner, Jenny and I imagined India as the ultimate in adventure tourism: a land of elephant-powered mass transit, of monkey pickpockets, of giant spiders guarding booby-trapped temples, and of heat that would melt our belt buckles even as the food melted our tongues. Adventure in the true Indiana Jones sense of the word. For many of our friends too, and for countless other Americans, the mere thought of visiting India got their eyes shining and their hearts pounding. (Except for Americans like my grandfather, for whom the same thought got their stomachs churning and their fingernails gripping even tighter to their living room armchairs.)

Knowing India only from the news, the movies and the posters affixed to the walls of Indian restaurants, we expected a land in which mosquito nets have to be worn at all times and even CEOs commute to work hanging off the side of a train. Risk! Danger! Excitement! Never mind moving there, even a two-week visit would be the adventure of a lifetime.

But the adventure Americans seek in India is not to raft the Himalayas, surf the Ganges, or rappel down the Taj Mahal. We seek far greater thrills: to ride in an autorickshaw! To shop in a spice market! To travel in an overnight train! To experience what a billion people live through every day, in other words. We fly twenty straight hours and pay thousands of dollars specifically to take pictures of ourselves doing what most Indians would consider chores. The American mindset when we step off the plane that very first time is an expectation that everything that happens from that moment onward would blow our conservative Midwestern relatives' minds.

And so, arriving in India with a sense of grandeur overinflated by the gasps of friends and family who can't believe we actually have the guts to make the trip, a very interesting phenomenon occurs in Western travelers: we refuse to notice all the other Western travelers around us. Americans in India collectively lose their ability to perceive the color white.

We've predicated our egos on the belief that we are the natural heirs to Magellan and De Soto wholly by virtue of buying those plane tickets and queuing up for visas in the India consulate. With our egos set on pioneer mode, it would actually be quite disappointing to walk around Delhi and see all those other Magellans and De Sotos with their khaki shorts, meticulous sunscreen, and *Lonely Planets* open to the exact same page as ours.

Which is why we'd pretend not to notice each other.

Jenny and I called this behavior "gora evasion." Goras are relatively rare in India, enough so that everyone wants a closer look when they spot one—even Jenny and I, after a few months in the country, would stare at them just like everyone else on the street. "Whoa, look—goras!" we'd whisper to each other, jerking our heads in their direction, the intensity of our ensuing stares (like that of every passing auto driver) increasing in direct proportion to the inappropriateness of their attire. And then the disappointment would set in. "This neighborhood isn't even listed in *Lonely Planet*. How the hell did *they* find it?"

The presence of goras in what we thought was an unknown neighborhood popped our bubble. It told us that we were not the cleverest travelers in all of India. So while we would stare at goras, we wouldn't let them catch us staring. We would surreptitiously study them as judgementally as we could, ridiculing them for any naïveté we could spot or manufacture ("Ha! They're looking at a map!" "Ha! They're, uh, wearing socks!") so we could congratulate ourselves on our own sophistication. If they happened to look over, we'd pretend we were studying the trees. No eye contact, that's for sure.

Nor would they want us to acknowledge them. Every American on a grand Indian adventure wants to think they're the only ones. Our self-images rest on the perception that there won't be any other American faces spoiling the photos we send to the folks back home. This is the American pioneer mythology drilled into us since grade school: the spirit of Columbus discovering a continent with millions of people already living on it. We strap on our backpacks and march boldly forward into the empty unknown, refusing to acknowledge our fellow travelers (much less the fact that the people who live in our empty unknown drink cappuccinos and watch *Friends*). The very last thing any American traveler wants is a reminder that India had over one million other American visitors in 2011 alone[1]— especially if that reminder comes in the form of insincere pleasantries exchanged with a smiling yokel whose son's girlfriend's sister turns out to have been in the rival high school marching band back home. Gora evasion is how we dismiss evidence of other goras already existing around us like so many indigenous civilizations.

Thus, when two goras converge on a Delhi road, there are no hellos. No polite nods. Not even the raised eyebrows and tight smiles of two co-workers meeting each other in the office restroom for the second time in one morning. If gora eyes happen to meet, all involved sets look quickly away.

Jenny and I have both experienced and practiced gora evasion in the alleys near Chandni Chowk, on passing houseboats in the Kerala backwaters, while jostling for viewing angles in the Bharatpur Bird Sanctuary, and even outside the Reebok Store in Saket Select Citywalk Mall,

---

1. http://tourism.gov.in/TourismDivision/AboutDivision.aspx?
   Name=Market%20Research%20and%20Statistics

where the two of us and the two of them mutually maintained our illusions of isolation while Kenny G. warbled at us over the mall's loudspeakers.

The more Frostian the point of convergence, the more comically awkward gora evasion becomes. On our visit to Mumbai, we found ourselves walking down a long, desolate road on the way down from Malabar Hill. It was twilight on that wooded lane, and the few people we saw were outnumbered by the giant bats swooping purposefully on two-foot wings. In the distance, at the bottom of the hill, two goras materialized: a guy and a girl, coming our way on the same sidewalk. Their very existence deflated the mystery of the trail we'd hoped to blaze, just as our very existence stripped their intended path of all the drama it might have held for them.

Jenny and I had been discussing our theory of gora evasion for weeks, and on this moment in Mumbai we decided to put it to the test. As we grew closer, we intentionally ignored our instinctual aversion to our counterparts, and we continued to gaze pleasantly ahead.

The other two, meanwhile, looked in all directions but ours. And then, just at the point where two pairs of polite people would smile and nod in every circumstance back home, that's when the guy elaborately pointed to something above and behind and to the left of Jenny and me. And they both studiously contemplated this point in space as the four of us passed each other, greetings not exchanged, illusion of adventure still unbroken. They were still the only goras in Mumbai.

★

All of which is to say that we stopped feeling like pioneers once we realized that Delhi's expat population, while a small percentage of the whole, was still far too big for us ever to be the first to discover a restaurant, explore a neighborhood, or find some unknown wonder of the world. Foreigners were certainly rare enough to be stared at, but they were plentiful enough that we were able to identify a number of patterns in our sightings of them. We came up with three categorizations of expats in Delhi, in fact: three broad stereotypes that were fairly accurate in predicting how people got here, what they were doing, and whether or not they'd be our friends.

The first category of expats was the short-term tourists. They were shell-shocked newbies wearing cameras that were too bulky and shorts that were too short. They were twenty-something girlfriends in town for the wedding of a college roommate, staying in the bride's house in south Delhi, insisting that they not be fussed over but secretly reveling in the maid turning down their beds and preparing fresh mango every morning. They were hippie travelers keeping it real in Paharganj flophouses, seeking bhang for Thursday night Sufi music at Nizamuddin, planning trips to Varanasi to smoke hash with actual sadhus, and resenting their dads for insisting they moved back to Long Island to work for the family investment bank. They were retired people on packaged tours grimacing at the beggars, shoving away the touts, pursing their lips to keep out the germs, and fantasizing about the bar back at the hotel.

This first category is expansive—let's not forget spinsters on chaperoned adventures, photographers on poverty tourism, brave Midwesterners hopped up on malaria pills—but there are a few shared behavior patterns: they stick to the main sights, they fear the tap water even more than we did, they go on day trips to Agra and come back disgusted, and then they board the train to Jaipur and return to Delhi only to fly out. These short-term expats were the most evasive of all, refusing to acknowledge their fellow foreigners even when the waiters at Karim's sat them directly across from us.

The next categorization of expats encompassed the medium-term postings: the NGO interns, the Hindi students, the Rhodes scholars, the blossoming corporate cogs, the middle managers, and anyone else living in Delhi longer than a few months but not long enough to have their furniture shipped over. Like me, most of these medium-term residents were worth a plane ticket to Delhi to their sponsoring organization but were not seen as valuable enough to receive the gold treatment. If we had one unifying factor beyond the duration of our residence, it was this: none of us could afford membership to American Community Support Association, which at the time opened up the US embassy's amenities to its members for around $1,400 a year. Members (and their lucky, lucky guests) got access to everything Delhi's Tucson-on-the-Yamuna has to offer: its swimming pool, its beef-serving restaurant, its Budweiser-serving bar, and its Western standards of cleavage acceptability.

The long-term folks relaxing at the embassy were our third categorization, and they were in a league beyond ours. They were the heads of NGOs, the country leads for big corporations, the diplomats, the bylined foreign correspondents, the teachers at the international schools, the Westerners who married Indians and moved back with them. They lived in tree-lined central Delhi, in "farmhouses" with private pools on the outskirts of the city, or above the fray in shining Gurgaon. These were the lucky expats with beautiful cars and articulate drivers. And they existed on a plane through which our Delhi vector rarely passed. We'd naïvely concluded that between attending a few Democrats Abroad meetings *and* being active on the foreigner email lists, we knew most of the expats in Delhi; but when we showed up at the embassy's Presidential Inauguration party, we couldn't believe how many non-Indians also lived in India.

Between Delhi's two resident categories, there were variations and outliers, of course: some NGO heads lived modestly in north Delhi while other medium-term students shacked up in luxurious service apartments. But one constant is that the two resident categories almost always kept to separate social circles, and only the most outgoing members of each group were able to bridge the gap.

This divide is due to one of the biggest perils facing foreigners living in Delhi: expat turnover. Every six months, it seemed, everyone left.

And this turnover meant that for expats—and for medium-term expats especially—it was a bad idea to grow complacent with one's social circle. Because the moment one looked around a dinner table and thought, "I've got all the friends I need in Delhi!" is the moment when the going-away parties would begin: dissertations would be complete, postings would conclude, businesses would reorganize, or people would just miss Arby's too much.

One guy I met told me a story of expats' lament that was the worst I'd heard: he'd gotten himself a girlfriend, spent six blissful months locked in his bedroom, broke up, and then returned to the Delhi social scene only to discover that everyone else he knew had moved away in the meantime.

We personally went through three rounds of expat friends. In round one, we'd hardly gotten to know Tony, Parker, Karem, and Samantha before they jetted off; and though we quickly replaced them with Mike and Dana, we were attending the second round of going away parties soon enough. We replaced Mike and Dana with Scott and Sally late enough in our stay in Delhi that we became their statistic: Scott and Sally were the ones attending our going away party, followed shortly by their goodbyes for Suzanne, Michelle, Cailin, and Leslie, the last of our round three crew. "We began to feel as if we were the last men standing in Delhi," Scott told me.

But Scott and Sally, who ended up putting in nineteen months in Delhi, learned from our experience. "After a while," Scott said, "we wouldn't consider friends who weren't going to be around for more than a year." Natrece and Ashwin became their new Dave and Jenny, but only after the intended duration of that couple's stay in Delhi satisfied Scott and Sally's vetting process.

This social reality is exactly why so few long-term expats socialized with medium-termers like us: it just wasn't worth it for them to befriend people who would disappear so soon. This wasn't snobbery, but rather the harsh lessons one learns in Delhi's social economics. Delhi's a challenging city for expats, so people living here naturally seek out those who are enduring the same sort of Delhi struggle. For the long-termers, that meant people who knew the names of the city's politicians, who recognized the city's foreign correspondents when they were spotted in the bars, and who could describe Delhi as it was before Café Coffee Day made air conditioning so easy to find. What insight could we offer them, those of us who tended to love Delhi vocally and intensely and then, just when our second summer began to kick in, pick up and move to Singapore?

The few times we met long-term expats, our pleasant conversations would degrade when our accidental greenhorn sentiments ("You're so brave to actually drive your own car in Delhi's traffic!") exposed our limited-time stay in the city. Even as they'd respond, we could see that we were already fading in their eyes like a photo of Marty McFly as they scanned the room for more relevant conversation partners. ("It's not so difficult as you . . . oops, excuse me, the *HT*'s man is here and I have to ask him about the referendum.")

Don't think that we only sought friendships with expats. Far from it. We were in India to meet Indians, and Jenny and I made great friends among neighbors, co-workers, and EOID members. But we needed expat friends as well, because we needed to talk to people who were going through the same challenges. Which is another reason the medium-term and long-term expat groups didn't mix very easily: we the medium-termers would want to commiserate about the awkwardness of ordering peons or to show off the faded kalavas still tied around our wrists from the pooja we'd attended months before. Long-term folks were far more interested in discussing techniques for acquiring a Delhi driver's license, determining whom to bribe to open a cupcake bakery, and sorting out passport issues for their newborns. We all needed friends who could empathize accordingly.

★

There is, however, one gloomy rite of passage that both medium-term and long-term expats can discuss with equal melancholy. But before I recite our tales of grief, I must first encourage any Indians reading this book to prepare their eye muscles for a great deal of rolling. Because I am indeed going to spend the next few pages complaining about the one instance that foreigners must deal with the Indian bureaucracy. And I won't once appreciate the fact that locals have to deal with a lifetime of it.

That being said: woe are we expats for having to endure the FRRO!

For expats with employment visas, our invitation to visit the Foreigner Regional Registration Office is printed on our passports and date-stamped the moment we set foot in the country. "Registration required within fourteen days of arrival in India," it says. Which means that no sooner do we get settled in our offices than we're required to abandon them for a day of stamping and shuffling and standing and squirming and sighing.

Delhi's FRRO office is located just a few hundred meters south of the Hyatt Hotel, mockingly close to the hotel's efficient air-conditioning and Italian espresso machines. Nevertheless, it's extremely difficult to locate for those foreigners whose companies haven't hired a tout to lead them through the maze and grease palms along the way. The pale blue sign that announces its presence is hidden behind another sign of some other agency that's been erected right in front of it. The building itself is one of many squat cement government buildings in the complex. To reach it, one must pass a burned-out hulk of a taxicab rusting in the parking lot; it's hard not to assign symbolic meaning to the wreck.

The first stop for registrants is the pre-queue: that is, the queue in which one waits to secure a spot in the actual queue. If one arrives before the office opens, there's even a queue for the pre-queue, with a sign-in sheet that is completely ignored when the doors are opened and everyone stampedes in. At the desk at the end of the pre-queue, a registrant is assigned to one of a handful of counters. And then it's just a matter of waiting as comfortably as possible on the hard plastic chairs, hopefully in front of a fan, with nothing to do but cringe at the loud Americans bemoaning their misery with the spittle-flecked bitterness of which Americans are so exceedingly capable (I find it so much more dignified to complain in literary form), and listen for the glorious sound of that magic number being called.

It's a long wait, though. Each counter is manned by an expressionless clerk with a fondness for unannounced chai breaks and a clear aversion against typing at a rate perceptible to the eye. Each transaction takes a minimum of fifteen minutes, assuming that each registrant's paperwork is in order, that his or her passport photographs are the acceptable width and height, and that everything is photocopied at least twice. I failed the latter two requirements my first time around—as it turns out, not all passport photographs are created equal and not all government offices are kind enough to have a photocopier behind the counter. I had to trek down the street to a small market where various entrepreneurs have set up photo booths and Xerox machines for this very purpose.

The FRRO has all the elements of the perfect bureaucracy: soulless lighting, chairs engineered for backaches, and automaton clerks drained of every last drop of empathy. It's like any American city's Department of Motor Vehicles, but without the joy. My co-workers had advised me to stash a few hundred-rupee notes in various pockets so I could pay bribes without revealing the full contents of my wallet, but the one element of bureaucracy the FRRO actually did seem to lack was corruption: at no point did I spot an opening to bribe my way out.

My conversations with other expats taught me that there was actually a method for defeating the FRRO: one can use the momentum of the bureaucracy against itself. Unfortunately, I learned of this bureaucratic judo only in time for the last of the four days I could have been contributing to India's GDP but was instead getting paid to stand in line at this office. Here's what I did: once I got my counter assignment from the clerk at the end of the pre-queue—my assignment was C18, the eighteenth person in line for counter C—I turned on my heels and walked out of the FRRO. I took an auto to Green Park and had lunch at Evergreen. I spent an hour on my computer at Barista. I took a walk through the nearby monuments. I relaxed in the shade and watched kids who should have been in school play cricket. And then I moseyed back to the FRRO, cut directly in front of C29 and C30 despite their glares, waited patiently for the clerk to finish with C28, and then showed her my number. Though I hadn't been there when she called my number two hours prior, this is the way bureaucracy sees the world: having a number is more important than actually waiting my turn.

★

Why did I have to go to the FRRO four times when foreigners are only required to register once? Officially, it was because my company changed its name when we split from our former sister company, which required a new visa and new registration; and then twice again because my tax papers were in question. But I believe the true reason I had to visit so many times is karmic retribution: I was being punished for the time I told Murali that I'd be spending a full day in a queue at the US embassy to drop off my passport for renewal, and another full day again two weeks later to pick it up. I knew that Murali's expectations of government bureaucracy would lead him to believe me when, in fact, those two transactions actually took fifteen minutes each.

So karma paid me back with four miserable visits to the FRRO. ("Four visits!" I can still hear Murali gasping in mock horror when I made the mistake of whining about this to him. "You should ask President Bush to invade us immediately!") And karma's divine will was manifested by a finicky clerk who decided that the FRRO's mandate to process my registration extended to making sure my taxes were paid. The little scribble she wrote in my registration book obliged me to return at the conclusion of the fiscal year with proof of my contribution to the Indian treasury; and another clerk's subsequent scribble on my third visit a few months later obliged me to return again with even more paperwork.

It would have been much easier to just slip my income through the treasury's cracks. After all, Edward Luce's *In Spite of the Gods* claims that only nineteen percent of Indians pay taxes. And no police officer ever visited my house to examine my FRRO registration booklet as they were supposed to, so nobody would have known if I hadn't gone back with my tax receipts. But I consider myself an honest fellow, so I made the effort necessary to contribute whatever I owed to fund the government's bodyguard regiments for VIP politicians and gardener corps for their taxpayer-supplied houses.

My company automatically withheld around twelve percent of my salary, but my tax bracket demanded more than that. So I relied on the accountancy services of one Mr. G., a certified accountant who was friends with the finance guy at my company. Mr. G. helped me get my PAN card (my taxpayer ID) when I first arrived and, at the end of the fiscal year a few months later, helped me bequeath what seemed like far too much money to the

Indian government considering how little of the year I'd been in the country.

For the next year's tax obligation, I knew I had to act in advance. The Indian fiscal year ends on March 31, and we were planning to leave the country for good on April 1. I was terrified that our timing might raise eyebrows at passport control, and I had visions of airport customs officials tying me to a chair in the basement of Indira Gandhi airport and demanding that I write an enormous check to the Income Tax Department of India right then and there. (Or, perhaps, simply deposit a lesser amount of cash directly to the Bank of Rajesh the Customs Officer.)

So when January rolled around, I duly informed Mr. G. of my leaving date, making it clear how critical it was to get my accounts settled before I departed. But despite my insistent emails, phone calls and SMSes, it wasn't until the second week of March—just two weeks before our departure—when I finally found myself in the same room with him. I handed over my papers and explained for the tenth time that my departure was growing more imminent by the second. His mouth formed a little shocked "o" as he looked up from my tax papers and said—and, dear reader, he actually said this—"April first? We should have started this a long time ago!"

Which is exactly why I'd hedged my bets against him. At that point, my meeting with Mr. G. was only out of courtesy, because the estimated payment he'd emailed me a few days earlier seemed so absurdly high that I had gotten a second opinion. I'd queried the expat email lists and found an accountant who specialized in foreigners. And while this new accountant's estimate for what I owed was still many multiples of India's average per capita income, it was many multiples less than what Mr. G. wanted me to pay.

So after Mr. G. assured me there was no possible way that my tax obligation could be any lower than his estimate, I handed him a check for his services and assured him that I'd send over my forms the next day. And then, once he was gone, coward that I am, I severed our business relationship via SMS, making up some story that my friend's uncle had volunteered to do my taxes for free. Still, my hand shook slightly as I signed the check for the amount my new accountant assured me I had to pay; it still seemed far too high when considered against the general cost of living in India and the specific state of our finances.

Because, believe it or not, our finances weren't doing as good as we'd hoped.

We'd calculated my monthly salary when we first arrived in India. And after we deducted our expected housing, food and transportation costs, we admired the amount we expected to save and then set about learning how to calculate the forty-to-one exchange rate on the fly. We successfully trained our minds to value mangoes in terms of Granny Smiths and samosas in terms of Big Macs, and then we never gave the exchange rate a second thought beyond sighing happily whenever we remembered to consider a Café Coffee Day double espresso on a Starbucks continuum. So it was a cruel bucket of fiscal water poured on heads happily ignorant of the dynamics of global finance when Dipankar slapped me heavily on the back one day and gleefully informed me that the exchange rate was now forty-four-to-one.

This was terrible news for me. Even though I saw life in dollars, I was getting paid in rupees. My salary—as expressed in US Treasury bonds, shares in Google stock, rides on the New York City subway, doughnuts purchased on Seventh Avenue in Brooklyn, bets on baseball with my brother Eric, birthday spa packages for my sister Susan, and anything else I'd use dollars to buy—had just gone down by ten percent.

What caused this shift? Economists might point to the global financial crisis, the price of oil, a butterfly flapping its wings outside the offices of the Reserve Bank of India, or the failure of Anoop Desai to win *American Idol*. Whatever the case, it all coalesced into a sudden macroeconomic buggering.

I refused to acknowledge this rate shift as permanent. For months I resisted changing the cell containing .025 in our financial spreadsheet, afraid to see what the new .0222 would mean for all the money we'd hoped to save. Instead, I began to watch the exchange rates for good news as closely as I watched Facebook for high school friends to post unflattering pictures of themselves. Reloading the finance sites dozens of times a day, I'd cheer a tenth-of-a-percentage movement in my favor and curse any hundredth-of-a-percentage plunge in the opposite direction. And I'd follow either shift with quick calculations as to how much (usually expressed in fives of dollars) our savings had gained or lost in that single day.

Jenny and I decided to delay transferring our money back to our US account while the exchange rate was forty-four-to-one. We feared locking in our losses. So naturally the rupee hit fifty-to-one a few months later, and we mourned for the good ol' days of forty-four.

I complain about my tax burden and my forex losses, but I'm also fully aware that I made far more money than most. My salary was justified in terms of the cost of living in the country I'd eventually return to—I had to save for life there, not here. But it still made me feel awkward with respect to the cost of living in the country I was in and with respect the co-workers who surely knew how much more I made than they. So my good fortune was accompanied by an overwhelming sense of guilt: guilt about my high salary, my nice apartment, my private taxi, my reliable air conditioning, my uninterrupted water supply, my precious Apple computer, and the fact that I could go back to New York City any time I wanted. I felt guilty about my very accident of being born an American, and the thirty years I'd spent being unaware of just how lucky I was.

Most of all, I felt guilty that I'd arrived in Delhi thinking that everyone's everyday struggle was going to be my grand adventure. It was Western privilege for me to take smiling tourist pictures in the back of an autorickshaw, because I could always call a cab, or lease a car, or fly to America. It was Western privilege for me to blog about how brave I was to eat in an actual dhaba, because I could afford McDonalds, or Park Balluchi in Hauz Khas village, or Masala Art in the Taj Palace Hotel. Given the sheer odds against being born into American privilege, the actions I perceived as broadening my cultural horizons—buying vegetables from an old lady! asking a poor tailor to repair a button on my shirt!—could justifiably be perceived by everyone else as poverty tourism.

My guilt manifested in an exaggerated pretence of humility that I wore as often as I could, as if arguing with the chaiwallah who withheld the single rupee of change he owed me would be too evocative of the world's geopolitical inequities. I'd play down my good fortune and my spendthrift ways. I'd deflate my salary, my rent, and the salary we paid Ganga to anyone who asked. I'd find myself fibbing when Indians would contrast my country with theirs, like when Birender asked if Europe had as much traffic as Delhi did. As we both stared at the sea of motionless tail lights stretched before us, my instinct was to dispel his national inadequacy; and not only did I not clarify my continent of origin, but I gently assured him that Europe's traffic problems were worse.

But I never felt more guilty about my country's place in the world than when Murali was unable to attend our company's annual creative directors' meeting in France. As an Indian, Murali had to apply a month in advance for his visa; whereas I, as an American, could cross the border at any time without prior permission. So when Murali's visa wasn't granted in time, I was sent to Nice in his place, bearing the presentation he'd intended to deliver along with such overwhelming guilt on top of my everyday guilt that it took all the Camembert and Pinot Noir I could consume to look him in the eyes when I got back to Delhi.

★

We didn't have it nearly as good as many of the expats in Delhi. For instance, we managed to score only a handful of the coveted invitations onto the US embassy grounds, and at no time did we experience the joy of swimming in the embassy's pool. So we had to find other ways to cool down on Delhi's hottest weekends. We considered at one point attending the Sunday night pool party at the Park Hotel near Connaught Place which, we'd heard, was open to non-guests; but I was sure there was a rule dictating the minimum bicep size necessary to gain entrance. So for those times when even the green waters of the ancient Hauz Khas village water tank started to look refreshing, we did two things: we bricked up our consciences against the inequities of swimming in a landlocked city with chronic water shortages, and then we shelled out a fortune to swim at one of the five-star hotels.

A few of Delhi's top hotels will, for what most Indians would consider a nice weekly salary, give outsiders a few hours' access to the facilities that their guests rarely make use of anyway. On those few times we splurged, the blue water and white lounge chairs were ours alone, empty but for the groundsmen discreetly watching Jenny from behind some hedges. There were 125 licensed swimming pools in the city[2] when we lived there, but nearly all of them were in the hands of hotels, embassies, or the exceedingly wealthy, so swimming was a rarefied pastime outside those who'd dive into the ancient stepwells or wade into the Yamuna.

The city does run a few pools, including one at Siri Fort, the sports complex near our flat. Demand is understandably high, though, so they only allowed one hundred people in the water during each of the eleven one-hour daily shifts.

2. http://timesofindia.indiatimes.com/articleshow/13201155.cms

Siri Fort's pool was both within walking distance and far more affordable than a five-star hotel, but Jenny assumed that the sheer number of boys and men to be found in the swimming complex—combined with the presumed rarity of foreigners wearing swimsuits—would be the ocular equivalent of her walk up the Jama Masjid minaret. For her, a cold shower was far less uncomfortable.

So we learned other ways to beat the heat. One of the best was Indian-style clothes: loose and flowing, they made the climate much more bearable, capturing cooling breezes without sticking to sweaty skin. Jenny took advantage of this much more than I: the kurtas I'd bought when I first arrived migrated to the back of my closet when I realized I'd be the only one at the office wearing one. But Jenny found Indian-style clothing to be fashionable, comfortable, and demure. And it was critical for Jenny that she cover her skin—not just to keep it out of the sun, but to ensure auto drivers kept their eyes where they belonged. In Mumbai or Pune, it might be slightly more acceptable to dress like Bollywood starlets, but Delhi's cultural conservatism meant that any skin she left bare would be burned both by the sun and by the concentrated attention of the city's men.

Although she really couldn't win either way. On her last day of work in Delhi, Jenny decided to mark the occasion by dressing in a full Indian ensemble: a bright blue salwar-kameez ensemble complete with a matching blue dupatta. As she and her co-workers walked through the neighborhood on their way to her farewell lunch, the men stared and made catcalls louder and more openly than they ever had when she just wore Western clothes.

★

Aside from buying Indian clothes, Jenny spent our first weeks in Delhi buying household goods for our new flat. Every day I'd solicit co-workers' opinions as to where to find certain household items, and every day Jenny would run all over the city following their suggestions: Lajpat Nagar for kitchen stuff, Amar Colony for furniture, Sarojini Nagar for carrom boards, and the roadsides near Saket for crockery. Sometimes our requests for assistance baffled my colleagues in their simplicity, like when I asked where I could buy superglue. "Everywhere!" was Dipankar's immediate, unhelpful, and entirely accurate response.

He was right: superglue was found in stationery stores, and stationery stores were found everywhere. But because we didn't have stationery stores where we came from (they'd long since been run out of business by office supply chains), we never thought to look in them.

Eventually, though we realized that almost everything Jenny searched for during those first few months was available within walking distance. In fact, nearly everything we could have wanted short of Old El Paso canned refried beans was available in Hauz Khas. It took us so long to figure this out, though, because we hadn't reached the second phase of awareness yet.

Our first phase of awareness began the moment we stepped out of the Delhi airport: we were immediately overwhelmed by everything that we saw. This first phase consisted of gape-mouthed staring while dodging beggars, skirting black puddles, scowling at those who stared back at us, cursing those who touched us, and being almost wholly unable to extend our attention beyond the honking, the traffic and the muck on the road. Hauz Khas market held more dangers to us in this phase than it did shopping opportunities: autos screeched around blind corners, water tankers barreled down the street with their payloads splashing out in their wake, holes in the sidewalk wanted nothing more than to turn our ankles, and electrical wires dangled at eye level, threatening to muss our hair at best and zap a million volts into it at worst.

This first phase was one of total sensory overload of wondering if certain grumpy family members hadn't been right: maybe we would have been better off if we'd stayed back home.

Eventually though, we began to understand the rhythm of the city, and we moved into our second phase of awareness. In this phase, the distractions no longer assumed cognitive priority. Now we could step around cows without noticing, brush off beggars without feeling guilty, ignore those who stared at us, and accept India's narrower definition of personal space. We stopped whirling our heads towards every bus barreling towards us. This new-found ability to passively process the foreground let us appreciate the background details that we'd missed the first dozen times: cryptic shrines, frangipani trees, street chai, hidden monuments, and conversations with people we would have previously dismissed as touts. Our feet could now navigate by instinct, and Hauz Khas market's hazards became a lower priority in our brains. This freed up enough cognitive bandwidth to actually process what we saw in store windows: hey, look, this place sells pillows!

In this phase of awareness, what had been shockingly foreign became comfortably mundane. That which once exhilarated us became white noise. And this let us see more of what the locals saw and experience more what the locals experienced. In fact, we'd often forget that the first phase of awareness had existed at all until we interacted with those who hadn't yet transcended it—like when my parents emerged pale from their first autorickshaw ride. Jenny and I looked at their ashen faces and realized that we no longer thought twice about reaching our destination un-splattered on the grill of an oncoming bus.

It was in this phase that we noticed something behind the India that was waving its arms to capture our attention: another India, a parallel India, that was quietly going about its business with no interest in us at all. Beyond the initial India that had shocked us, and beyond the subsequent India that we now had the context to appreciate, there was a further India still. It was active in the vacant lots, bustling in the alleyways, and occupying any vacuum of formal retail. In fact, anywhere we least expected to find commerce, that's exactly where this parallel India would be. Like between a fence and the bumpers of the cars parked outside the Café Coffee Day in Hauz Khas market. That's the last place we'd expect to find a parallel café, but that's exactly where a chaiwallah was squatting at his burner, dispensing tea at four rupees a cup.

He was a complement to Café Coffee Day, not a competitive threat. His target market would never spend half their day's wages on imported Italian espresso. In fact, his whole revenue stream probably came from drivers who were waiting for their bosses enjoying the air conditioning inside. There, in the last place people like us would think to look, that's exactly where his customers would expect him to be.

Our eyes were now opened wider, and we began to see this parallel economy everywhere. We saw tailors and barbers in the alleys behind clothing stores and day spas. We saw dhabas just around the corner from five-star restaurants. Clothes-laden wagons were parked only a few hundred meters past Saket Citywalk Mall. On the rear side of the brand-name storefronts at Yusuf Sarai market was a bustling alley with a much different clientele shopping in much cheaper stores. Even across the street from Khan Market was a run-down collection of hardware stores and electronics vendors. Inexperienced tourists would wander over, get confused, glance behind them at the recognizable brands, and hustle back to the appropriate side of the road.

Once we saw these parallel patterns, we realized why a pushcart vendor laden with fashion and electronics accessories always set up his shop on the road between our flat and the market. "What a poor location for a business!" Jenny and I had said to each other when we first saw him. We'd never shop for socks, belts and mobile phone cases at the location where he stood. He should be in the shade. He should be in the market.

But because a sun-baked spot on a busy road was the least attractive place for us, that's exactly where his customers would think to look for him.

The parallel India extends far beyond clothes, food, sidewalk haircuts, and alley dentistry. Though Westerners are eternally obsessed with finding the "real" India, our holy *Lonely Planet* offered no hints that there existed an India not aligned to Western tourists. Like Govardhan, for instance: a city near Agra where ten million people converge each year to hike thirteen miles around a hill that Lord Krishna lifted with his little finger to protect his people from the rains.[3] There's nothing about Govardhan in any of the tourist books we owned—which isn't a dig at *Lonely Planet*, but rather an illustration of how separately the two Indias run. Govardhan must have a huge tourist infrastructure to feed and house and transport ten million people less than ninety miles from where we lived, but we never noticed any hint of it.

The more we experienced life in India, the clearer it became how very little we actually understood of it. This was the lesson of our second phase of awareness: greater context actually meant less comprehension.

And this was a very liberating lesson, because once we knew how much we'd never know, we were able to appreciate India simply for what it was.

For instance, just before we left India for Singapore, we decided to spend three weeks touring south India. It was three weeks of local buses, five-dollar hotel rooms, and thirty-five-rupee all-you-can-eat bus station thalis to give us our fill of India before we moved on. And it was on the longest of our long bus rides around Tamil Nadu (an eight-hour journey from Pondicherry to Karaikkudi) that I had an experience that made me realize just how comfortable I'd grown with India and just how much I'd miss it: the bus's conductor spent five minutes leaning on me while conversing with another passenger.

---

3. http://www.thaindian.com/newsportal/uncategorized/annual-fair-at-goverdhan-ends_100215091.html

I'll make this picture clearer. Jenny was sitting in the window seat, I was sitting in the aisle seat, and the conductor—perhaps thirty years old, thin, with a bushy mustache and an even more impressive pompadour rising a few dramatic inches above his forehead—planted his right buttock on my seatback and his left buttock on my shoulder, and he spent five minutes discussing with the guy across from me the fare, the destination and, I assume, mutual friends, distant relations, the BJP's prospects for the next election, the Reserve Bank of India's latest economic forecasts, and the potential impact of Twitter on Indian political discourse.

I was not uncomfortable. I was not upset. In fact, it was the opposite: for the full five minutes, I was flattered to be treated as one of the guys instead of as a delicate American tourist demanding special consideration lest I decide to sue somebody. Two weeks after leaving the workplace in which I'd spent so many grueling hours, I suddenly felt an intense nostalgia for Murali putting his arm around me as he told a dirty joke, for Soumya squished into my side as we rode to a client meeting, and for Dipankar and his impromptu back rubs. My co-workers were my brothers in those instances, and I was the conductor's brother in this one. Had I not had those wonderful eighteen months with my co-workers, I doubt I'd have appreciated that stranger's butt so much.

★

The third phase of awareness began only when we left India: we're now terrifically nostalgic for the stuff that terrified us in phase one.

12

The Change We Wish
to See

Our second-to-last day living in India was spent selling our excess possessions. Our exercise bike went to a guy from the Austrian embassy, who drove off with it jammed precariously in his trunk and cantilevered a few unsteady feet over the road; I'm sure it fell out on his way home. Our potted plants went to a Gurgaon housewife who sent her driver to pick them up despite our warnings that she should probably see them first. ("Our bamboo tree is either recovering or dying," we told her. "We're not sure which.") Our stereo went to Scott and Sally's yoga instructor, who casually negotiated my asking price down to half of what I'd wanted and still somehow made me feel guilty about charging so much.

Everything we hadn't been able to sell went to Ganga: our bathroom scale, our unwanted paperbacks, our floor pillows, our plastic stools, our broken iPod speakers, a few black trash bags worth of bedding, and all our leftover canned goods and spices. We helped Ganga and her husband carry it all downstairs and watched as they strapped as much as they could to her husband's scooter. She stuffed the rest into an autorickshaw that precariously bounced Ganga out of our lives. As we waved sadly, we thought about the solitary container of palak paneer in our refrigerator: our final taste of Heaven, already half consumed.

With all our belongings either sold off, packed up, or trundling south towards Ganga's place, all that was left was to begin throwing stuff out. We'd tried to live with a small footprint in Delhi—not only because Ganga and Shilpa trained us to temper our consumption, but also because we knew that anything we wanted to keep would have to fit in our suitcases when we moved out. Still, we ended up dragging a surprising amount of trash out to the terrace. (The detritus of a modern expat's Delhi existence include dozens of photocopies of our passport, corrupted DVDs from Palika Bazaar, and handmade village crafts bought on trips around the country that didn't survive the flight back to Delhi.) And though none of it seemed ostentatiously wasteful, it was still no surprise when Shilpa rang our doorbell. We figured something would slip into one of the garbage bags to rouse her ire.

I opened the door for her just as I had on so many mornings, my head already nodding in false understanding of whatever it was she was going to shout at me. But on this morning, she showed none of her usual aggressiveness. She pulled her headscarf down gently, humbly, and asked a shy question. "Kya aap ja rahain hai?"

I smiled sadly at her, hoping my face returned her dignified goodbye with the respect it deserved. "Yup, we're leaving."

And then I broke into a grin—I'd actually understood her. For the first time in the eighteen months this woman had been shouting words I didn't understand about deeds I hadn't known I'd done wrong, we were actually communicating!

And then, as quickly as my elation came on, uncertainty replaced it. Was this really the time to be leaving Delhi? Now, in the midst of a global recession? Now, when we didn't have proper jobs or housing anywhere else in the world? Now, when I'd somehow learned Hindi by osmosis and finally connected with this dear, sweet woman about to bare her soul before me?

I gazed at Shilpa with sudden love, realizing that she had a heart of gold under her gruff exterior and knowing that we were about to achieve a deep, meaningful connection that would last long after I'd left India. "Hamlog Singapore jata hoon," I babbled happily. "Hamlog Singapore meh naukri deko."

Shilpa cocked her head and evaluated me for a second. Suddenly the softness in her eyes disappeared. "Kya?" she snorted. Then, sputtering with laughter, she launched into a stream of Hindi, her shoulders shaking as she turned and walked towards the terrace. When she reached the door she turned back to me and raised her hand, placing her thumb to her ear and her pinky to her mouth. "Something something something!" she giggled. Then she walked out to the terrace, either to take away our garbage bags or to start looking through them for things to yell at us about.

As I closed the door, I puzzled over her gesture. Of all the head bobbles and hand motions I'd grown familiar with in Delhi, this gesture was new. Unless it had the same meaning as it did in America: was she really asking me to call her sometime?

★

We resigned our jobs and said our goodbyes anyway, of course. But because we had no jobs to move on to, there was no reason not to take some time for ourselves. So we embarked upon a week in Nepal and then three weeks in south India that together gave us a month of ear infections, heat rash, cold showers, and some of the most captivating sights we'd ever seen. And when the month was over, we flew back to Delhi to pay our taxes, close our bank account, and visit our favorite restaurants one last time.

Seeking a sort of poetic reprise—I like stories that end where they begin—I returned on my last day in Delhi to the GK-II main market to retrace some of the steps I'd taken on my very first day. I went to Nathu's Sweets for one last south Indian thali, where the waiter's head bobble of acknowledgement didn't confuse me in the slightest. I went into one of the salons, where five dollars got my hair cut, my hippie travel beard shaved off, and my head massaged into blissful jelly. And because the weather was springtime perfect—as if the city knew we'd be writing a book about it and wanted us to remember it at its best—I took a coffee from Café Coffee Day into the market's central park to sit in the shade, watch the boys play cricket, and organize my thoughts on Delhi, this city of hallucinatory optimism and irrational pessimism, this city that is at once delighted by and hysterical about the present because of the dueling visions of the future it promises.

A shout from the boys at some athletic feat brought back memories of cricket matches on the office television. Murali's sudden howls of joy would bring every male in the office dashing to the television to see what national triumph they'd just missed. They'd cheer and clap each other's backs as the replay showed someone doing something cricket-wise in a manner significant to everyone in the room but me; I'd jump up and down with them anyway, waiting for the din to die so I could ask Anurag what was so exciting. This memory in turn reminded me that I wanted to call Murali because, in the four brief weeks since I'd left the company, he'd suddenly resigned, and I wanted to get the gossip.

This is how fast New Delhi changes. In less than a month, Murali was on his way out. Paul had already entered his transition period before I'd left; he, too, would soon be gone. And in just a few more months, so many of my co-workers would have resigned or been laid off that the company would be nearly unrecognizable to me had I walked back through its doors.

And as my company, so too the city. The airport terminal was renovated and sparkling. Work had abruptly commenced on that Outer Ring Road flyover that had sat idle for so much of my commute. The disconnected overhead vectors of the Metro had fused like synapses above M.G. Road. And the government had stepped up its 'beautification' campaign:

street vendors were being bustled off the streets, street-side encampments were disappearing, and slums were being walled off from the sensitive eyes of polite society. The city in which I was currently chatting with Murali was no longer the city we'd known. Nor will it be the same city when we return. Delhi exists uniquely in each moment of time. Its constant renewal means continuity lies only in the memory of what was there last time we looked.

What's more, our flight back from Trivandrum had made it clear just how little we'd known of this city in the first place. I had a pen and paper in hand as we began our descent, ready to list the landmarks I recognized from the airplane window in preparation to write this very paragraph. It was going to be a terrifically clever literary technique that would introduce our concluding thoughts on the city. But I didn't recognize anything. I didn't spot Ansal Plaza, Deer Park, Safdarjung Airport, or any of the other sights I usually used on the flights home to triangulate our house from above. Instead, I gaped at an impenetrable colony of dense houses and narrow lanes that was dotted with a few striking blue ponds that could only be old quarries. Houses were pressed up against those quarries on all sides, which meant that the only people who knew that those quarries existed were those whose back windows looked out upon them. Then I saw a sprawling neighborhood of glorious mansions with tennis courts, swimming pools and impossibly green lawns, all of which were surrounded by thick trees that hid their luxuries from the street. I saw faint columns of smoke coming from the center of a forested area: someone cooking? Someone working? And I even saw a giant statue of

Hanuman—but not *the* giant statue of Hanuman near Karol Bagh, because I looked for the Metro tracks in a vain attempt to figure out where it was. Imagine a city that has *two* towering statues of the monkey god and I'd only seen one of them?

So many treasures still unseen. And would any of them be there when we returned? Delhi changes at a rate we can't comprehend. Just thirty years ago, according to Jenny's boss Renuka, one of the highest points in the city was the Defence Colony flyover near Nehru Stadium. Renuka, who ran Pardada Pardadi's Delhi office, told us that it was her favorite childhood destination for her family's morning walks. They'd go there to look over the city and wonder why Delhi needed a flyover at all. After all, Renuka told us, traffic was hardly a problem: the waiting lists for Bajaj motorscooters was years long, anyone who didn't have a bicycle just took the bus, and where would anyone want to go anyway? There may have been a handful of restaurants, she said, but no one she knew considered visiting them. "We had no concept of going out to eat." And in this Delhi before Café Coffee Day, there were just two coffee shops in the city, both in Connaught Place; to go out for coffee would be even more eccentric than going out to eat.

Perhaps I'm being dramatic—thirty years is a long time. But Delhi is apparently unrecognizable even on a ten-year scale. One night, while driving home from a restaurant with Hemanshu, the founder of Eating Out in Delhi, we asked him what changes he'd seen in the last decade. "It would have been unbelievable ten years ago," he responded, "to think anyone could consider a career as a food critic." It was an understated answer, and it left unsaid all the changes over the last ten years necessary for such a career path to be viable: an explosion in newspapers, magazines, advertisers and readers; an explosion in restaurants, lounges, coffee shops and dessert bars; and an explosion in disposable income necessary to patronize them and in palates discriminating enough to demand professional criticism. Ten years ago, there were just four "remunerative career paths," as Hemanshu phrased it: engineer, lawyer, doctor and civil servant. But today, in this city of sudden possibilities . . . !

The three of us fell silent as Hemanshu drove down Aurobindo Marg. And then another thought struck him. "Even this," he said, gesturing out of the window at the construction of the Delhi Metro. It was nearly midnight but work was in full swing, lit by steaming lamps that were being swarmed by suicidal insects. "Hard hats, safety barriers . . . Ten years ago, there would have been nothing like this!"

Nor would there have been mobile phones, obviously, which Jenny and I spotted even in the poorest villages of Pardada Pardadi's students, where handsets dangled from chargers that were affixed to jugaad electrical outlets. Nor would there have been escalators, apparently, which explains the distrust so many grandmothers showed as they rode to the third level of the mall. Nor would there have been glass doors, we suppose, which explains why on three separate occasions I saw men walk into the ones at our office: a disquieting thud, a gasp of pain, and then a man sitting on the chair by the door for twenty minutes, rubbing his nose and looking miserable. (Given how little time I spent hanging around the office lobby, it's possible that those doors claimed dozens of other victims I never heard about.)

According to author Sam Miller, the modernization of Delhi's infrastructure began with the city's preparations for the 1982 Asian Games. That event kick-started a construction binge of stadiums, flyovers and five-star hotels.[1] But until the 1990s, there were still no malls, no Café Coffee Days, and nothing in Gurgaon but farms and the occasional homestead. ("In 1986, when we moved to Gurgaon, we were scared of the bandits at the edge of the city," our friend Anirban told us. "We had to come back by four p.m. or else we'd be attacked.") Economic change—and the escalators and glass doors that accompany it—didn't really begin until the liberalization of the 1990s. Soon malls were being built,[2] McDonalds opened up,[3] construction began on the Metro, and Cheerios came out of hiding from under shopkeepers' counters.

In 2003, Delhi was awarded hosting duties for the 2010 Commonwealth Games, and everything was thrown into overdrive: a sense of urgency and an infusion of funds led to the marathon of transformation that was in full swing during our time in Delhi.

But change will be Delhi's dominant narrative long after the last Commonwealth javelin lands quivering in the

---

1. Sam Miller, *Delhi: Adventures in a Megacity*, Penguin Books India, p.155.
2. http://www.3isite.com/articles/twilight.htm
3. http://mcdonaldsindia.net/about/our_journey.htm

earth. Every other day the papers would announce a new proclamation that would revolutionize the city: that Delhi will plant 250,000 new trees, eliminate slums, ensure a city-wide power surplus, shrink the protected area around Lutyens's Delhi, create incentives to encourage high-rise residential development, and actually develop some of the Yamuna's riverfront real estate for recreational purposes. If even a fraction of these developments come to pass (and every day that the papers weren't proudly reporting some new plan, they were criticizing the failure of an old one), change is sure to remain the essence of the Delhi experience for years to come.

*

Except for one problem: what the city builds, the people take away. The city is perpetually eroded by the impact of Delhi's glacial traffic—not "glacial" in the sense that it's slow, but in the sense that every Delhiite inflicts imperceptible damage simply by joining the flow of traffic. On a municipal–geological scale, this amalgamated impact forces the city to continuously rebuild everything it's already modernized, just to keep pace.

When Americans think of traffic, we picture a four-lane highway at a standstill, an orderly queue of tail lights stretching into infinity. Everyone in the American jam fantasizes about driving down the shoulder to bypass it, but the threat of traffic tickets and social condemnation keeps us waiting within the lanes. Delhi's traffic jams, though, create pressure in two dimensions: not only do they stretch into the distance, but they also impose tremendous outward force even beyond the roads' shoulders. In a Delhi traffic jam, the bigger vehicles commandeer the inner lanes, smaller cars jostle among the outer lanes, and motorcyclists and bicyclists are pushed past the shoulders, into the gutters and onto the sidewalks. And just as pebbles dragged by glaciers become geological sandpaper as they flow, so too are the lightest elements of Delhi's traffic causing the most damage. Bicycle pedals are scraping curbs, motorcyclists are spinning wheels and spraying abrasive gravel, and everyone's knocking debris into storm drains that will one day cause them to stop up, flood and undermine the pavement. The occasional bus slamming into a telephone pole doesn't help, but the long-term damage comes from every dragged foot, every kicked rock, and every horseshoe sparking along the pavement. Millions of pedestrians, bicyclists, motorcyclists, cars, buses, trucks, horses, cows, camels, and elephants aggregate into unrelenting infrastructure erosion, one nick in the concrete at a time.

But it's not just the pressure of jammed roads that's eroding Delhi's infrastructure. There's also the tendency of traffic to find the quickest route between two points regardless of where the infrastructure intends for them to go. Shortly after we moved to Hauz Khas, the city built new medians down a stretch of nearby Aurobindo Marg. These concrete islands were raised a full foot off the ground, and they prevented cars from making the illegal U-turns they'd been enjoying ever since the old medians had worn down into rubble. Unfortunately for those new medians, though, traffic coming off the Ring Road really wanted to make those illegal U-turns, because the first legal U-turn was one long half-mile beyond where traffic entered this stretch of Aurobindo Marg. And in evening traffic, that single half-mile could take fifteen minutes. Similarly, pedestrians and bicyclists certainly weren't going to walk all the way to the U-turns when they could just cross directly over the medians. And that's how it began: in less than eighteen months, pedestrians and bicyclists had instigated fissures in the median that scooters and motorcycles had widened and shaped, creating a half-dozen holes through which autorickshaws and even cars were eventually passing.

I'd shake my head at the cars crossing these rubble strips, but I'd also silently hope my driver would follow their lead to shave precious minutes off my commute home.

Even beyond the traffic, other beavers are gnawing at the city's infrastructure. The sun bakes the concrete. The monsoon floods undermine it. And the bureaucracy contributes poor planning, thoughtless execution, and rampant corruption that overlooks sub-par materials and construction. Again I bemoan the fate of Aurobindo Marg: a few months after we left, the city decided to replace a nearby open storm-water drain with a buried 1,200mm drainage pipe. This on its own would be a perfectly satisfactory capital investment if only they hadn't decided to channel the outflow of three 1,800mm sewage pipes into this single 1,200mm conduit.[4] I'm certainly no engineer, but basic addition suggests an error in their planning. And

---

4. http://timesofindia.indiatimes.com/Cities/More-leaks-so-road-closed/articleshow/4610265.cms

sure enough, the new pipe couldn't handle all that run-off during one day of heavy rain: the water back-flowed, causing so much damage that whole sections of the street caved in. Northbound Aurobindo Marg was closed for over a month for repairs.[5]

Poor, hapless Aurobindo Marg! How we wept for that beleaguered street.

But there's hope. Aurobindo Marg is a symbol of all that ails Delhi's infrastructure—but it also represents the bright promise of Delhi's eventual future. Because all those construction barriers, jackhammers and men wearing hard hats had a higher purpose: the city was lifting Aurobindo Marg up so it could slip the Delhi Metro underneath. Phase II of the Metro (which now connects the city's southern sprawl with the system already so successfully unifying the northern, western, and eastern stretches) was inching forward the whole time we drove grumpily over it. And it was imperceptibly transforming this beaten boulevard into a model of urban infrastructure.

We felt genuine pride when we first saw the map of the future Metro displayed in the Central Secretariat station. Our fingers traced the green line, feeling sudden ownership of the planned route by virtue of its proximity to our home as it followed Aurobindo Marg south from INA Market, past AIIMS and Green Park, until it deviated from our now-beloved street with a gentle left in the direction of Malviya Nagar. We did have a moment of worry when we

---

5. http://www.expressindia.com/latest-news/aurobindo-marg-reopens-for-traffic/485519/

realized that that left turn took it directly under our flat, imagining that our ICICI-ruined mornings might be preceded by the nighttime lullaby of a seventy-two-ton tunneling machine pummeling bedrock below our pillows. But the team building the Delhi Metro had a world-class reputation for good reason: absolutely no noise or vibration ever disturbed our slumber.

With the Metro's construction now complete, Aurobindo Marg has been sewn up and topped off with a fresh layer of asphalt. And Delhi's future rolls on well-oiled wheels underneath it as proof that the city can accomplish great things. I imagine the Metro pulling smoothly out of the Green Park station and passing silently beneath our flat, and that the loudest sounds to disturb our former neighbors are still Anya's dogs barking at passing cars and Mr. M. yelling at parking ones. Somewhere near Qutub Minar, the Metro blinks into the sunshine above M.G. Road, with each one of its passengers representing one less point of pressure on the road below. Meanwhile, the merchants of M.G. Road reclaim their sidewalks, entice their patrons to return, and rehabilitate the half-destroyed buildings that remain as reminders of darker times.

We have no doubt that this sort of leap forward will occur all across Delhi in the years and decades to follow. Isolated accomplishments—an overpass here, a footbridge there—will ease the pressures at particular points until, on a geological scale, Delhi moves forward faster than its progress can be eroded away. In fact, by 2021, Delhi's Metro will cover almost 275 miles, giving it more route-miles than New York's subway. Already it stretches from the

northernmost poles of the city to eastern and western
satellite cities; it connects the airport directly to New Delhi
Railway station; it reaches deep into central Gurgaon; and
it has many more lines under frantic construction.

Delhi's geographic sprawl makes the Metro experience
very unlike New York. In the central areas of the New
York's boroughs—and especially in Manhattan—the subway
is rarely more than a brisk walk away. But Delhi's stations
tend to follow the main roads, which means that other
forms of transportation are necessary to get from the
neighborhoods to the stations. This has changed the character
of getting around Delhi: instead of forty-five terrifying
minutes in an auto, there's now just ten terrifying minutes
on either side of an air-conditioned train ride. Progress!

And more progress: with the Metro construction
complete, M.G. Road is back to its intended width. Rush-
hour traffic has been upgraded from singularly cataclysmic
to routinely traumatic. It's enough to reinstate the feasibility
of leaving the office before seven p.m.

(But even as some pressures are alleviated, new ones are
created. Every train into Gurgaon spills thousands of riders
into a city without an infrastructure for getting them to
their offices. Which is why Gurgaon is now hastily building
a Metro of its own. And meanwhile, over at the NH-8 toll
plaza—well, that's a situation that can't be discussed in
polite company.)

★

Our optimism about Delhi's future does not stem from a
belief that the city is an extraordinary model of development.

We're optimistic for precisely the opposite reason: that there's no reason to think Delhi is different from any other city. In fact, all of the problems we saw in Delhi just reminded us of New York City.

Not today's New York City, but rather the New York City from Jacob Riis's 1890 book *How the Other Half Lives*. A pioneering work of photojournalism, Riis's book exposed the more fortunate classes to the terrible things happening in neighborhoods that are today among the hippest in the city. Looking through the pictures[6] of bygone New York, we see children sewing shirts in sweatshop conditions, women huddled miserably with blankets wrapped around their shoulders, alleys strewn with trash, blind beggars, squatters' camps, shoeless men with rags wrapped around their feet, and the expressionless faces of people who stoically endure it all. The poor were stuffed into squalid slums in this old New York, and the city was tortured by issues of pollution and sewage. Hogs were its primary method of waste disposal, horses plagued it with four million pounds of manure every single day, and one visitor famously described the whole of New York as a "nasal disaster, where some streets smell like bad eggs dissolved in ammonia."[7]

All of which mirrors the issues Delhi is coping with today. Glancing through the pictures and reading the text of Riis's book, the parallels between these two cities separated

---

6. http://www.authentichistory.com/1865-1897/progressive/riis/
illustrations.html

7. http://www.astc.org/exhibitions/rotten/timeline.htm

by oceans and decades are striking, down to the same method with which one elderly man in one of Riis's photos wraps a scarf around his head to stay warm. His scarf, his scraggly beard, his defeated eyes: he's identical to the poor souls we saw huddled on Delhi's cold sidewalks.

Nor is New York the only city with this historical parallel. Glancing through history, it emerges that almost all of today's world-class cities rose from similarly dismal conditions. Paris, for instance, brought us the word "loo" because Parisians would shout "*gardez-loo*" before emptying their chamber pots onto the sidewalks below their windows. Edinburgh had a similar reputation, and its stench was even given the ironic nickname "The Flowers of Edinburgh." Cleveland's Cuyahoga River was so polluted that it regularly caught fire in the 1960s. As late as 1977, Singapore's government had to convene extraordinary action to clean up its filthy namesake river. London, Boston, Shanghai— most of today's world-class cities were once defined by a small upper class, a huge lower class, and terrible problems from their oversupply of labor. We admit that our understanding of developmental economics is loose, but it does look like there's a pattern: for all these cities, the solutions came as the middle class emerged.

Obviously, there are significant differences between New York and New Delhi. First and foremost, New York has that human-scale street grid which Jenny and I hold in such esteem. But the parallels extend even beyond the mere fact of poverty. Consider the Yamuna against New York's Hudson River: a century ago, the Hudson was cut off from the city by docks and warehouses, just like the Yamuna today is cut off by farmland. New York's rivers were glimpsed from bridges or buildings, but few people interacted with them in any way beyond those who worked on the docks or those who dumped bodies off of them.

But as New York's economic structure changed, so did the city. Today, the Hudson River boasts parkland running almost unbroken along Manhattan's entire west side. Paris and Edinburgh are similarly magnificent, Cleveland is planning its waterfront revival, and Singapore's reputation is without peer. ("I got your holiday card and it made me somewhat of a celebrity in my neighborhood," Anurag emailed me after I'd left India. "Everyone was like, 'Ooooohhh a gora sent him a postcard, that too from Singapore!'") London, Boston, Shanghai—they've all emerged from their low points. And there's no reason to think that Delhi won't do the same.

★

Jenny and I aren't alone in seeing a bright future for distant Delhi. The phrase we heard over and over again was "world-class city." It was a goal enunciated by the politicians, the papers and the people. Most Delhiites to whom we spoke eagerly anticipate the city reaching this standard, even if it's unclear exactly what this benchmark entails beyond the hazy promise of something better.

Many people are ushering in this new era in their own way. Mr. M., for instance, wouldn't do so much shouting at passers-by if he didn't think he was helping. Nor would Anya chastise urinating men. Nor would Sam Singh return to India to start his school when he could have just as easily saved his fortune and retired in comfort. Delhiites are well aware of the challenges, of course, but that doesn't change their optimism. When I asked Anurag about his vision, he rattled off a half-dozen examples of things that were catastrophically wrong in the city and then expressed unflagging optimism that they'll figure it out eventually.

As long as the middle class keeps growing, we agree. The rich always insulate themselves from their city's problems, and the poor are always too busy trying to eat to worry about what's around them. The middle class is development's catalyst: it has the incentive to care about what's around it along with the influence to agitate for change. The middle class will vote, it will write letters to the editor, it will spend money in malls that encourage markets to clean up. The middle class will grow, Delhi's labor surplus will move towards equilibrium, and Delhi will develop in the model of so many other cities before it.

But while everyone predicts good things for Delhi, there's one particular bright spot that I suspect Jenny and I are among the first to have noticed. It's too bad that it's currently so difficult for foreigners to invest in property, because we'd love to buy some real estate before we make this prediction public: we believe that the Daryaganj neighborhood will one day be the most vibrant in Delhi.

Three quarters of a mile long and a quarter mile wide, Daryaganj is perfectly situated to evolve into Delhi's cultural nerve center. It's smack in the middle of the city and surrounded on three sides by major tourist draws: the Old City to the west, the Red Fort to the north and Raj Ghat to the east. It will be well served by transit—not only is it bordered by major boulevards that make it easily accessible, but Phase III of the Metro plans a Daryaganj stop.[8] Most promising of all, Daryaganj is a full-scale municipal miracle hidden under a few decades of neglect. Its blocks are short, walkable and laid out at right angles, but it still contains enough unpredictability to keep things interesting. It has a surprising number of open spaces for such a small area. And, most importantly, it's filled with grand old Art Deco buildings that evoke glamour and elegance, with bold forms and sweeping curves that are hidden today behind signs for photocopy shops or textbook printers. According to historian Lucy Peck, Daryaganj's buildings were built in the 1930s, probably by Indian merchant families who thrived during British rule. The architecture is perfectly suited to amplify the optimism and glorious promise of modernity that we think Daryaganj will represent.

These days, Daryaganj is a hub for the publishing industry. It's bustling during the workdays and desolate on the weekends. But its geography, street design, throwback architecture, and potential for human-scale vibrancy make it easy to imagine sidewalk cafés, trendy hotels, fashion boutiques, loft apartments, art galleries and coffee shops. Compared to south Delhi's isolation and sprawl, Daryaganj faces a much easier transition to becoming a twenty-four-hour neighborhood in which artists live, tourists play, writers work, musicians jam, culture is developed, trends are set, and decent espresso is served.

---

8. http://www.indianexpress.com/news/metro-set-to-start-work-on-challenging-red/796970/

We're basing this on nothing more than a gut feeling, a bias towards walkable streets, and an overdeveloped sense of optimism, but we believe Daryaganj will one day be Delhi's Greenwich Village.

★

After eighteen months in Delhi, the extent of our experience can be plotted in a diamond shape laid out upon the map of the city that hung in our living room. The diamond's northern apex is squarely in Old Delhi, with threads marking our wanderings that extend up the minar at Jama Masjid, over to Karol Bagh, through Civil Lines and into Majnu Ka Tila, but always retreating to Connaught Place for dinner before night fell and the shadows came out. The sides of our diamond widen along the borders of Central and South Delhi (NH-8 to the west, Mathura Road to the east) before narrowing to join the traffic inching into Gurgaon. Discreet polyps hang off our diamond that represent brief trips to Noida, Faridabad, Ghaziabad and Dwarka to attend meetings or visit friends, where we'd scrunch our faces at the concrete apartment buildings, unable to appreciate their appeal despite the obvious middle-class happiness that so many people were finding inside.

It's clear that our experience covers relatively little of the city. More was unseen than seen, that's for sure. It was a difficult choice to leave Delhi, with so much still to explore within the shapeless borders of the National Capital Territory and so much further still in diamond-shaped India itself. But an even larger geography beckoned. And given the choice between scattershot appreciation of the Asian continent or focused exploration around our home in Delhi, we chose breadth over depth. All signs pointed to this being a bad idea, from the stock market's miseries to the various corporate officers in my parent company assuring me that there were no job opportunities east of Dubai. We resigned our jobs anyway, confident that optimism alone would provide for us.

And it did. We found a two-month volunteer gig with a Singaporean charity in exchange for housing and a stipend big enough to buy lunch while we looked for jobs that actually paid. The first of April rolled around and off we went, fools in everyone's eyes but our own, flying from New Delhi to Singapore's Dunlop Street. That's where housing had been arranged for us—coincidentally enough, right in the heart of Singapore's Little India.

This neighborhood instantly felt like home to us. Though it did not become our actual home (we moved out in a matter of hours when we discovered that our proposed flat had no electricity, no furniture, no shower, and that its toilet was padlocked behind metal shutters in the unoccupied storefront on the ground floor), we returned to Little India as often as we could. And we felt like we were discovering Singapore through Indian eyes more than Western ones: we gaped at the acreage of supermarkets, we were scandalized by the skimpiness of skirts, and we engaged in an immediate hunt for Indian food that was comparable to what we'd just left behind. (This hunt compounded in intensity once we discovered that Singapore's branch of Saravana Bhavan was as disappointing as Delhi's was good.) And we continued to apply the assertiveness we'd learned in India. I crossed the street wherever I pleased, for instance, flicking my hands to stop oncoming cars as I had with Delhi drivers. That practice had worked so well in Delhi because Indian drivers expect anything to prance into their path and possess the instincts to brake accordingly; it was a bad idea in Singapore's tamer traffic, where a driver suddenly confronted by a crazy *ang mo* doing a Luke Skywalker impression is far less likely to stop in time.

But I couldn't help my hubris. Man, we'd lived in *Delhi*—and *that* is a real city!

We were high on our sense of municipal superiority after living in Delhi. If we could make it there, we could make it anywhere, so I think I can handle crossing your quiet little street, Singapore. You call this traffic? Let me tell you about traffic . . .

Just like living in New York had made us appreciate elements of America's suburbs we'd taken for granted while growing up (front lawns, parking lots, drugstore employees who don't strangle us with their eyes), so too did moving to Singapore spotlight elements of Delhi life that we hadn't realized we'd miss so much: street life that was actually lively, shopkeepers who knew who we were and remembered what we liked, neighbors who were always eager to chat, and the friendly curiosity shown by everyone who encountered us about who we were and what the heck we were doing in their city.

Singapore is as modern and spotless and perfect as everyone thinks. The future here is scripted, though, for better or for worse. Even as we were scrambling to find a flat to replace the toiletless one in Little India, we knew we'd eventually find good jobs, move into a condo with a swimming pool, meet a bunch of other expats, and fly off to other parts of

Asia whenever we craved excitement. And that's exactly how things progressed. Every so often, though, we'd stumble upon a Chinese wedding, or poke our heads inside a circus tent containing some sort of community celebration, or stand in front of a food stall with no English menus. We'd pause at the periphery and peer in—and nobody would acknowledge us.

And this is where our homesickness for Delhi would really kick in. Because if we ever peeked inside a tent in Delhi, a half-dozen people would immediately wave us in, give us food, introduce their aunties, pose their babies for pictures, and extend heartfelt invitations for us to visit their home villages.

As Delhi moves inexorably towards some amorphous "world-class" end point that nobody can define but everyone eagerly anticipates, we know that its spirit will remain constant. Strangers will always wave at us in strange neighborhoods, and every time we stick our noses somewhere it doesn't belong, someone will always appear to make us feel welcome anyway.

We don't expect to move back to Delhi in the immediate future. The world is too big, and there are too many other cuisines we still want to immerse ourselves in. But maybe, one day, the stars will align, and we'll find ourselves living in Delhi once again. Maybe we'll wake up in a Hauz Khas market that's now a cosmopolitan neighborhood of wine bars and art galleries and designer furniture outlets. Maybe we'll get to discover it all over again. And maybe on this first morning, the bicycle vendor who wakes us up will also reflect Delhi's new sophistication: he really will be selling paella.

Acknowledgments

I deeply appreciate everyone who shaped this book. First and foremost are the readers and commentators on our blog who shared their views of India and helped influence our own. I can't emphasize enough how wonderful it feels to get so much unsolicited positive feedback. (And as for the trolls, the joke's on you: the negative feedback helped just as much.)

Knowing full well that I've surely forgotten somebody, I'll start down the list of people I need to thank. I'll begin with Harneet Bhatia, Deep Bisht, Nobin Dutta, Pankaj Kashyup, Tapan Khurana, Dipankar Paul, Prajakta Samant, Kasturi Sengupta, Silky Sethi and Bharat Tiwari for answering my strange questions. Thanks to Tarn Kaur, Monali Shah Saraiya, Renuka Gupta, Murali Gopal and Anirban Mukherjee for sharing their memories and visions of Delhi with me. Thanks to Linda Blake for hunting that bottlewallah in vain, to Sachin Kalbag for explaining what lies beneath, and to Amba for answering so many questions without asking why I was writing everything down.

Thanks to Sam Singh for introducing us to the village. Thanks to Prashant Gandhi for helping ensure I didn't offend Hinduism. And thanks to everyone in New York who helped me get to Delhi in the first place—Toni Iacono, Joan Colten, Bill Manfredi, Tamara Smith and Nick Moore—and to Pete Pierce for reaching through the network and pulling me over.

Even bigger thanks to Sam Miller and Hemanshu Kumar for fact-checking chapter two and answering so many of my municipal questions, and to Edward Luce and Lucy Peck for being there on those rare occurrences when neither Sam nor Hemanshu knew the answer. Thanks to Sharbani Pal for sharing her lovely story, to Robb Selander and Sonia Khurana for remembering office anecdotes, to Nishant Gambhir for giving me the full-on sense of the optimism of Delhi's youth, and to Daphne for taking over that other aspect of my career when I ran out of time for it. Thanks to Tony Susi for abusing his office printing privileges, reading the manuscript, and convincing me to remove the ill-conceived murder sequence. (I'll email it to anyone who asks.)

I couldn't have completed this book without Anurag Giri and Govind Mukundan helping me spell simple Hindi, translate scrawled notes, put names to mantras, and track down endless bits of trivia. Nor could I have done it without Mom, Dad, and especially Mahua Ray Chaudhuri providing insight, feedback and opinions as they reviewed each and every page of each and every chapter.

Subcontinental thanks go to the great team at HarperCollins India: Saugata Mukherjee for sealing the deal, V.K. Karthika for moving it forward, and Ajitha G.S. for making it perfect. And global thanks go to Cal Barksdale and everyone at Arcade and Skyhorse Publishing for everything they have done and will do for me, for this book, and for Delhi.

Most of all, thanks to Jenny for starting the blog, for letting me horn in on it, for convincing me that a book could be written at all (although she says the suggestion came from Mark Vitelli, so I'll send a bowling fist bump over to him as well), for reading it, for critiquing it, for supporting it, for supporting me, and for being the perfect wife, collaborator and friend.

Index